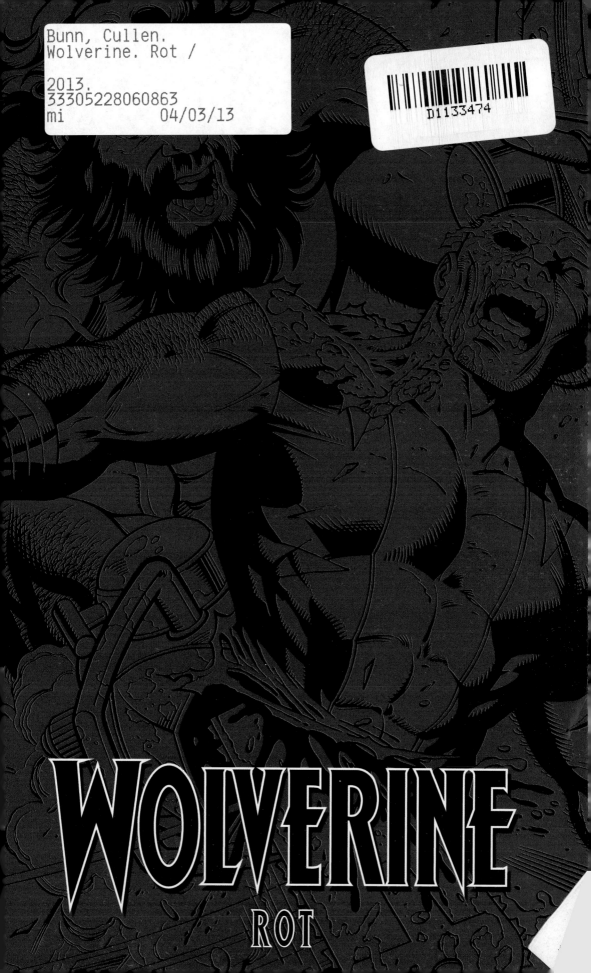

WOLVERINE

ROT

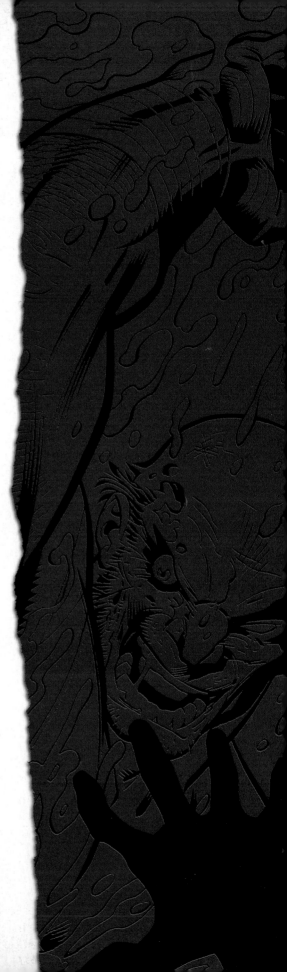

WOLVERINE

— ROT —

WRITER **CULLEN BUNN**

PENCILS **PAUL PELLETIER**

INKS **DAVE MEIKIS** WITH **CAM SMITH**
(ISSUES #306-308)

COLORS **RAIN BEREDO**

— UNDERNEATH —

WRITER **IVAN BRANDON**

ART **RAFAEL ALBUQUERQUE**
& JASON LATOUR

COLOR ART **JOHN RAUCH**
& JASON LATOUR

LETTERS **VC'S CORY PETIT**

COVER ART **JIM CHEUNG** WITH **JASON
KEITH** (ISSUE #305), **CHRIS SAMNEE** WITH
JAVIER RODRIGUEZ (ISSUES #306-308)
& ESAD RIBIC (ISSUE #309)

ASSISTANT EDITOR **JAKE THOMAS**

EDITOR **JEANINE SCHAEFER**

WITH **JOHN BARBER**

GROUP EDITOR **NICK LOWE**

Collection Editor CORY LEVINE
Assistant Editors ALEX STARBUCK & NELSON RIBEIRO
Editors, Special Projects JENNIFER GRÜNWALD & MARK D. BEAZLEY
Senior Editor, Special Projects JEFF YOUNGQUIST
Senior Vice President of Sales DAVID GABRIEL
SVP of Brand Planning & Communications MICHAEL PASCIULLO
Book Design JEFF POWELL
Editor in Chief AXEL ALONSO · Chief Creative Officer JOE QUESADA
Publisher DAN BUCKLEY · Executive Producer ALAN FINE

WOLVERINE: ROT. Contains material originally published in magazine form as WOLVERINE #305-309. First printing 2012. Hardcover ISBN# 978-0-7851-6145-5. Softcover ISBN# 978-0-7851-6146-2. Published by MARVEL WORLDWIDE, INC., a subsidiary of MARVEL ENTERTAINMENT, LLC. OFFICE OF PUBLICATION: 135 West 50th Street, New York, NY 10020. Copyright © 2012 Marvel Characters, Inc. All rights reserved. Hardcover: $24.99 per copy in the U.S. and $27.99 in Canada (GST #R127032852). Softcover: $19.99 per copy in the U.S. and $21.99 in Canada (GST #R127032852). Canadian Agreement #40668537. All characters featured in this issue and the distinctive names and likenesses thereof, and all related indicia are trademarks of Marvel Characters, Inc. No similarity between any of the names, characters, persons, and/or institutions in this magazine with those of any living or dead person or institution is intended, and any such similarity which may exist is purely coincidental. **Printed in the U.S.A.** ALAN FINE, EVP - Office of the President, Marvel Worldwide, Inc. and EVP & CMO Marvel Characters B.V.; DAN BUCKLEY, Publisher & President - Print, Animation & Digital Divisions; JOE QUESADA, Chief Creative Officer; TOM BREVOORT, SVP of Publishing; DAVID BOGART, SVP of Operations & Procurement, Publishing; RUWAN JAYATILLEKE, SVP & Associate Publisher, Publishing; C.B. CEBULSKI, SVP of Creator & Content Development; DAVID GABRIEL, SVP of Publishing Sales & Circulation; MICHAEL PASCIULLO, SVP of Brand Planning & Communications; JIM O'KEEFE, VP of Operations & Logistics; DAN CARR, Executive Director of Publishing Technology; SUSAN CRESPI, Editorial Operations Manager; ALEX MORALES, Publishing Operations Manager; STAN LEE, Chairman Emeritus. For information regarding advertising in Marvel Comics or on Marvel.com, please contact Niza Disla, Director of Marvel Partnerships, at ndisla@marvel.com. For Marvel subscription inquiries, please call 800-217-9158. **Manufactured between 7/16/2012 and 8/27/2012 (hardcover), and 7/16/2012 and 2/25/2013 (softcover), by R.R. DONNELLEY, INC., SALEM, VA, USA.**

9 8 7 6 5 4 3 2 1

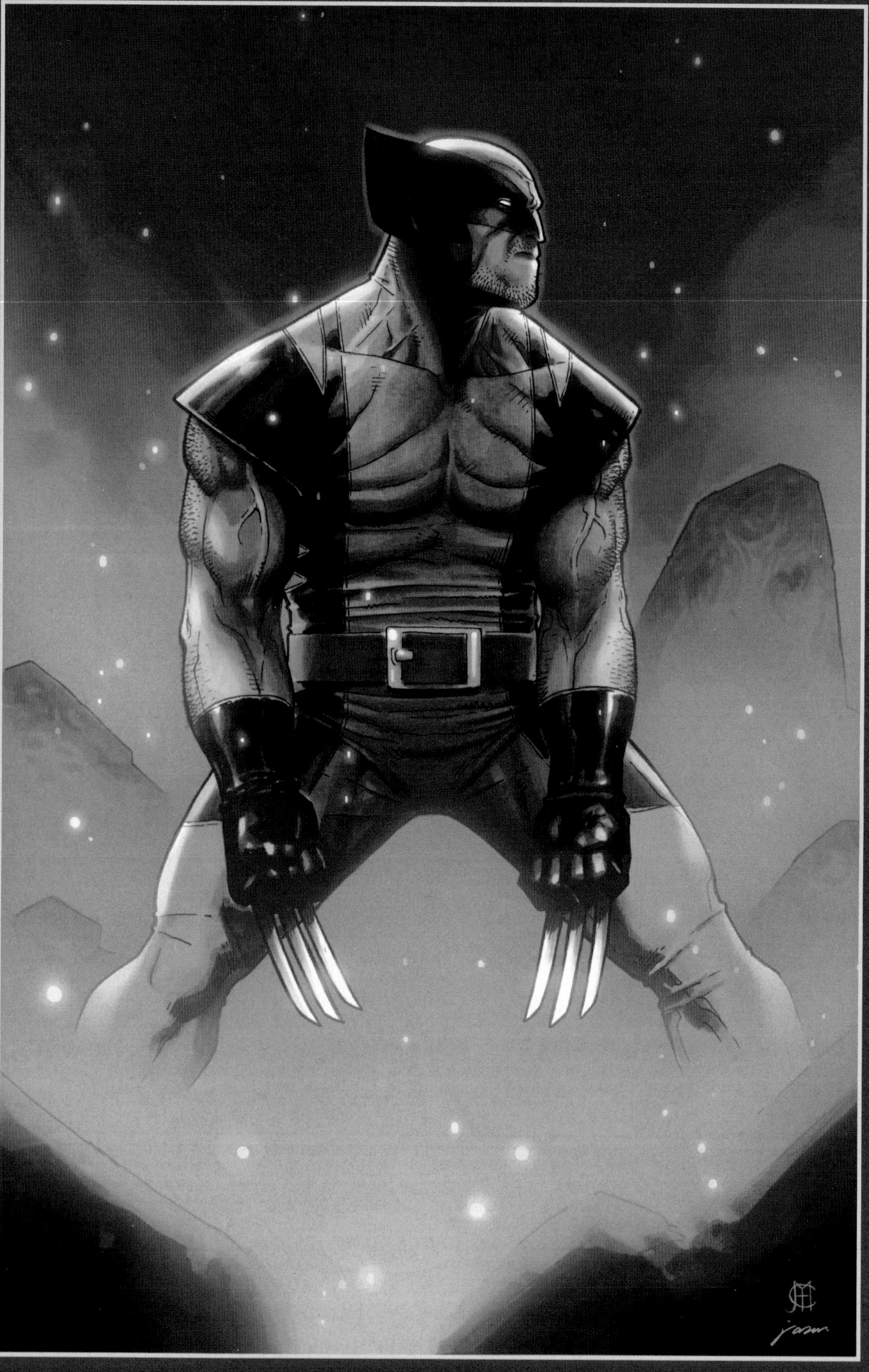

305

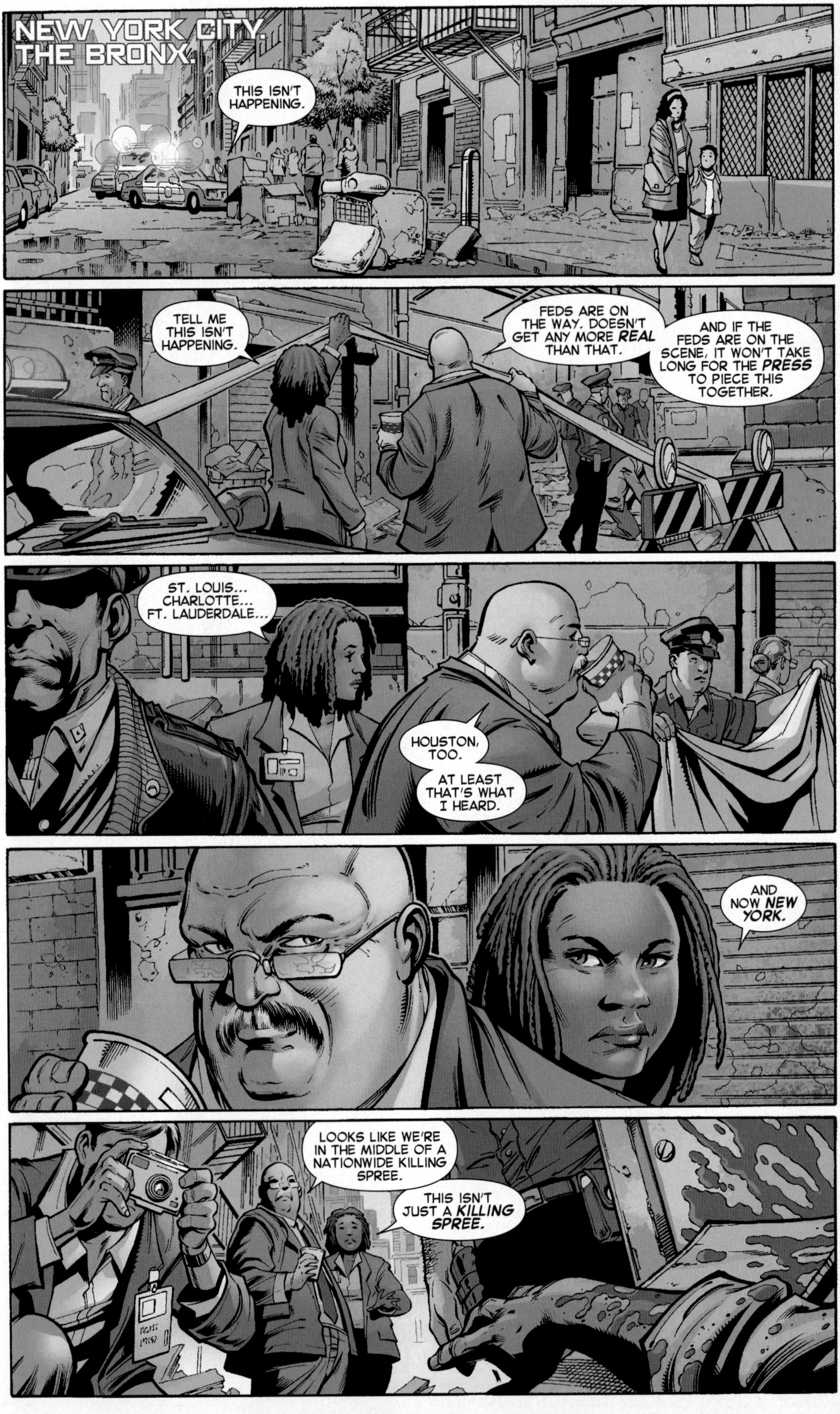
NEW YORK CITY.
THE BRONX.
THIS ISN'T HAPPENING.
TELL ME THIS ISN'T HAPPENING.
FEDS ARE ON THE WAY. DOESN'T GET ANY MORE REAL THAN THAT.
AND IF THE FEDS ARE ON THE SCENE, IT WON'T TAKE LONG FOR THE PRESS TO PIECE THIS TOGETHER.
ST. LOUIS... CHARLOTTE... FT. LAUDERDALE...
HOUSTON, TOO.
AT LEAST THAT'S WHAT I HEARD.
AND NOW NEW YORK.
LOOKS LIKE WE'RE IN THE MIDDLE OF A NATIONWIDE KILLING SPREE.
THIS ISN'T JUST A KILLING SPREE.

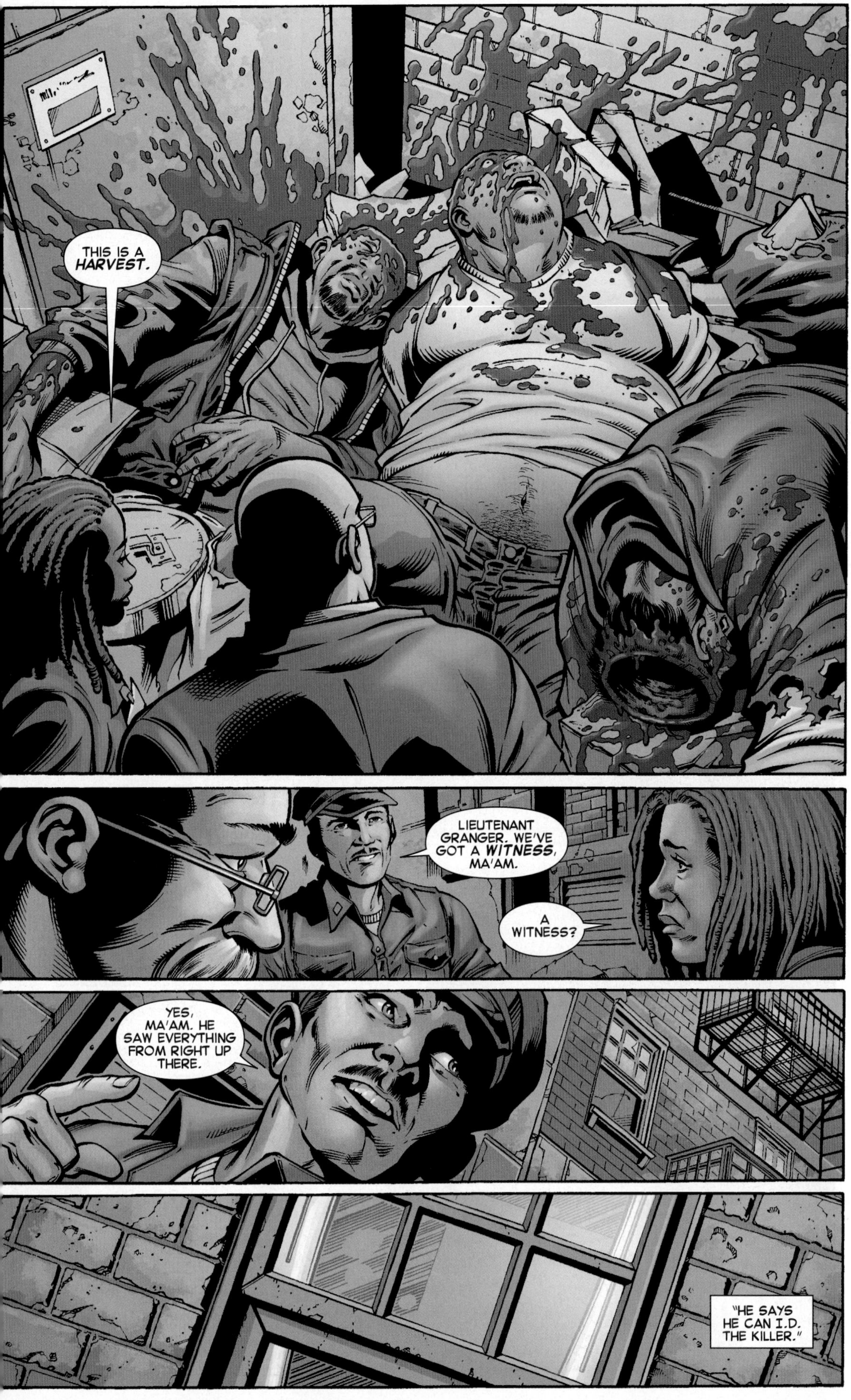
THIS IS A HARVEST.
LIEUTENANT GRANGER. WE'VE GOT A WITNESS, MA'AM.
A WITNESS?
YES, MA'AM. HE SAW EVERYTHING FROM RIGHT UP THERE.
"HE SAYS HE CAN I.D. THE KILLER."

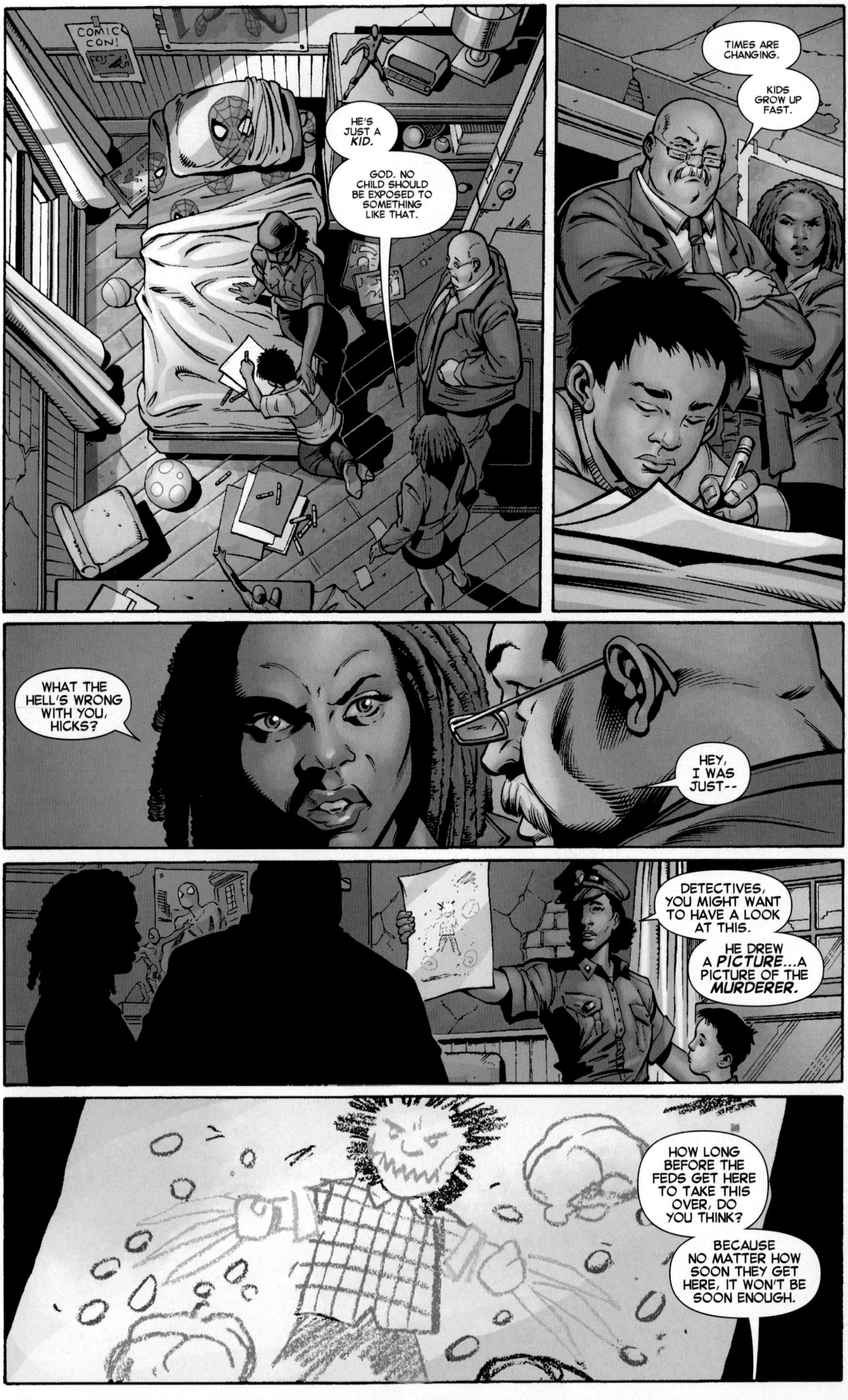
COMIC CON!
HE'S JUST A *KID.*
GOD. NO CHILD SHOULD BE EXPOSED TO SOMETHING LIKE THAT.
TIMES ARE CHANGING.
KIDS GROW UP FAST.
WHAT THE HELL'S WRONG WITH YOU, HICKS?
HEY, I WAS JUST--
DETECTIVES, YOU MIGHT WANT TO HAVE A LOOK AT THIS.
HE DREW A *PICTURE...*A PICTURE OF THE *MURDERER.*
HOW LONG BEFORE THE FEDS GET HERE TO TAKE THIS OVER, DO YOU THINK?
BECAUSE NO MATTER HOW SOON THEY GET HERE, IT WON'T BE SOON ENOUGH.

Many years ago, a secret government organization abducted the man called Logan, a mutant possessing razor-sharp bone claws and the ability to heal from any wound. In their attempt to create the perfect living weapon, the organization bonded the unbreakable metal Adamantium to his skeleton. The process was excruciating and by the end, there was little left of the man known as Logan. He had become...

WOLVERINE

PREVIOUSLY...

Wolverine's had quite a life. A mutant with an extraordinary healing factor, he's fought in wars, had his memory erased and was turned into a living weapon by a secret Canadian super-soldier program, been in an insane asylum, married and had a son in Japan (his wife was murdered and his son keeps trying to kill him) and recently fought his way out of Hell.

Now he's founded and is the headmaster of a school for mutants called the Jean Grey School for Higher Learning, where he's teaching young mutants that they don't have to resign themselves to a life of violence and fear.

Surely, that will run smoothly...

ROT

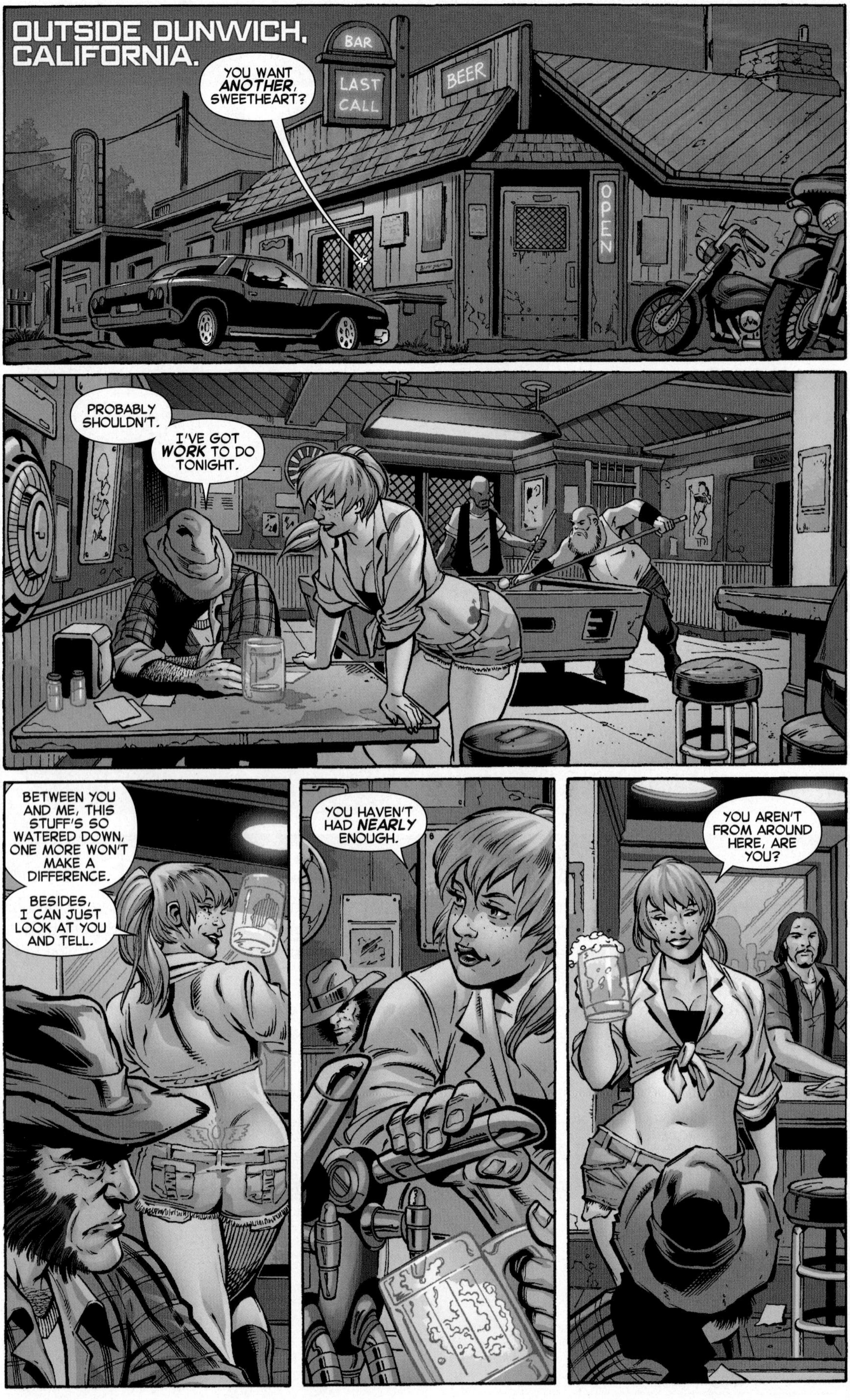
OUTSIDE DUNWICH, CALIFORNIA.
BAR
LAST CALL
BEER
OPEN
YOU WANT ANOTHER, SWEETHEART?
PROBABLY SHOULDN'T.
I'VE GOT WORK TO DO TONIGHT.
BETWEEN YOU AND ME, THIS STUFF'S SO WATERED DOWN, ONE MORE WON'T MAKE A DIFFERENCE.
BESIDES, I CAN JUST LOOK AT YOU AND TELL.
YOU HAVEN'T HAD NEARLY ENOUGH.
YOU AREN'T FROM AROUND HERE, ARE YOU?

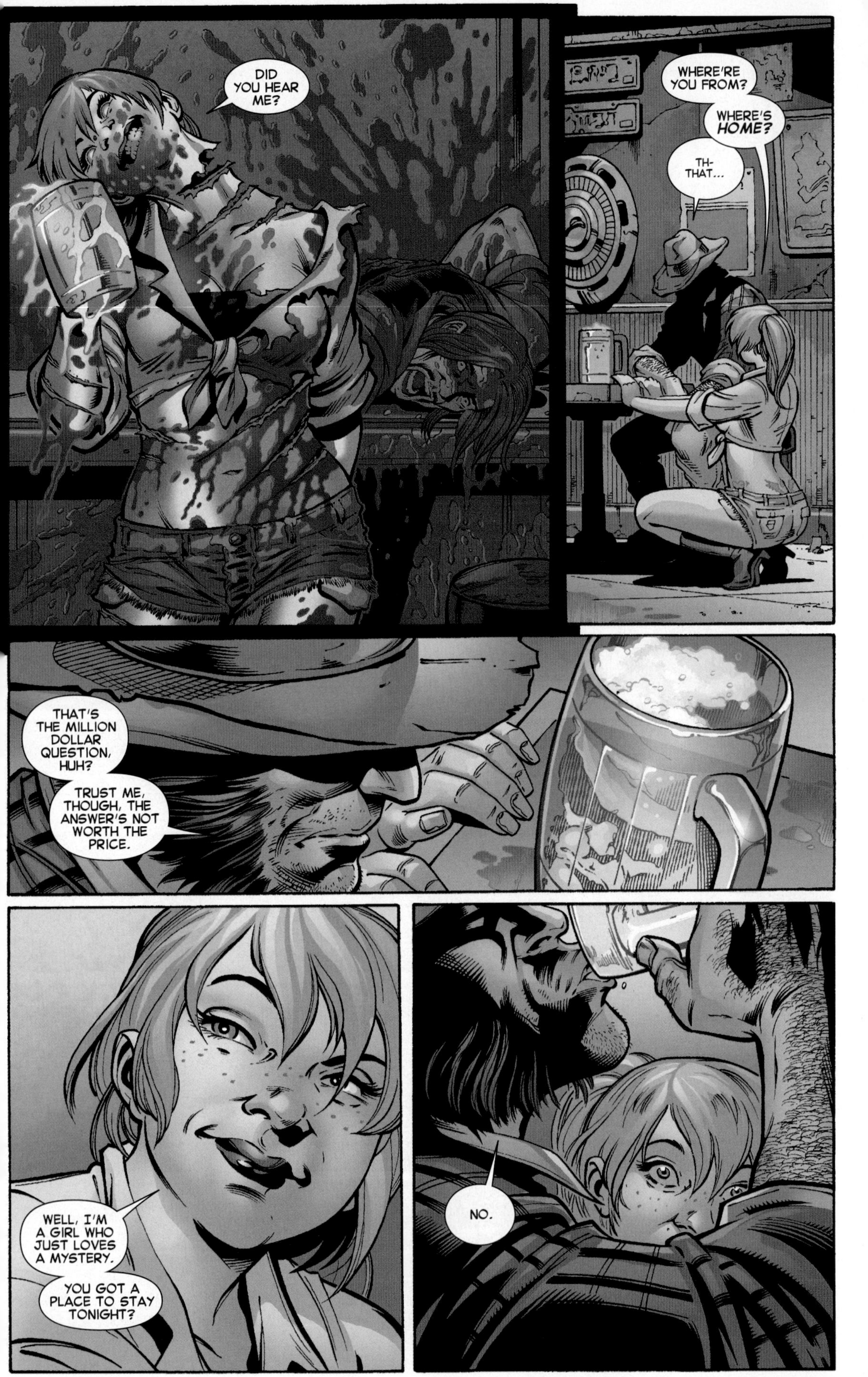
DID YOU HEAR ME?
WHERE'RE YOU FROM?
WHERE'S *HOME?*
TH- THAT...
THAT'S THE MILLION DOLLAR QUESTION, HUH?
TRUST ME, THOUGH, THE ANSWER'S NOT WORTH THE PRICE.
WELL, I'M A GIRL WHO JUST LOVES A MYSTERY.
YOU GOT A PLACE TO STAY TONIGHT?
NO.

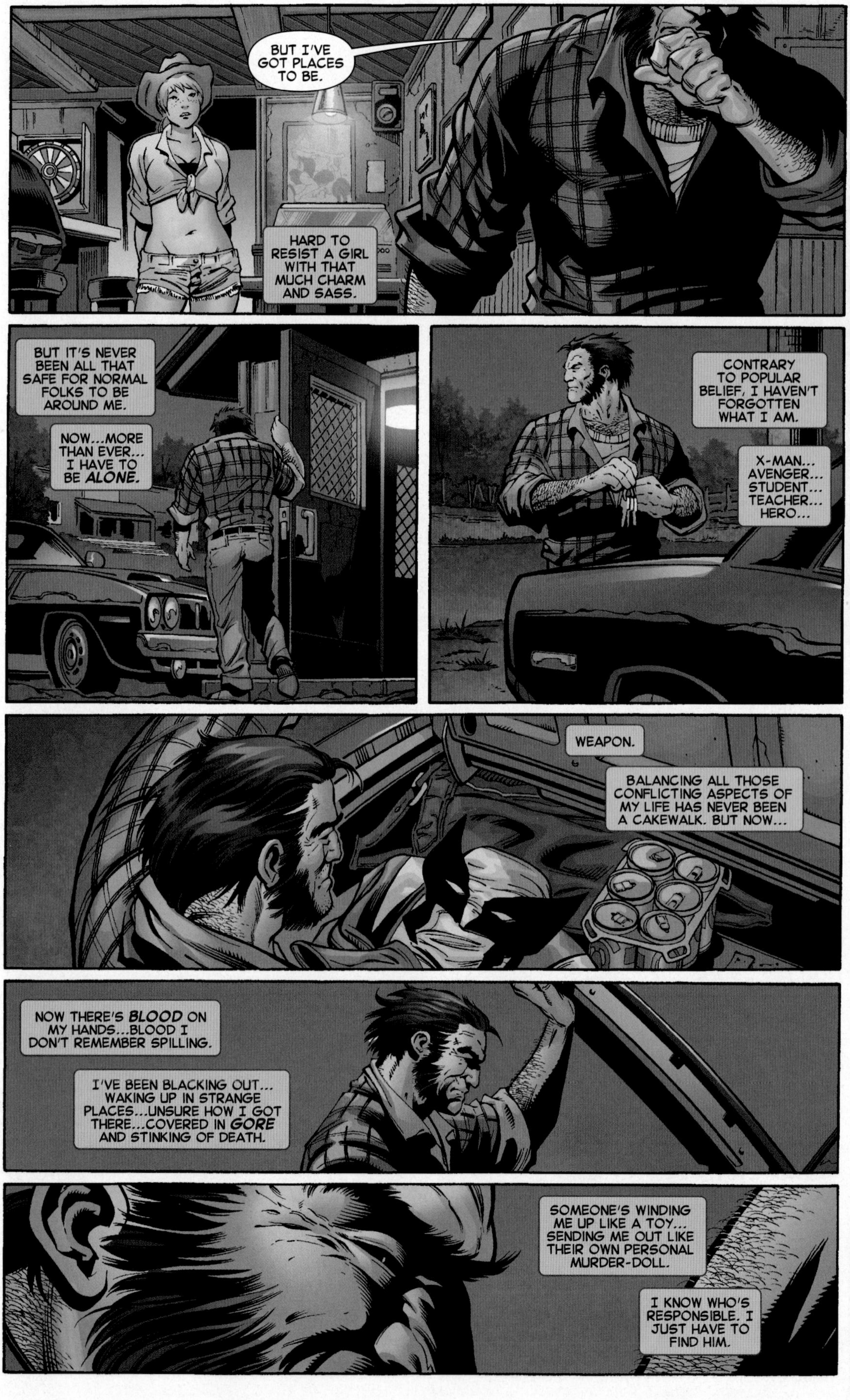
BUT I'VE GOT PLACES TO BE.
HARD TO RESIST A GIRL WITH THAT MUCH CHARM AND SASS.
BUT IT'S NEVER BEEN ALL THAT SAFE FOR NORMAL FOLKS TO BE AROUND ME.
NOW...MORE THAN EVER... I HAVE TO BE ALONE.
CONTRARY TO POPULAR BELIEF, I HAVEN'T FORGOTTEN WHAT I AM.
X-MAN... AVENGER... STUDENT... TEACHER... HERO...
WEAPON.
BALANCING ALL THOSE CONFLICTING ASPECTS OF MY LIFE HAS NEVER BEEN A CAKEWALK. BUT NOW...
NOW THERE'S BLOOD ON MY HANDS...BLOOD I DON'T REMEMBER SPILLING.
I'VE BEEN BLACKING OUT... WAKING UP IN STRANGE PLACES...UNSURE HOW I GOT THERE...COVERED IN GORE AND STINKING OF DEATH.
SOMEONE'S WINDING ME UP LIKE A TOY... SENDING ME OUT LIKE THEIR OWN PERSONAL MURDER-DOLL.
I KNOW WHO'S RESPONSIBLE. I JUST HAVE TO FIND HIM.

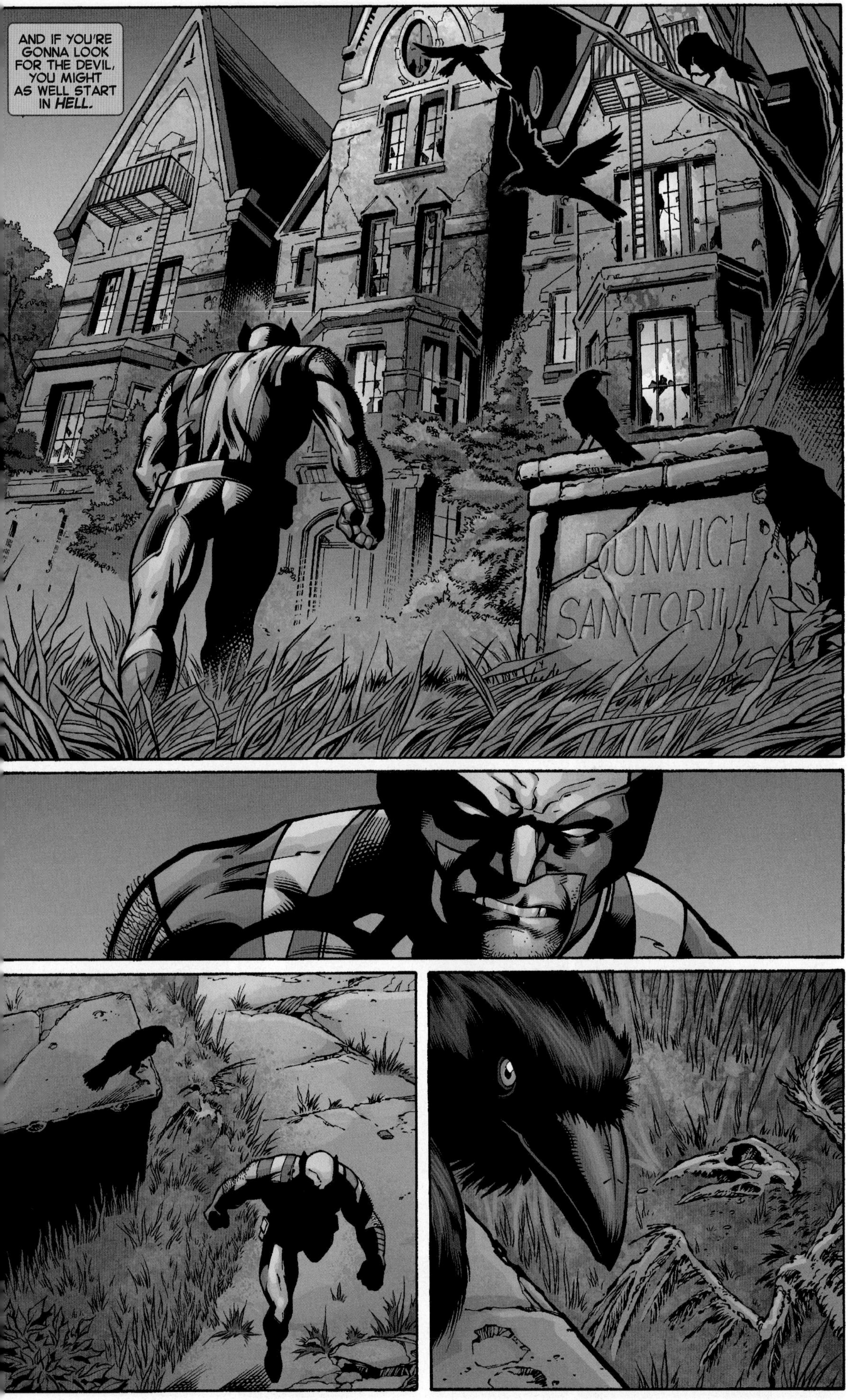
AND IF YOU'RE GONNA LOOK FOR THE DEVIL, YOU MIGHT AS WELL START IN HELL.
DUNWICH SANITORIUM

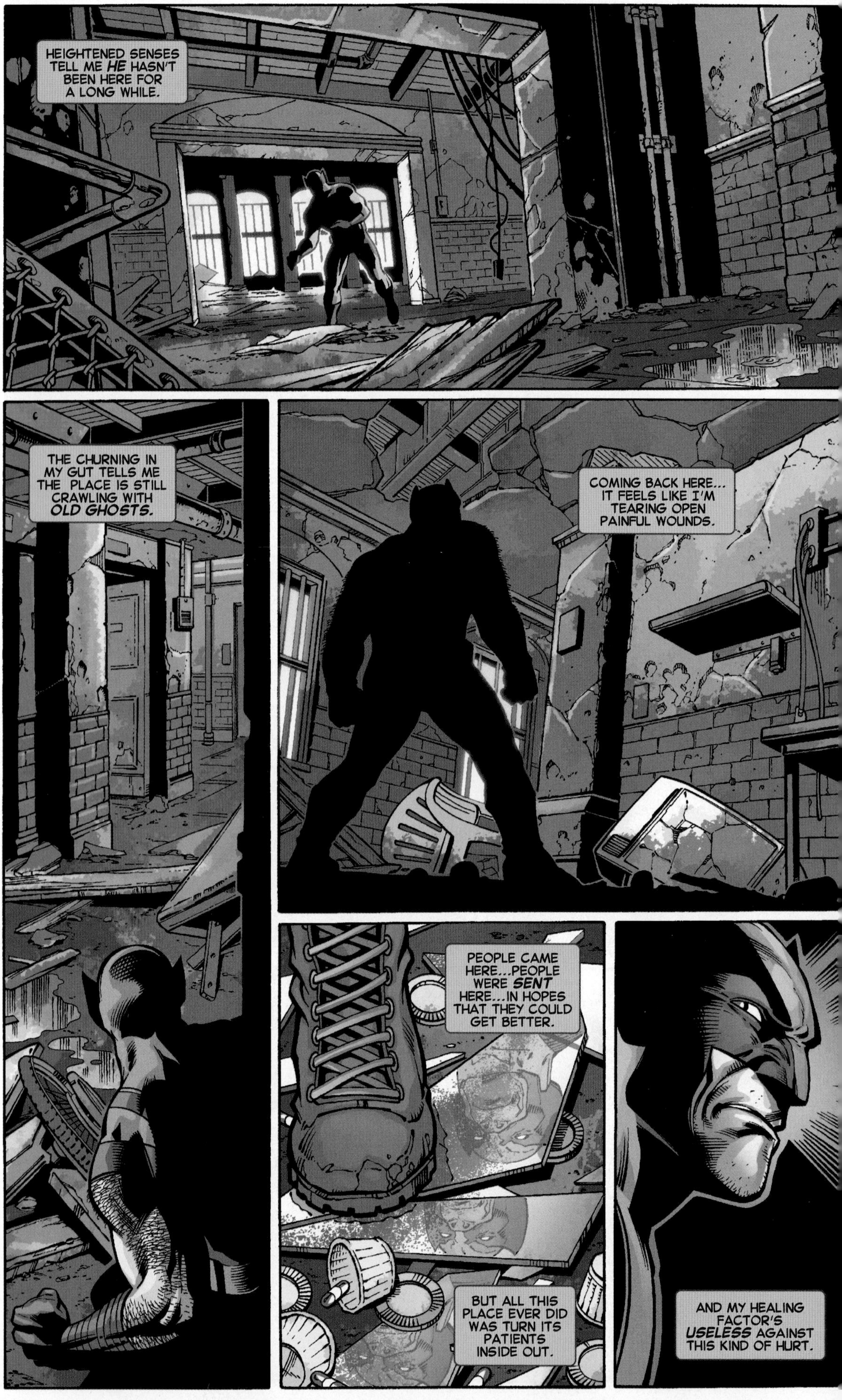
HEIGHTENED SENSES TELL ME HE HASN'T BEEN HERE FOR A LONG WHILE.
THE CHURNING IN MY GUT TELLS ME THE PLACE IS STILL CRAWLING WITH OLD GHOSTS.
COMING BACK HERE... IT FEELS LIKE I'M TEARING OPEN PAINFUL WOUNDS.
PEOPLE CAME HERE...PEOPLE WERE SENT HERE...IN HOPES THAT THEY COULD GET BETTER.
BUT ALL THIS PLACE EVER DID WAS TURN ITS PATIENTS INSIDE OUT.
AND MY HEALING FACTOR'S USELESS AGAINST THIS KIND OF HURT.

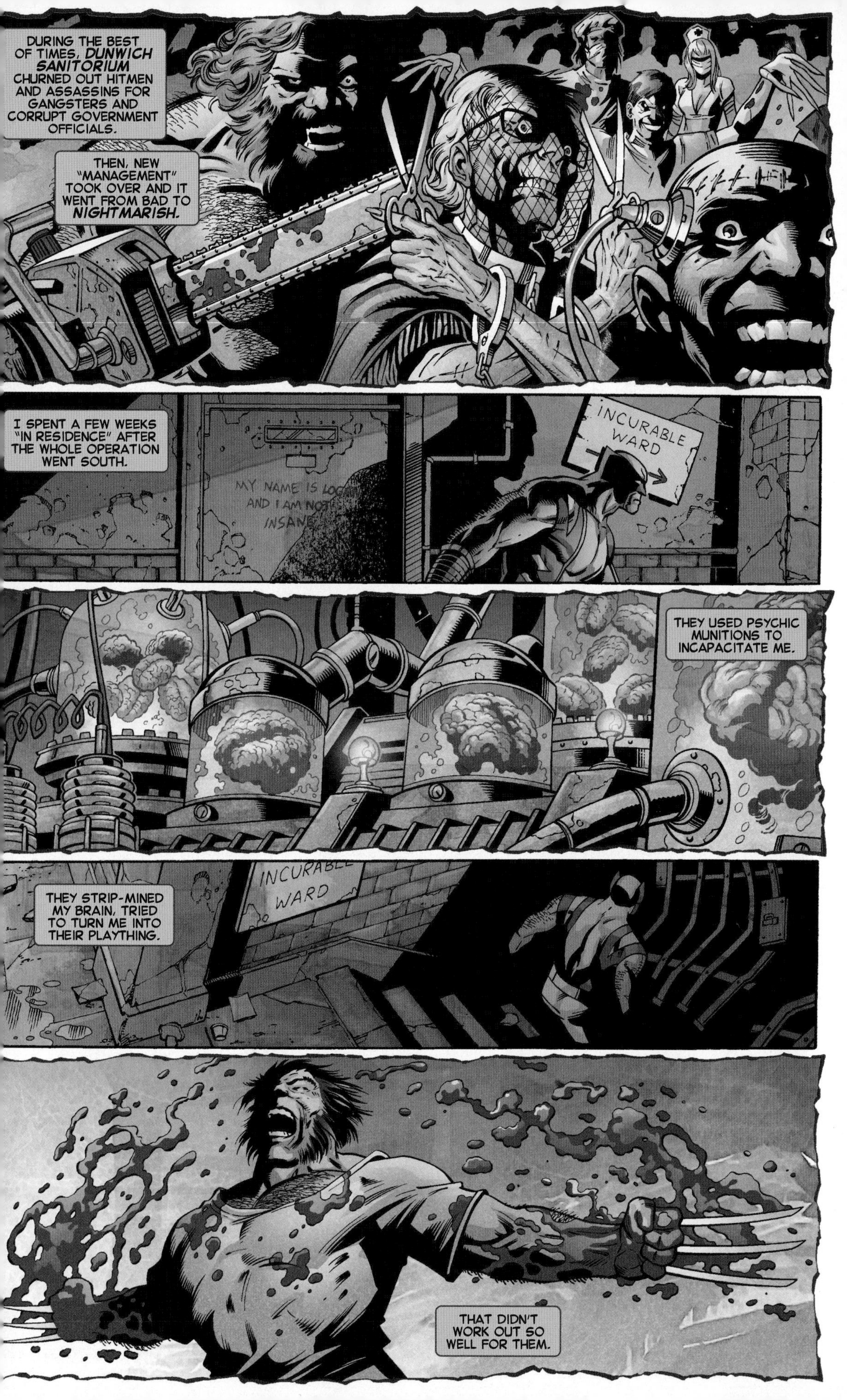

DURING THE BEST OF TIMES, DUNWICH SANITORIUM CHURNED OUT HITMEN AND ASSASSINS FOR GANGSTERS AND CORRUPT GOVERNMENT OFFICIALS.
THEN, NEW "MANAGEMENT" TOOK OVER AND IT WENT FROM BAD TO NIGHTMARISH.
I SPENT A FEW WEEKS "IN RESIDENCE" AFTER THE WHOLE OPERATION WENT SOUTH.
MY NAME IS LOGAN AND I AM NOT INSANE
INCURABLE WARD
THEY USED PSYCHIC MUNITIONS TO INCAPACITATE ME.
INCURABLE WARD
THEY STRIP-MINED MY BRAIN, TRIED TO TURN ME INTO THEIR PLAYTHING.
THAT DIDN'T WORK OUT SO WELL FOR THEM.

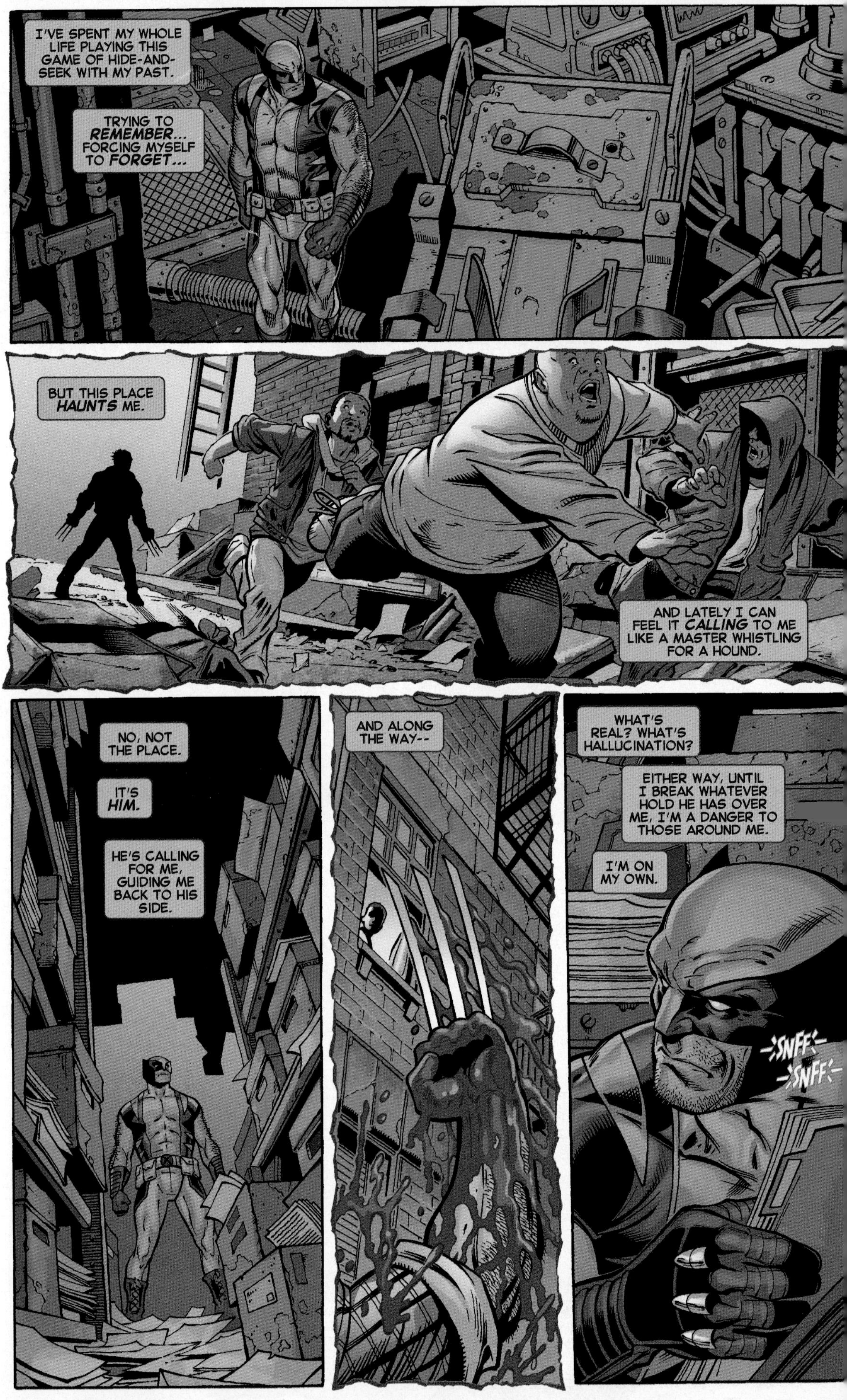
I'VE SPENT MY WHOLE LIFE PLAYING THIS GAME OF HIDE-AND-SEEK WITH MY PAST.
TRYING TO *REMEMBER*... FORCING MYSELF TO *FORGET*...
BUT THIS PLACE *HAUNTS* ME.
AND LATELY I CAN FEEL IT *CALLING* TO ME LIKE A MASTER WHISTLING FOR A HOUND.
NO, NOT THE PLACE.
IT'S *HIM.*
HE'S CALLING FOR ME, GUIDING ME BACK TO HIS SIDE.
AND ALONG THE WAY--
WHAT'S REAL? WHAT'S HALLUCINATION?
EITHER WAY, UNTIL I BREAK WHATEVER HOLD HE HAS OVER ME, I'M A DANGER TO THOSE AROUND ME.
I'M ON MY OWN.
SNFF
SNFF

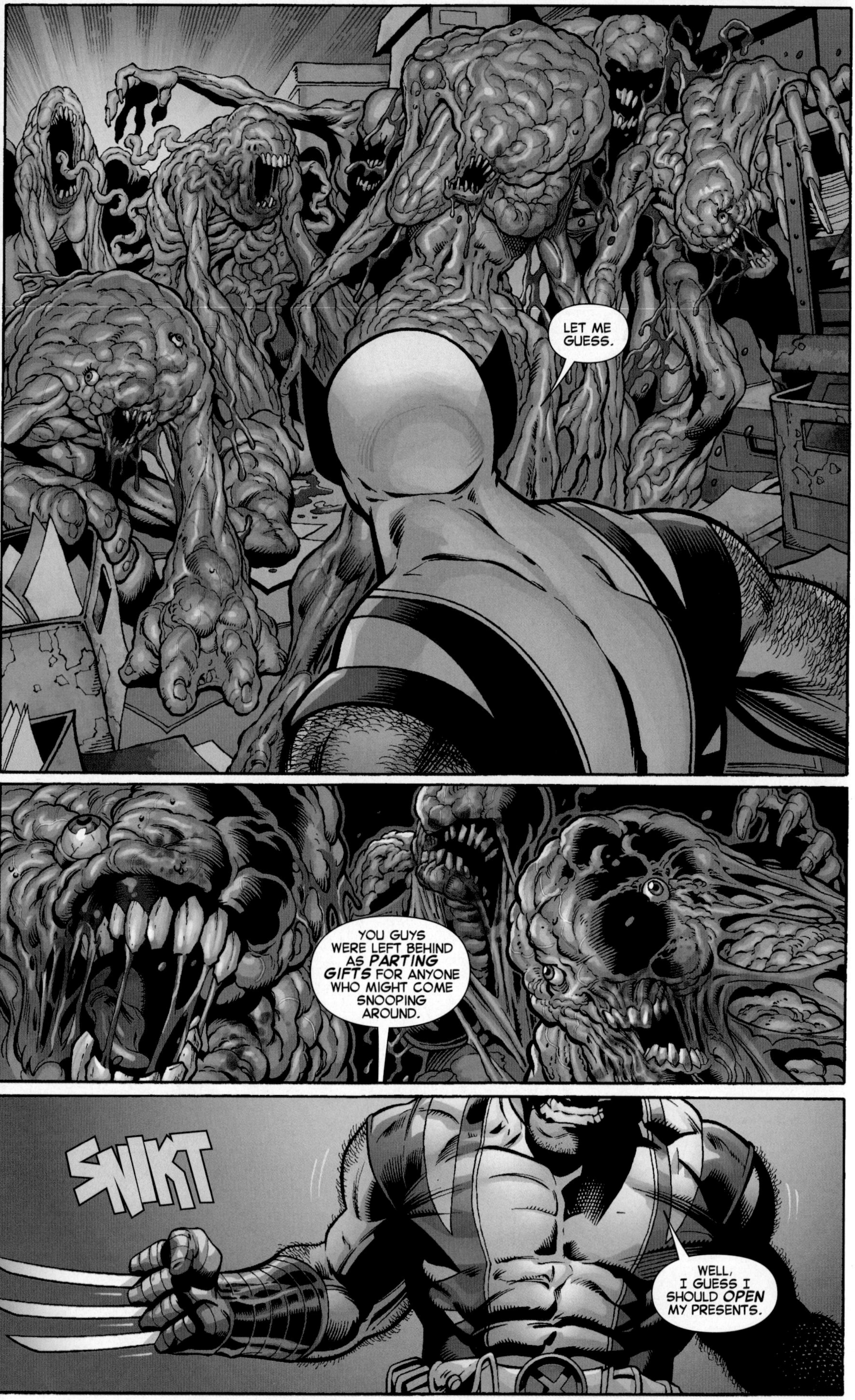
LET ME GUESS.
YOU GUYS WERE LEFT BEHIND AS PARTING GIFTS FOR ANYONE WHO MIGHT COME SNOOPING AROUND.
SNIKT
WELL, I GUESS I SHOULD OPEN MY PRESENTS.

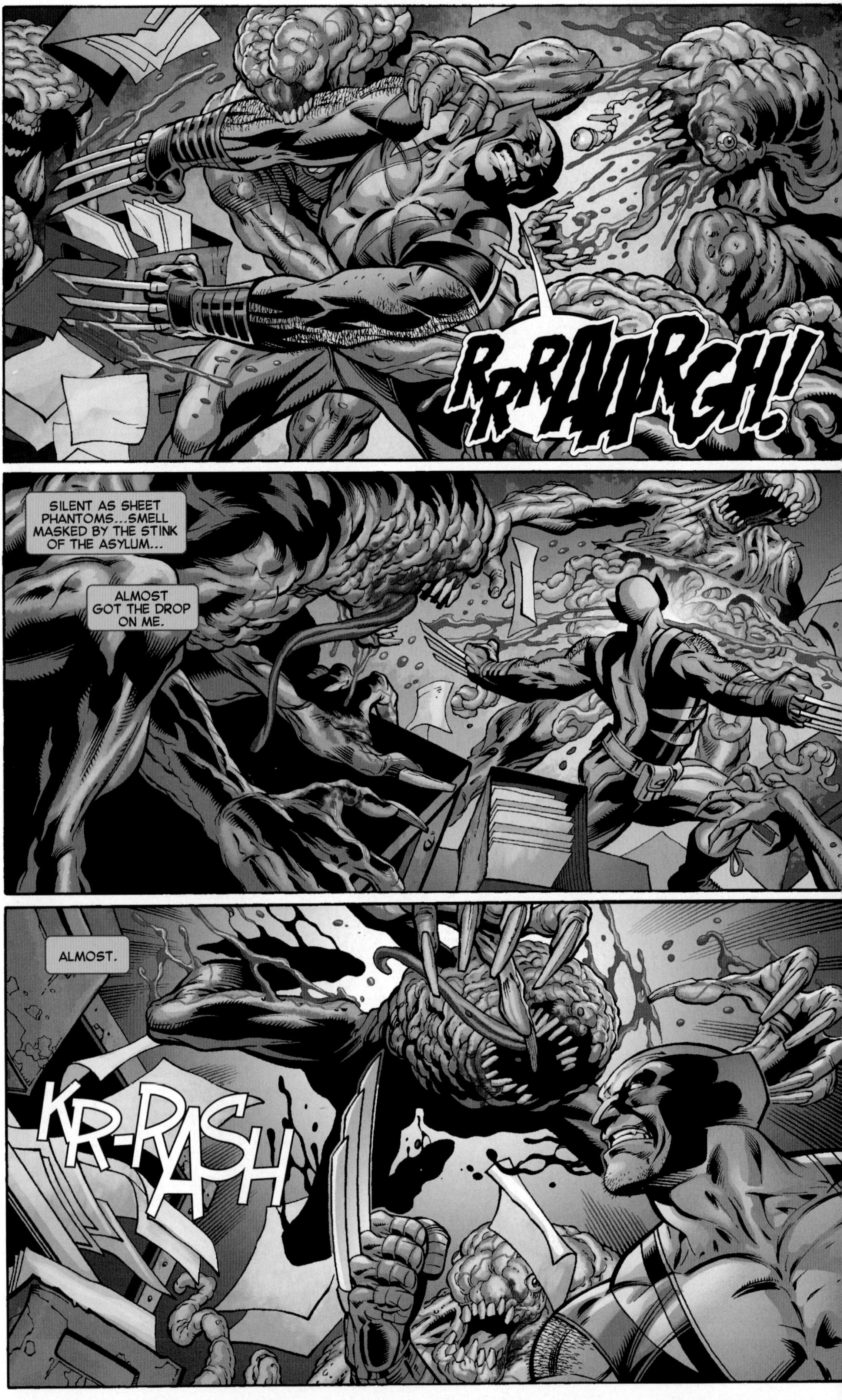
RRRAAARGH!
SILENT AS SHEET PHANTOMS...SMELL MASKED BY THE STINK OF THE ASYLUM...
ALMOST GOT THE DROP ON ME.
ALMOST.
KR-RASH

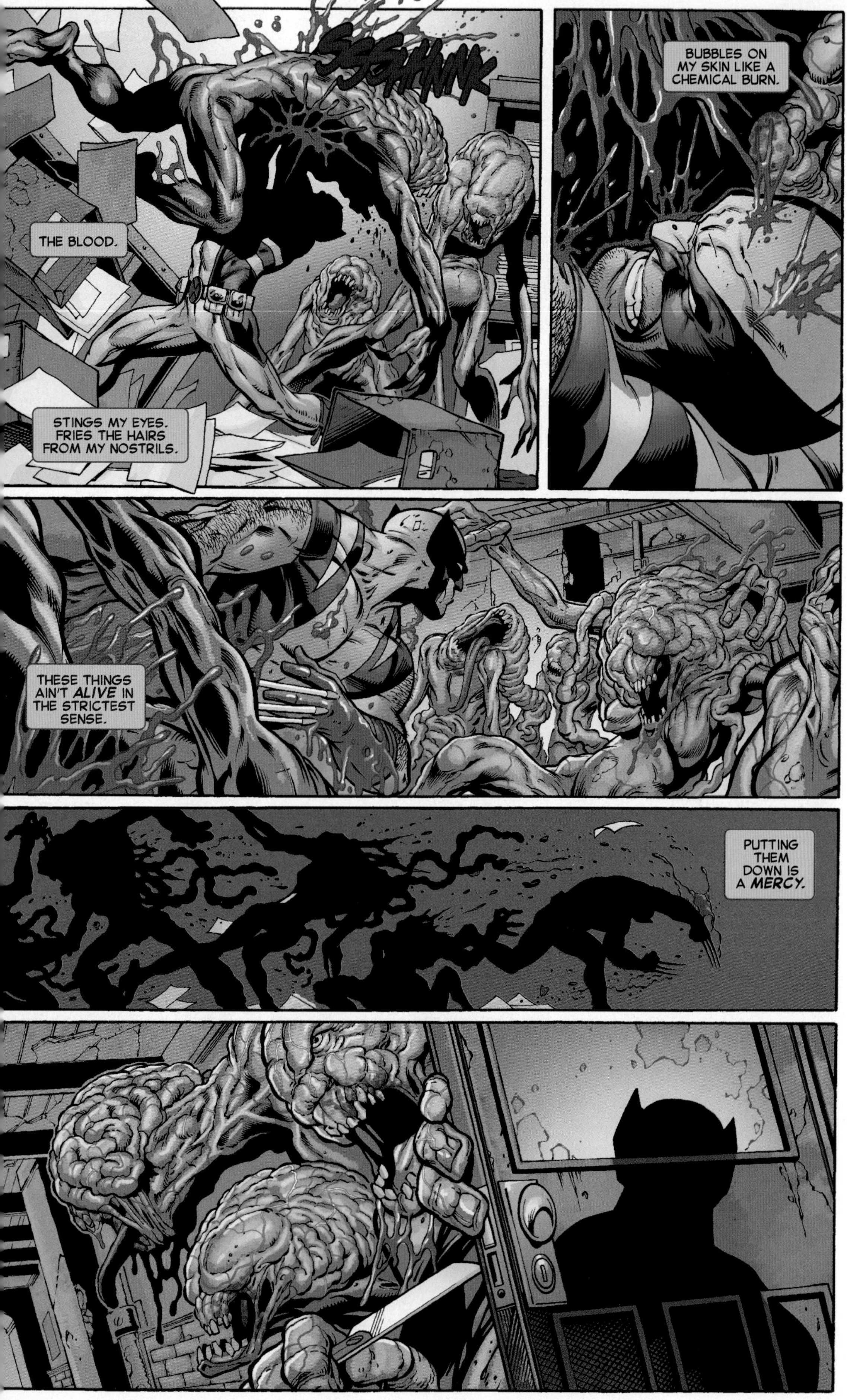
SSSHHNNK
THE BLOOD.
STINGS MY EYES. FRIES THE HAIRS FROM MY NOSTRILS.
BUBBLES ON MY SKIN LIKE A CHEMICAL BURN.
THESE THINGS AIN'T ALIVE IN THE STRICTEST SENSE.
PUTTING THEM DOWN IS A MERCY.

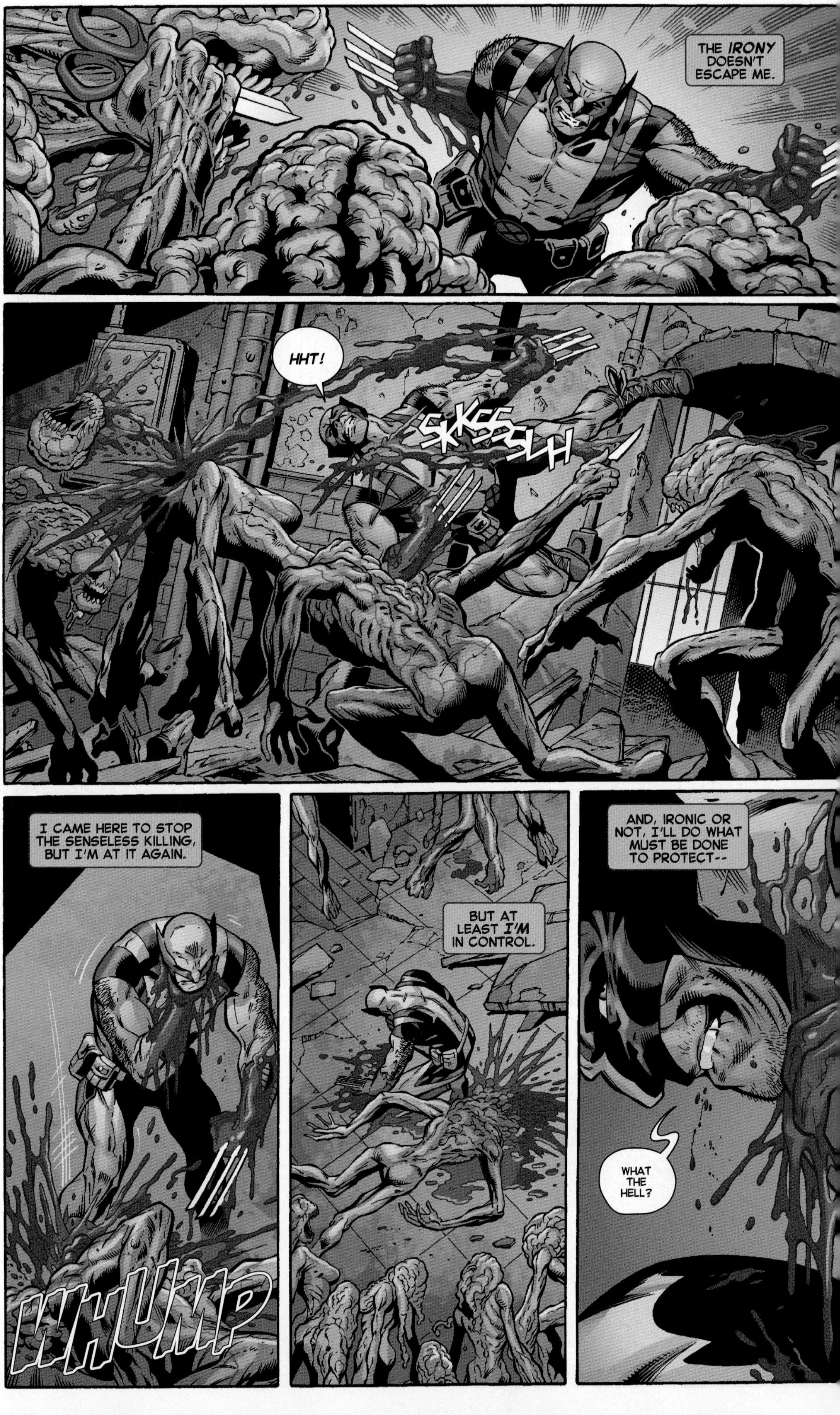
THE IRONY DOESN'T ESCAPE ME.
HHT!
SKKSSSLH
I CAME HERE TO STOP THE SENSELESS KILLING, BUT I'M AT IT AGAIN.
WHUMP
BUT AT LEAST I'M IN CONTROL.
AND, IRONIC OR NOT, I'LL DO WHAT MUST BE DONE TO PROTECT--
WHAT THE HELL?

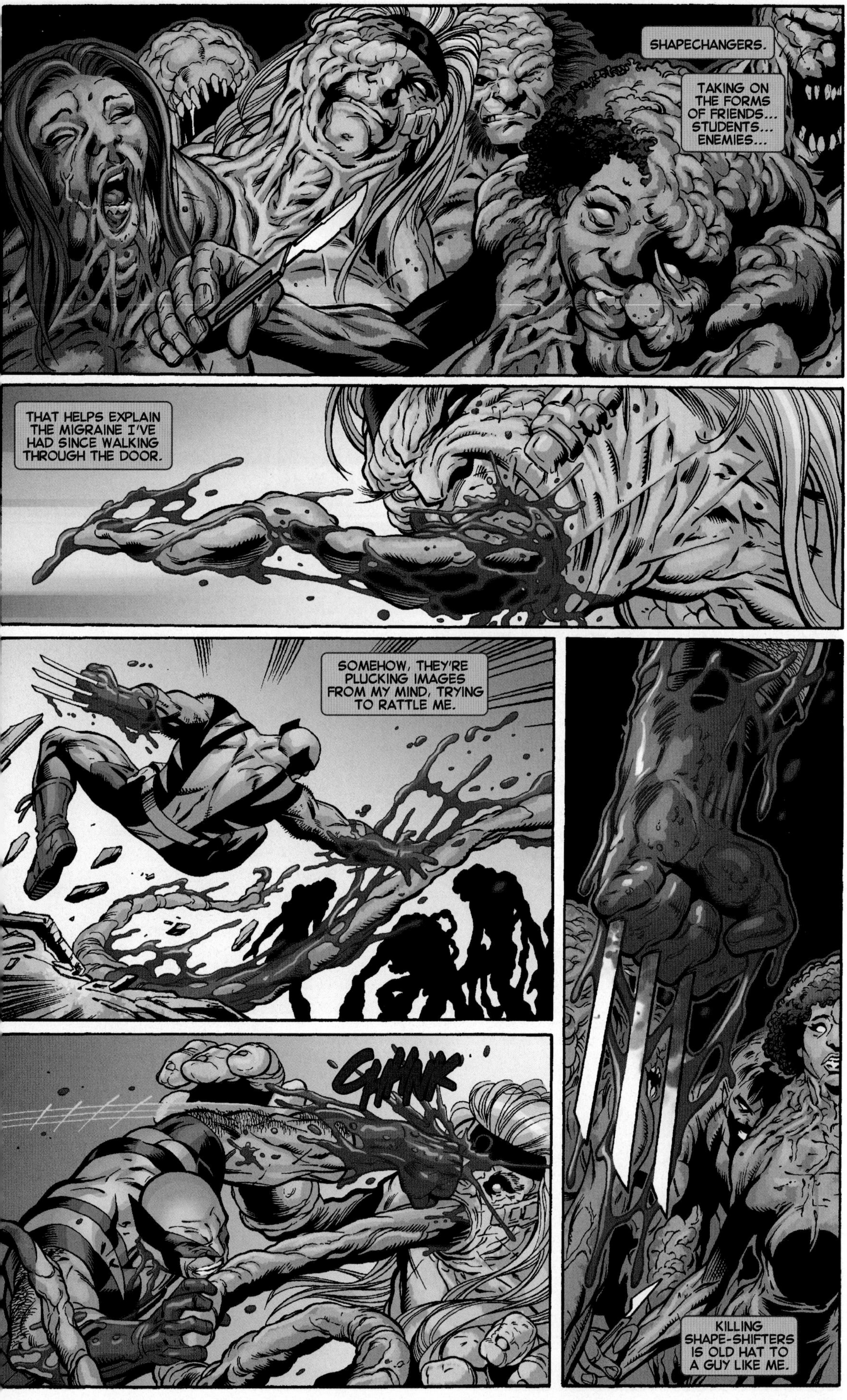
SHAPECHANGERS.
TAKING ON THE FORMS OF FRIENDS... STUDENTS... ENEMIES...
THAT HELPS EXPLAIN THE MIGRAINE I'VE HAD SINCE WALKING THROUGH THE DOOR.
SOMEHOW, THEY'RE PLUCKING IMAGES FROM MY MIND, TRYING TO RATTLE ME.
CHUNK
KILLING SHAPE-SHIFTERS IS OLD HAT TO A GUY LIKE ME.

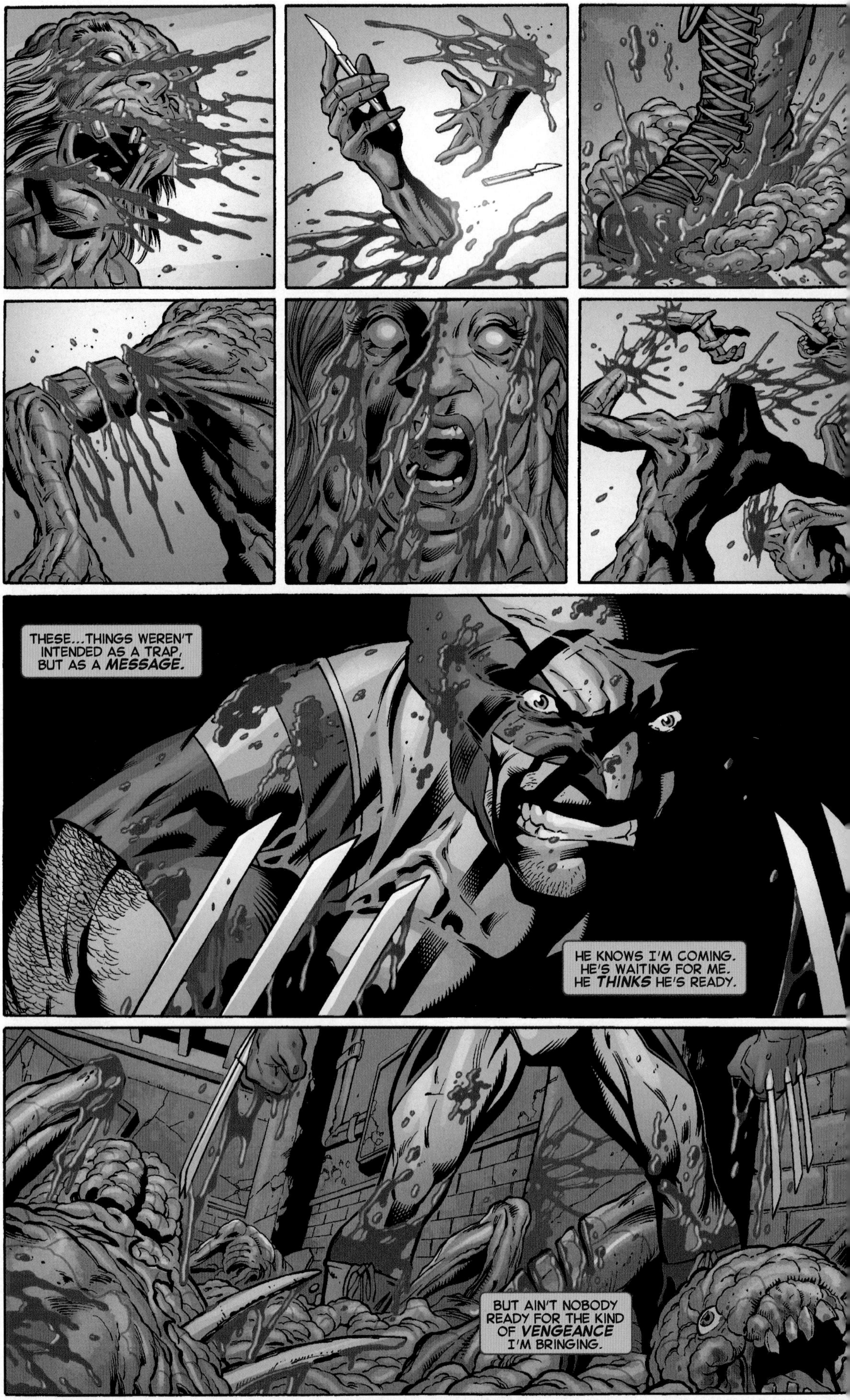
THESE...THINGS WEREN'T INTENDED AS A TRAP, BUT AS A MESSAGE.
HE KNOWS I'M COMING. HE'S WAITING FOR ME. HE THINKS HE'S READY.
BUT AIN'T NOBODY READY FOR THE KIND OF VENGEANCE I'M BRINGING.

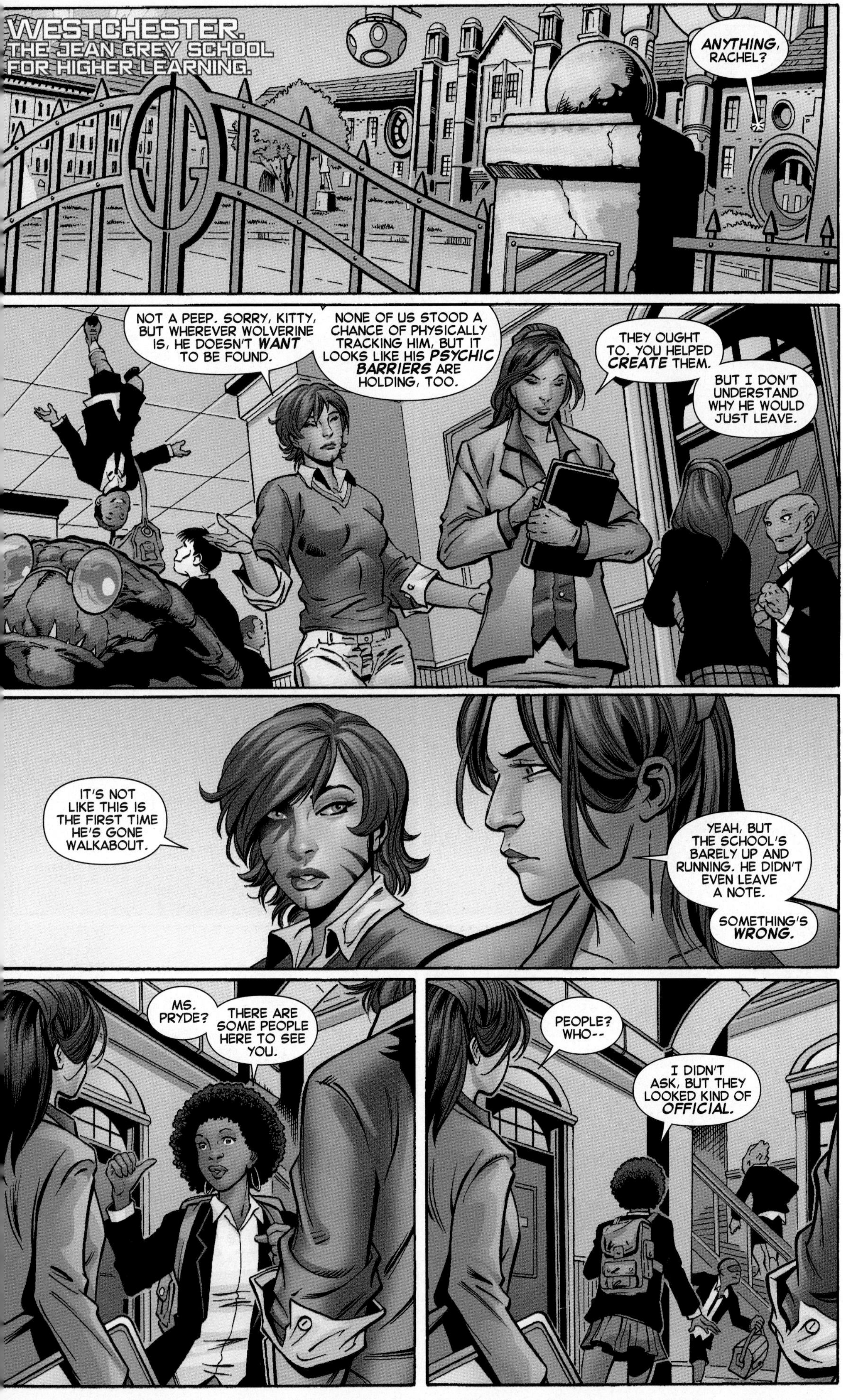
WESTCHESTER.
THE JEAN GREY SCHOOL FOR HIGHER LEARNING.
ANYTHING, RACHEL?
NOT A PEEP. SORRY, KITTY, BUT WHEREVER WOLVERINE IS, HE DOESN'T WANT TO BE FOUND.
NONE OF US STOOD A CHANCE OF PHYSICALLY TRACKING HIM, BUT IT LOOKS LIKE HIS PSYCHIC BARRIERS ARE HOLDING, TOO.
THEY OUGHT TO. YOU HELPED CREATE THEM.
BUT I DON'T UNDERSTAND WHY HE WOULD JUST LEAVE.
IT'S NOT LIKE THIS IS THE FIRST TIME HE'S GONE WALKABOUT.
YEAH, BUT THE SCHOOL'S BARELY UP AND RUNNING. HE DIDN'T EVEN LEAVE A NOTE.
SOMETHING'S WRONG.
MS. PRYDE?
THERE ARE SOME PEOPLE HERE TO SEE YOU.
PEOPLE? WHO--
I DIDN'T ASK, BUT THEY LOOKED KIND OF OFFICIAL.

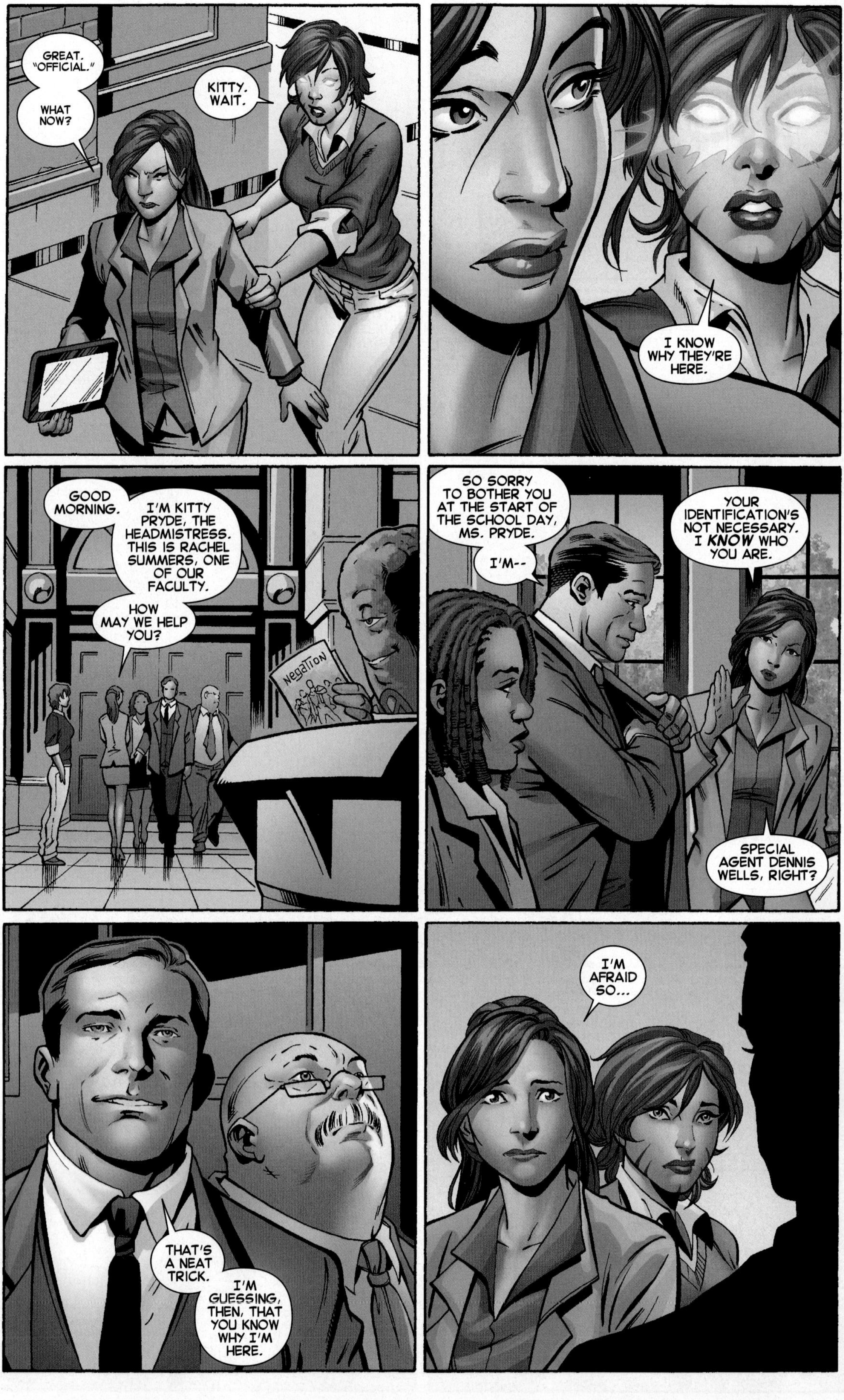
GREAT. "OFFICIAL."
WHAT NOW?
KITTY. WAIT.
I KNOW WHY THEY'RE HERE.
GOOD MORNING.
I'M KITTY PRYDE, THE HEADMISTRESS. THIS IS RACHEL SUMMERS, ONE OF OUR FACULTY.
HOW MAY WE HELP YOU?
NEGATION
SO SORRY TO BOTHER YOU AT THE START OF THE SCHOOL DAY, MS. PRYDE.
I'M--
YOUR IDENTIFICATION'S NOT NECESSARY. I KNOW WHO YOU ARE.
SPECIAL AGENT DENNIS WELLS, RIGHT?
THAT'S A NEAT TRICK.
I'M GUESSING, THEN, THAT YOU KNOW WHY I'M HERE.
I'M AFRAID SO...

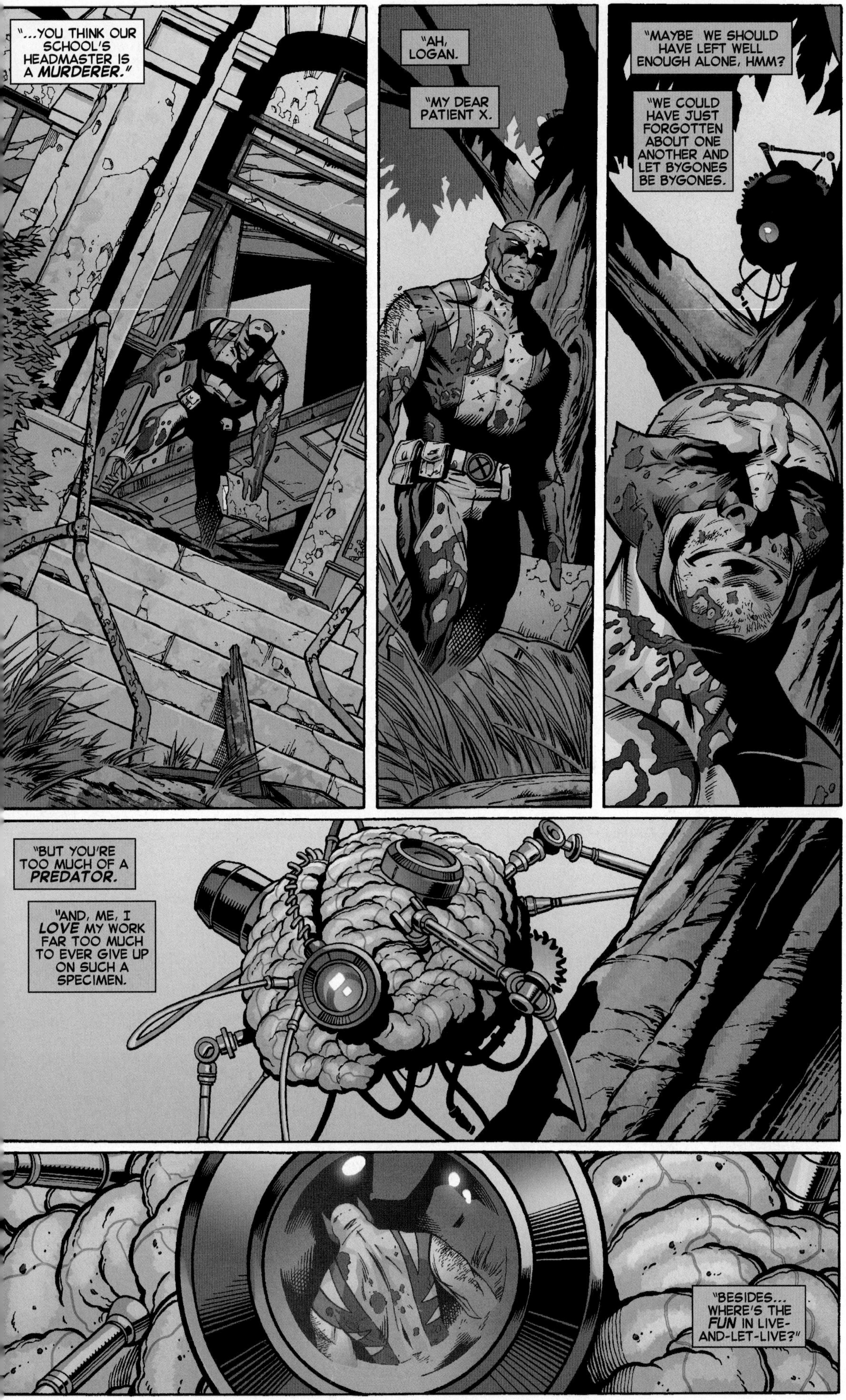
"...YOU THINK OUR SCHOOL'S HEADMASTER IS A *MURDERER.*"
"AH, LOGAN.
"MY DEAR PATIENT X.
"MAYBE WE SHOULD HAVE LEFT WELL ENOUGH ALONE, HMM?
"WE COULD HAVE JUST FORGOTTEN ABOUT ONE ANOTHER AND LET BYGONES BE BYGONES.
"BUT YOU'RE TOO MUCH OF A *PREDATOR.*
"AND, ME, I *LOVE* MY WORK FAR TOO MUCH TO EVER GIVE UP ON SUCH A SPECIMEN.
"BESIDES... WHERE'S THE *FUN* IN LIVE-AND-LET-LIVE?"

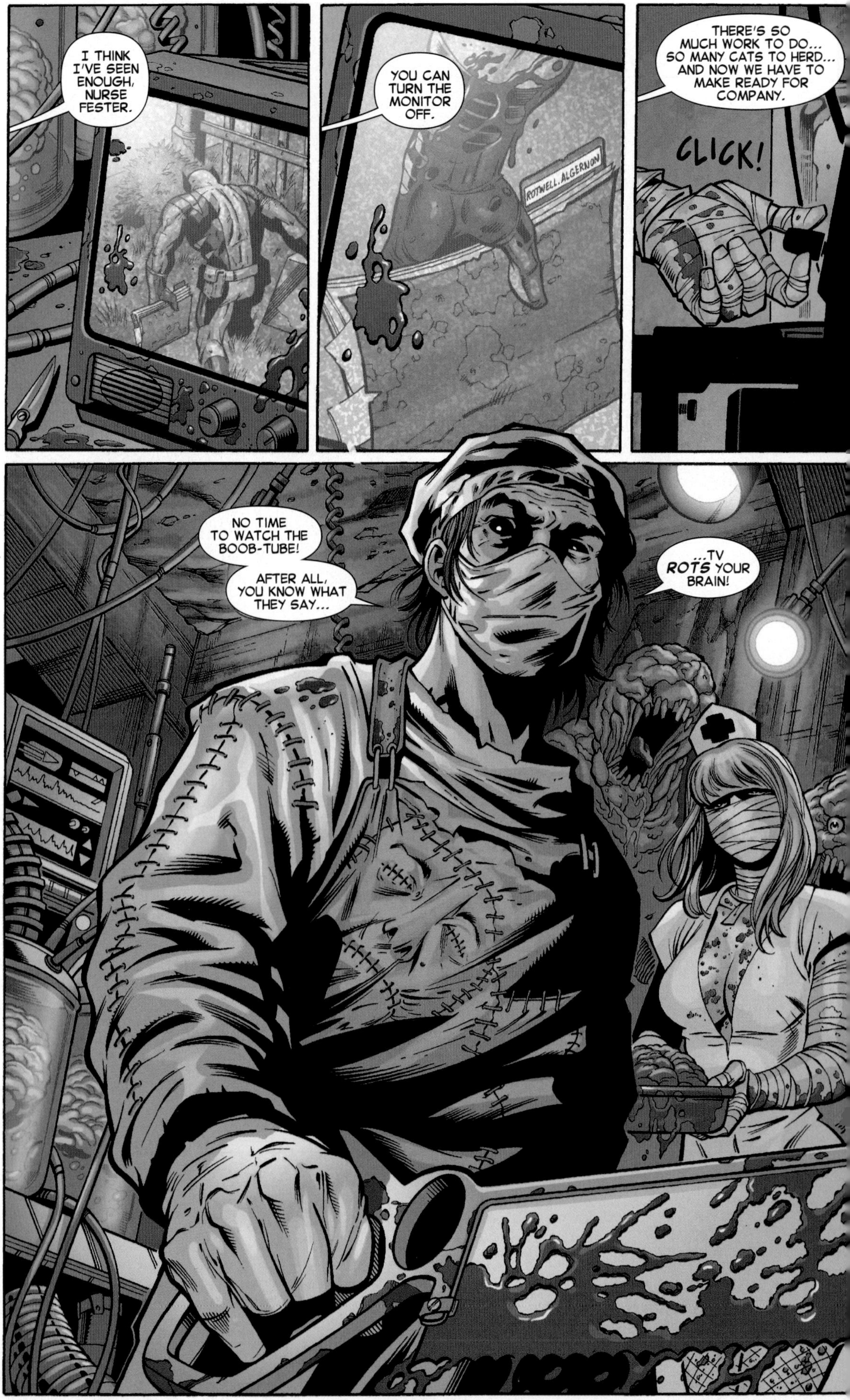
I THINK I'VE SEEN ENOUGH, NURSE FESTER.
YOU CAN TURN THE MONITOR OFF.
ROTWELL, ALGERNON
THERE'S SO MUCH WORK TO DO... SO MANY CATS TO HERD... AND NOW WE HAVE TO MAKE READY FOR COMPANY.
CLICK!
NO TIME TO WATCH THE BOOB-TUBE!
AFTER ALL, YOU KNOW WHAT THEY SAY...
...TV ROTS YOUR BRAIN!

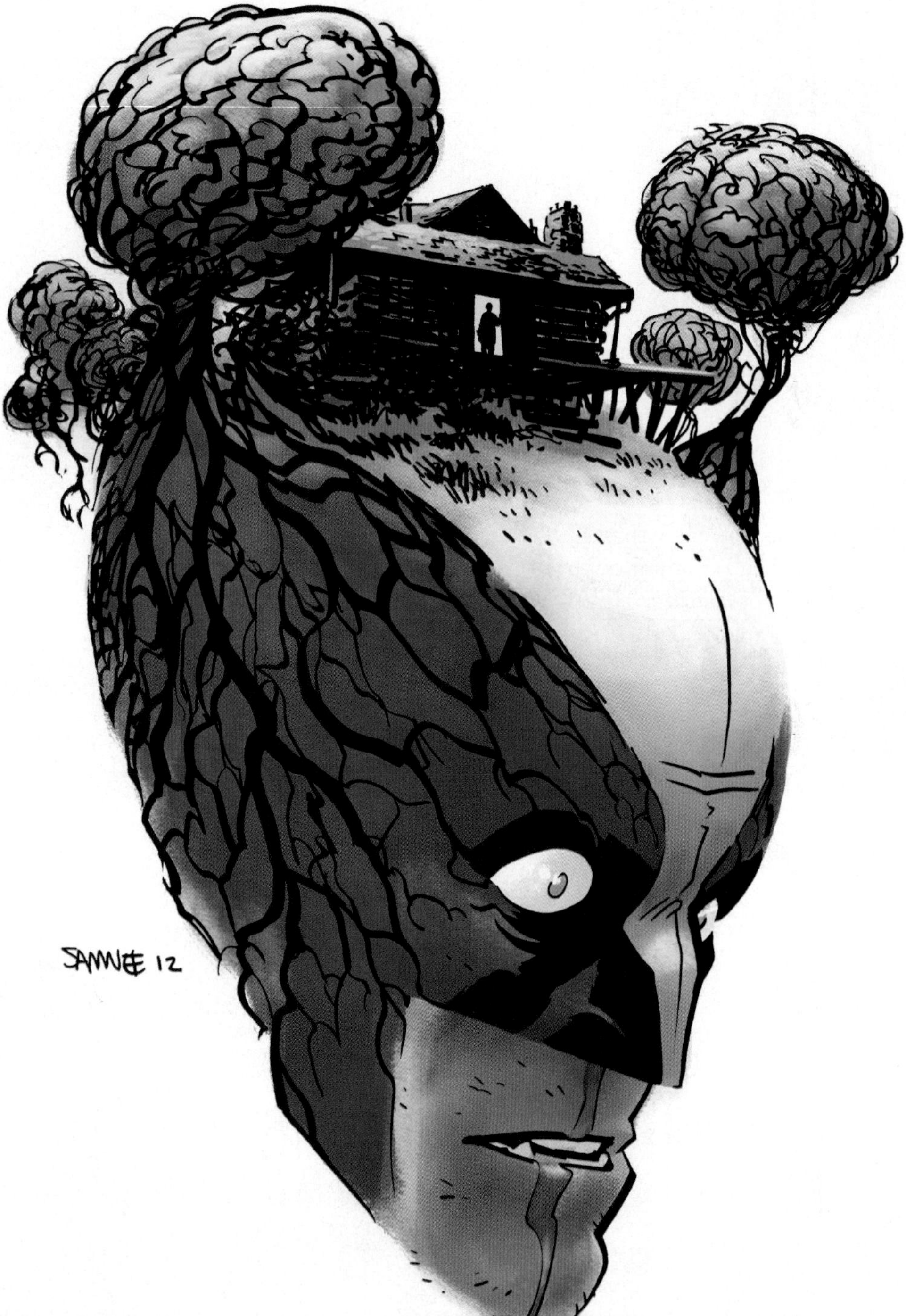
SAMNEE 12

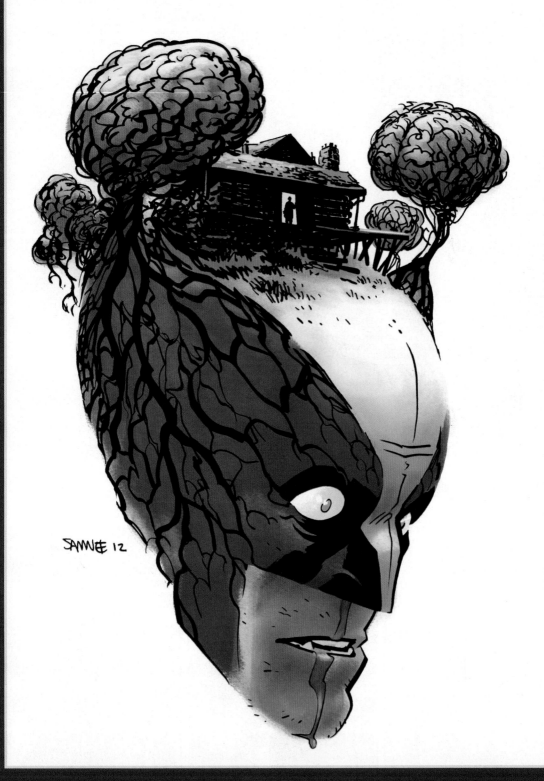

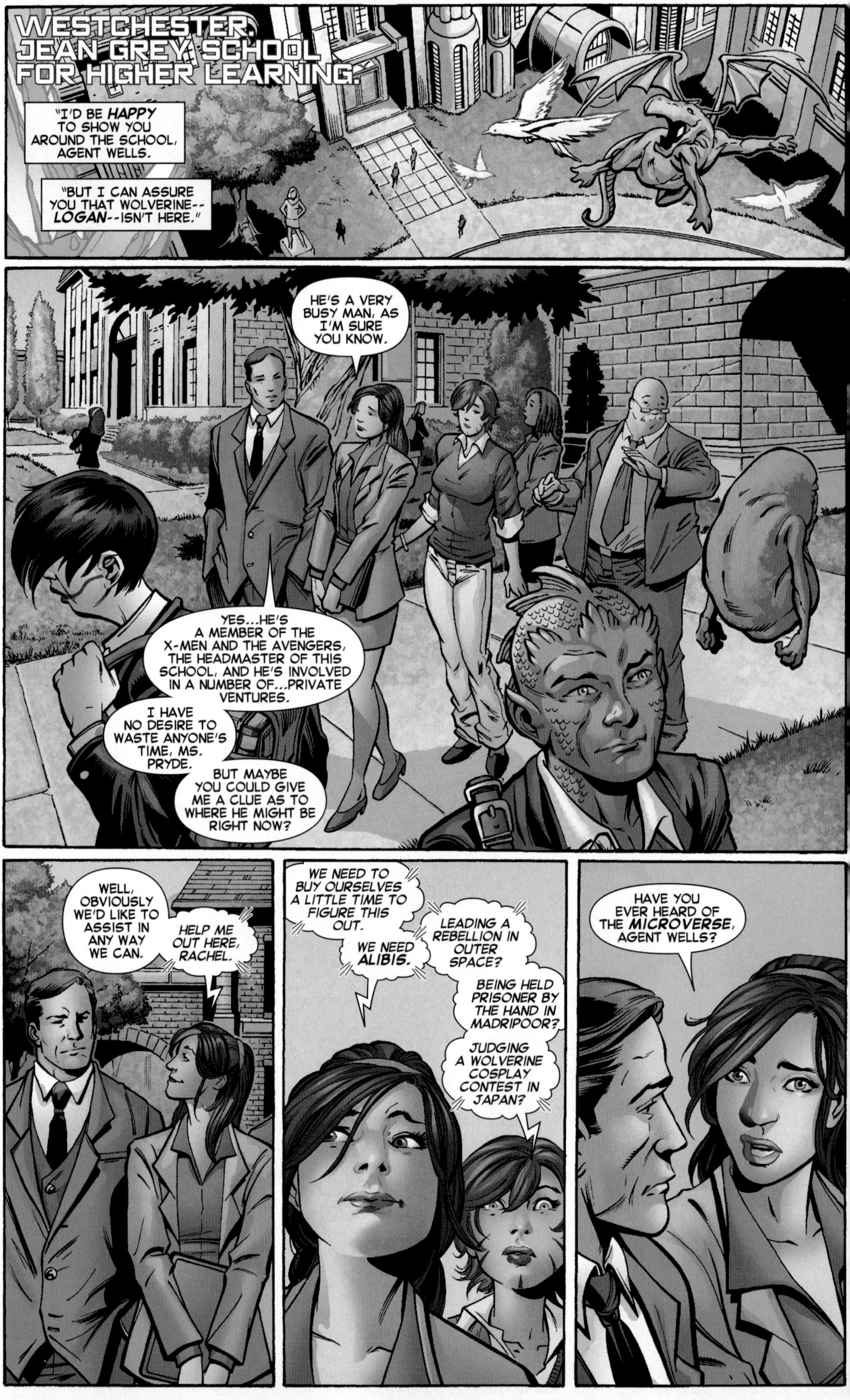
WESTCHESTER. JEAN GREY SCHOOL FOR HIGHER LEARNING.
"I'D BE HAPPY TO SHOW YOU AROUND THE SCHOOL, AGENT WELLS.
"BUT I CAN ASSURE YOU THAT WOLVERINE-- LOGAN--ISN'T HERE."
HE'S A VERY BUSY MAN, AS I'M SURE YOU KNOW.
YES...HE'S A MEMBER OF THE X-MEN AND THE AVENGERS, THE HEADMASTER OF THIS SCHOOL, AND HE'S INVOLVED IN A NUMBER OF...PRIVATE VENTURES.
I HAVE NO DESIRE TO WASTE ANYONE'S TIME, MS. PRYDE.
BUT MAYBE YOU COULD GIVE ME A CLUE AS TO WHERE HE MIGHT BE RIGHT NOW?
WELL, OBVIOUSLY WE'D LIKE TO ASSIST IN ANY WAY WE CAN.
HELP ME OUT HERE, RACHEL.
WE NEED TO BUY OURSELVES A LITTLE TIME TO FIGURE THIS OUT.
WE NEED ALIBIS.
LEADING A REBELLION IN OUTER SPACE?
BEING HELD PRISONER BY THE HAND IN MADRIPOOR?
JUDGING A WOLVERINE COSPLAY CONTEST IN JAPAN?
HAVE YOU EVER HEARD OF THE MICROVERSE, AGENT WELLS?

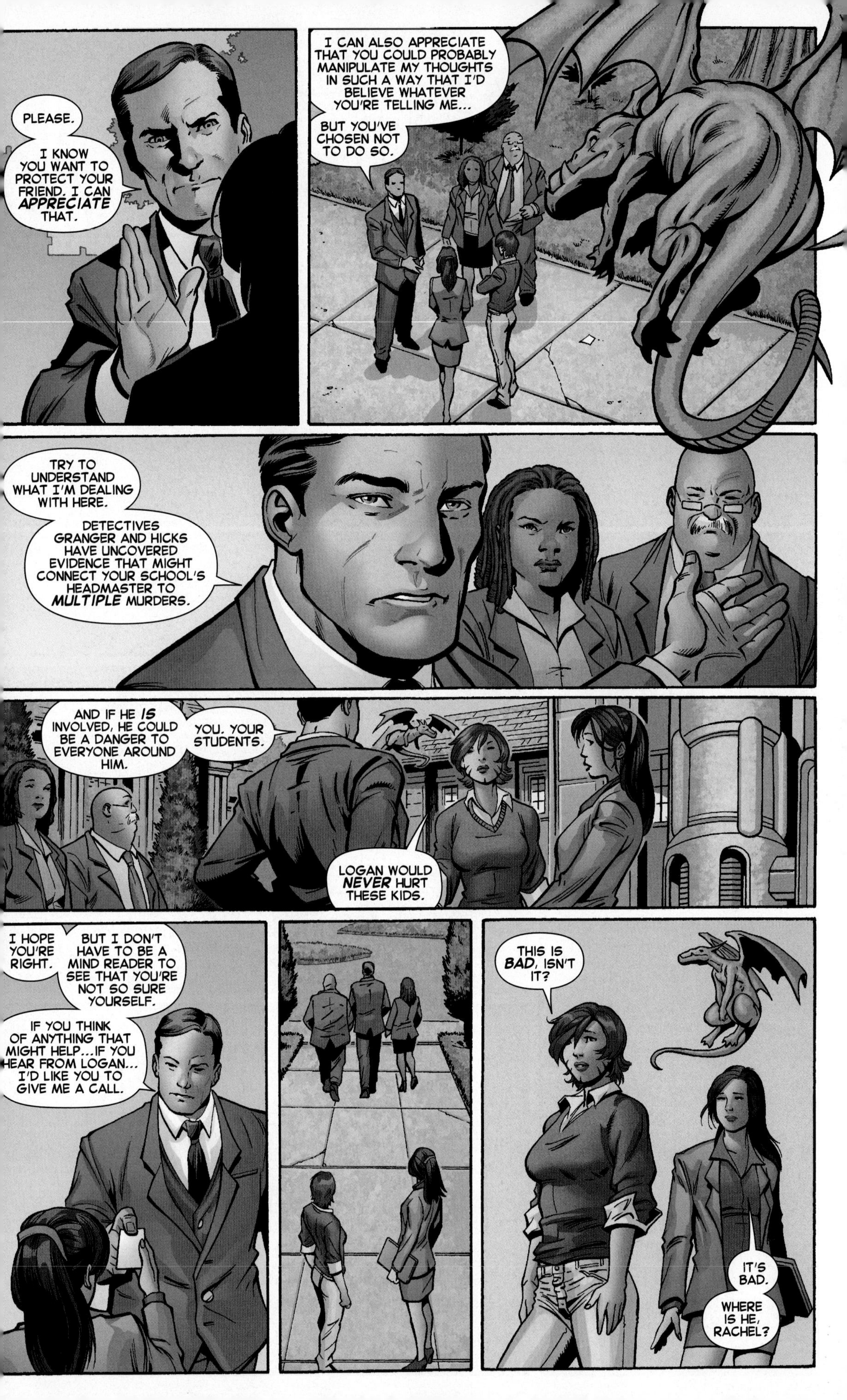
PLEASE.
I KNOW YOU WANT TO PROTECT YOUR FRIEND. I CAN *APPRECIATE* THAT.
I CAN ALSO APPRECIATE THAT YOU COULD PROBABLY MANIPULATE MY THOUGHTS IN SUCH A WAY THAT I'D BELIEVE WHATEVER YOU'RE TELLING ME...
BUT YOU'VE CHOSEN NOT TO DO SO.
TRY TO UNDERSTAND WHAT I'M DEALING WITH HERE.
DETECTIVES GRANGER AND HICKS HAVE UNCOVERED EVIDENCE THAT MIGHT CONNECT YOUR SCHOOL'S HEADMASTER TO *MULTIPLE* MURDERS.
AND IF HE *IS* INVOLVED, HE COULD BE A DANGER TO EVERYONE AROUND HIM.
YOU. YOUR STUDENTS.
LOGAN WOULD *NEVER* HURT THESE KIDS.
I HOPE YOU'RE RIGHT.
BUT I DON'T HAVE TO BE A MIND READER TO SEE THAT YOU'RE NOT SO SURE YOURSELF.
IF YOU THINK OF ANYTHING THAT MIGHT HELP...IF YOU HEAR FROM LOGAN... I'D LIKE YOU TO GIVE ME A CALL.
THIS IS *BAD*, ISN'T IT?
IT'S BAD.
WHERE IS HE, RACHEL?

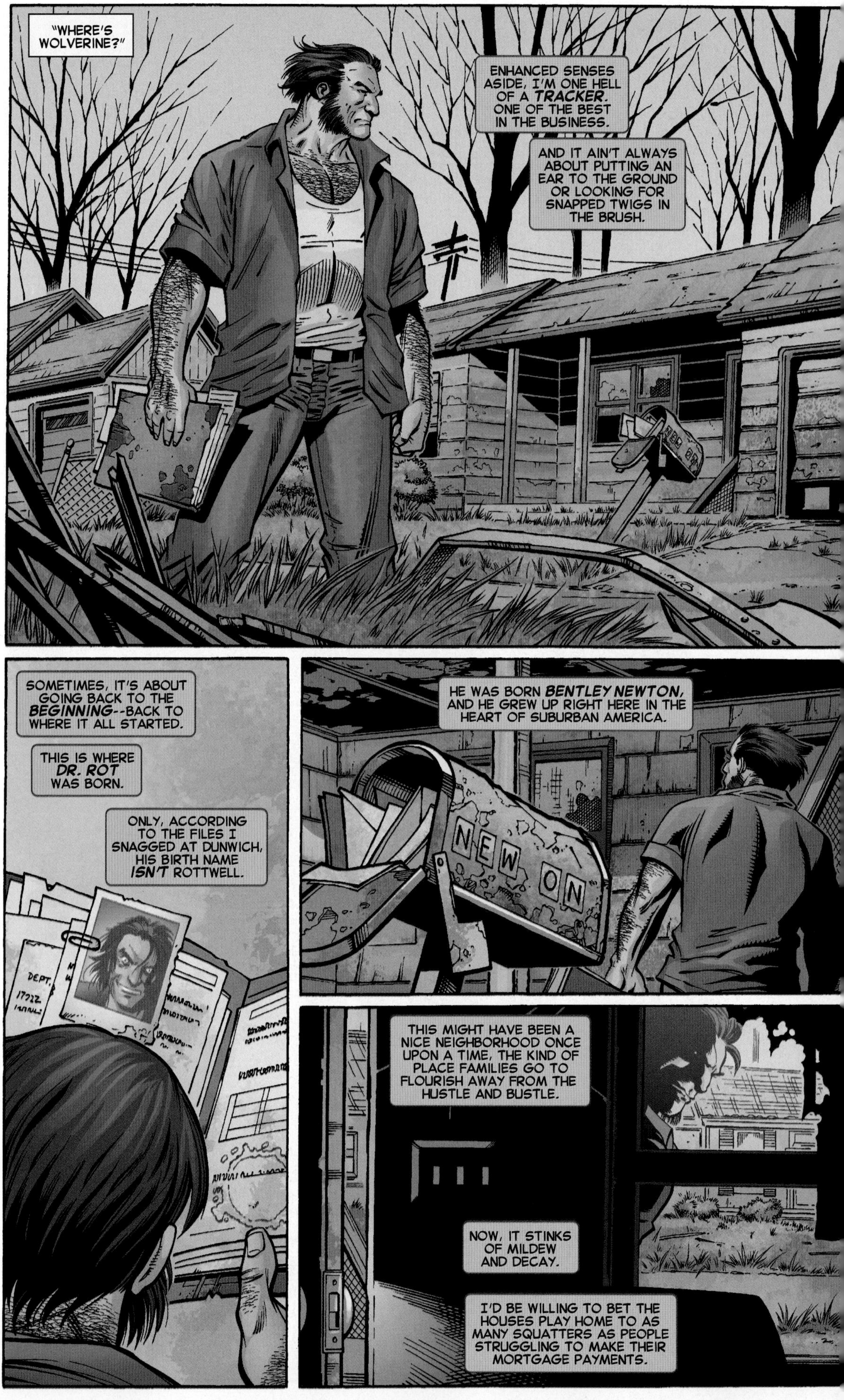
"WHERE'S WOLVERINE?"
ENHANCED SENSES ASIDE, I'M ONE HELL OF A TRACKER. ONE OF THE BEST IN THE BUSINESS.
AND IT AIN'T ALWAYS ABOUT PUTTING AN EAR TO THE GROUND OR LOOKING FOR SNAPPED TWIGS IN THE BRUSH.
SOMETIMES, IT'S ABOUT GOING BACK TO THE BEGINNING--BACK TO WHERE IT ALL STARTED.
THIS IS WHERE DR. ROT WAS BORN.
ONLY, ACCORDING TO THE FILES I SNAGGED AT DUNWICH, HIS BIRTH NAME ISN'T ROTTWELL.
HE WAS BORN BENTLEY NEWTON, AND HE GREW UP RIGHT HERE IN THE HEART OF SUBURBAN AMERICA.
NEW ON
THIS MIGHT HAVE BEEN A NICE NEIGHBORHOOD ONCE UPON A TIME, THE KIND OF PLACE FAMILIES GO TO FLOURISH AWAY FROM THE HUSTLE AND BUSTLE.
NOW, IT STINKS OF MILDEW AND DECAY.
I'D BE WILLING TO BET THE HOUSES PLAY HOME TO AS MANY SQUATTERS AS PEOPLE STRUGGLING TO MAKE THEIR MORTGAGE PAYMENTS.

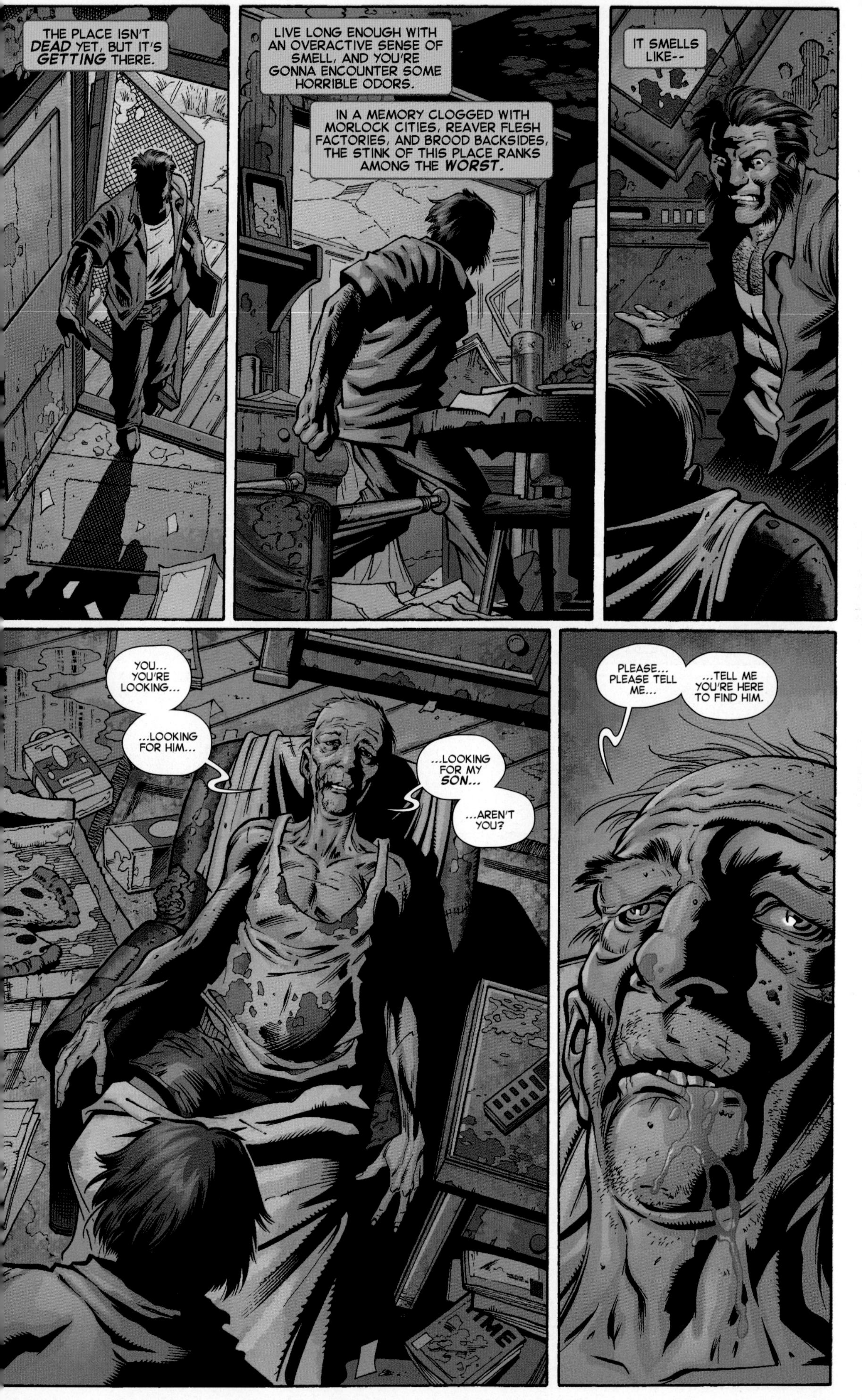
THE PLACE ISN'T DEAD YET, BUT IT'S GETTING THERE.
LIVE LONG ENOUGH WITH AN OVERACTIVE SENSE OF SMELL, AND YOU'RE GONNA ENCOUNTER SOME HORRIBLE ODORS.
IN A MEMORY CLOGGED WITH MORLOCK CITIES, REAVER FLESH FACTORIES, AND BROOD BACKSIDES, THE STINK OF THIS PLACE RANKS AMONG THE WORST.
IT SMELLS LIKE--
YOU... YOU'RE LOOKING...
...LOOKING FOR HIM...
...LOOKING FOR MY SON...
...AREN'T YOU?
PLEASE... PLEASE TELL ME...
...TELL ME YOU'RE HERE TO FIND HIM.

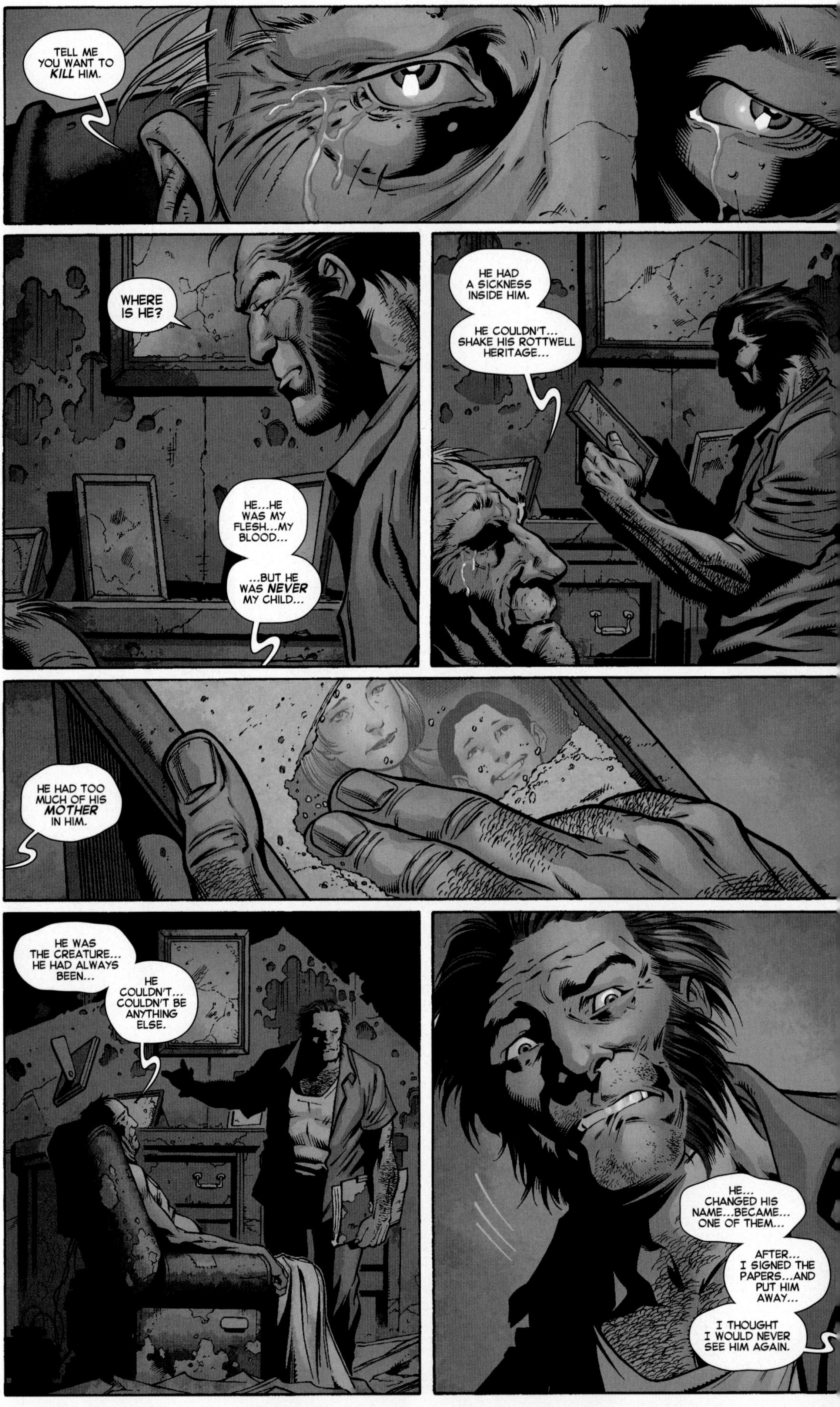
TELL ME YOU WANT TO KILL HIM.
WHERE IS HE?
HE...HE WAS MY FLESH...MY BLOOD...
...BUT HE WAS NEVER MY CHILD...
HE HAD A SICKNESS INSIDE HIM.
HE COULDN'T... SHAKE HIS ROTTWELL HERITAGE...
HE HAD TOO MUCH OF HIS MOTHER IN HIM.
HE WAS THE CREATURE... HE HAD ALWAYS BEEN...
HE COULDN'T... COULDN'T BE ANYTHING ELSE.
HE... CHANGED HIS NAME...BECAME... ONE OF THEM...
AFTER... I SIGNED THE PAPERS...AND PUT HIM AWAY...
I THOUGHT I WOULD NEVER SEE HIM AGAIN.

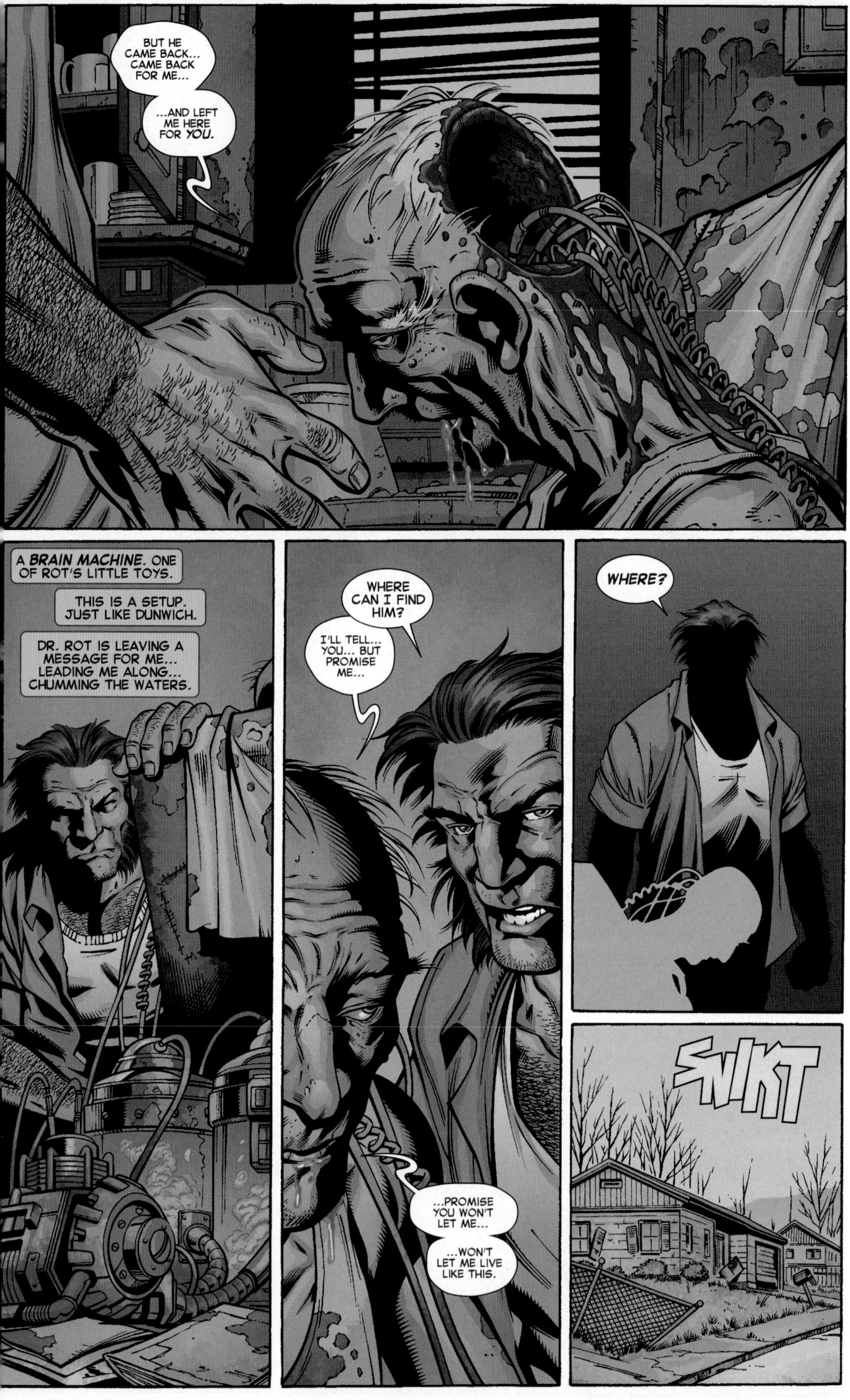

BUT HE CAME BACK... CAME BACK FOR ME...
...AND LEFT ME HERE FOR YOU.
A BRAIN MACHINE. ONE OF ROT'S LITTLE TOYS.
THIS IS A SETUP. JUST LIKE DUNWICH.
DR. ROT IS LEAVING A MESSAGE FOR ME... LEADING ME ALONG... CHUMMING THE WATERS.
WHERE CAN I FIND HIM?
I'LL TELL... YOU... BUT PROMISE ME...
...PROMISE YOU WON'T LET ME...
...WON'T LET ME LIVE LIKE THIS.
WHERE?
SNIKT

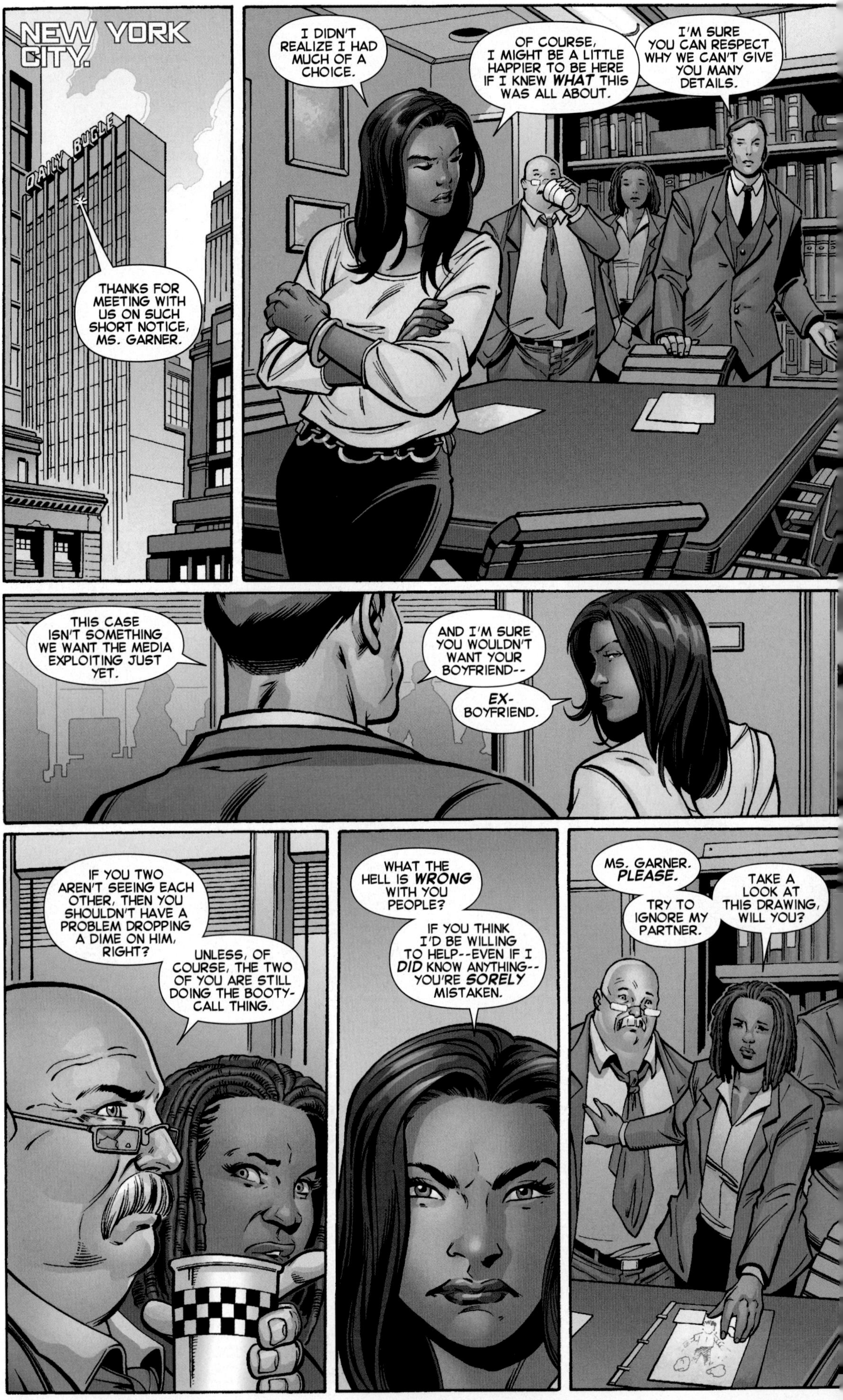
NEW YORK CITY.
DAILY BUGLE
THANKS FOR MEETING WITH US ON SUCH SHORT NOTICE, MS. GARNER.
I DIDN'T REALIZE I HAD MUCH OF A CHOICE.
OF COURSE, I MIGHT BE A LITTLE HAPPIER TO BE HERE IF I KNEW WHAT THIS WAS ALL ABOUT.
I'M SURE YOU CAN RESPECT WHY WE CAN'T GIVE YOU MANY DETAILS.
THIS CASE ISN'T SOMETHING WE WANT THE MEDIA EXPLOITING JUST YET.
AND I'M SURE YOU WOULDN'T WANT YOUR BOYFRIEND--
EX-BOYFRIEND.
IF YOU TWO AREN'T SEEING EACH OTHER, THEN YOU SHOULDN'T HAVE A PROBLEM DROPPING A DIME ON HIM, RIGHT?
UNLESS, OF COURSE, THE TWO OF YOU ARE STILL DOING THE BOOTY-CALL THING.
WHAT THE HELL IS WRONG WITH YOU PEOPLE?
IF YOU THINK I'D BE WILLING TO HELP--EVEN IF I DID KNOW ANYTHING--YOU'RE SORELY MISTAKEN.
MS. GARNER. PLEASE.
TRY TO IGNORE MY PARTNER.
TAKE A LOOK AT THIS DRAWING, WILL YOU?

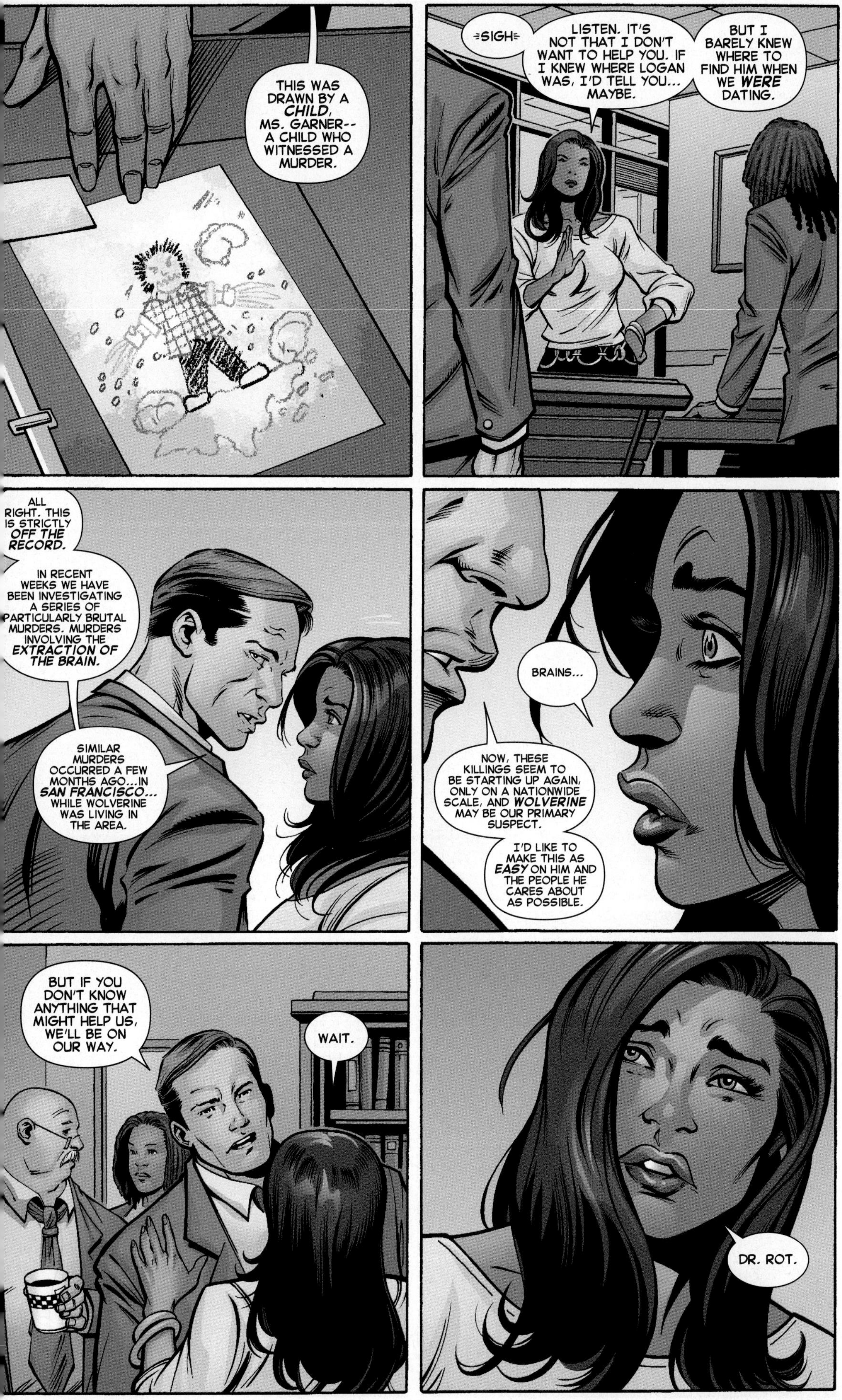

THIS WAS DRAWN BY A CHILD, MS. GARNER-- A CHILD WHO WITNESSED A MURDER.
SIGH
LISTEN. IT'S NOT THAT I DON'T WANT TO HELP YOU. IF I KNEW WHERE LOGAN WAS, I'D TELL YOU... MAYBE.
BUT I BARELY KNEW WHERE TO FIND HIM WHEN WE WERE DATING.
ALL RIGHT. THIS IS STRICTLY OFF THE RECORD.
IN RECENT WEEKS WE HAVE BEEN INVESTIGATING A SERIES OF PARTICULARLY BRUTAL MURDERS. MURDERS INVOLVING THE EXTRACTION OF THE BRAIN.
SIMILAR MURDERS OCCURRED A FEW MONTHS AGO...IN SAN FRANCISCO... WHILE WOLVERINE WAS LIVING IN THE AREA.
BRAINS...
NOW, THESE KILLINGS SEEM TO BE STARTING UP AGAIN, ONLY ON A NATIONWIDE SCALE, AND WOLVERINE MAY BE OUR PRIMARY SUSPECT.
I'D LIKE TO MAKE THIS AS EASY ON HIM AND THE PEOPLE HE CARES ABOUT AS POSSIBLE.
BUT IF YOU DON'T KNOW ANYTHING THAT MIGHT HELP US, WE'LL BE ON OUR WAY.
WAIT.
DR. ROT.

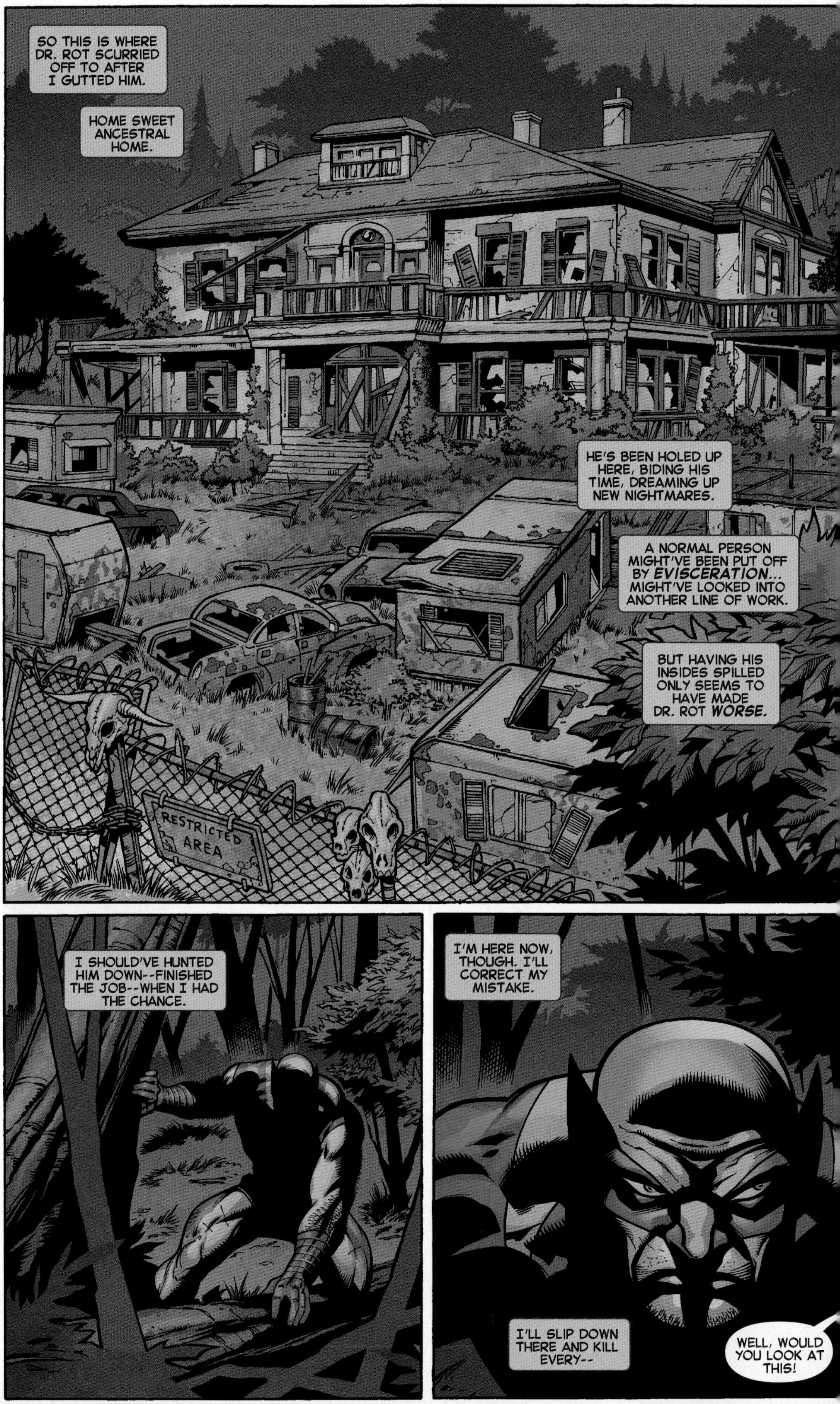
SO THIS IS WHERE DR. ROT SCURRIED OFF TO AFTER I GUTTED HIM.
HOME SWEET ANCESTRAL HOME.
HE'S BEEN HOLED UP HERE, BIDING HIS TIME, DREAMING UP NEW NIGHTMARES.
A NORMAL PERSON MIGHT'VE BEEN PUT OFF BY EVISCERATION... MIGHT'VE LOOKED INTO ANOTHER LINE OF WORK.
BUT HAVING HIS INSIDES SPILLED ONLY SEEMS TO HAVE MADE DR. ROT WORSE.
RESTRICTED AREA
I SHOULD'VE HUNTED HIM DOWN--FINISHED THE JOB--WHEN I HAD THE CHANCE.
I'M HERE NOW, THOUGH. I'LL CORRECT MY MISTAKE.
I'LL SLIP DOWN THERE AND KILL EVERY--
WELL, WOULD YOU LOOK AT THIS!

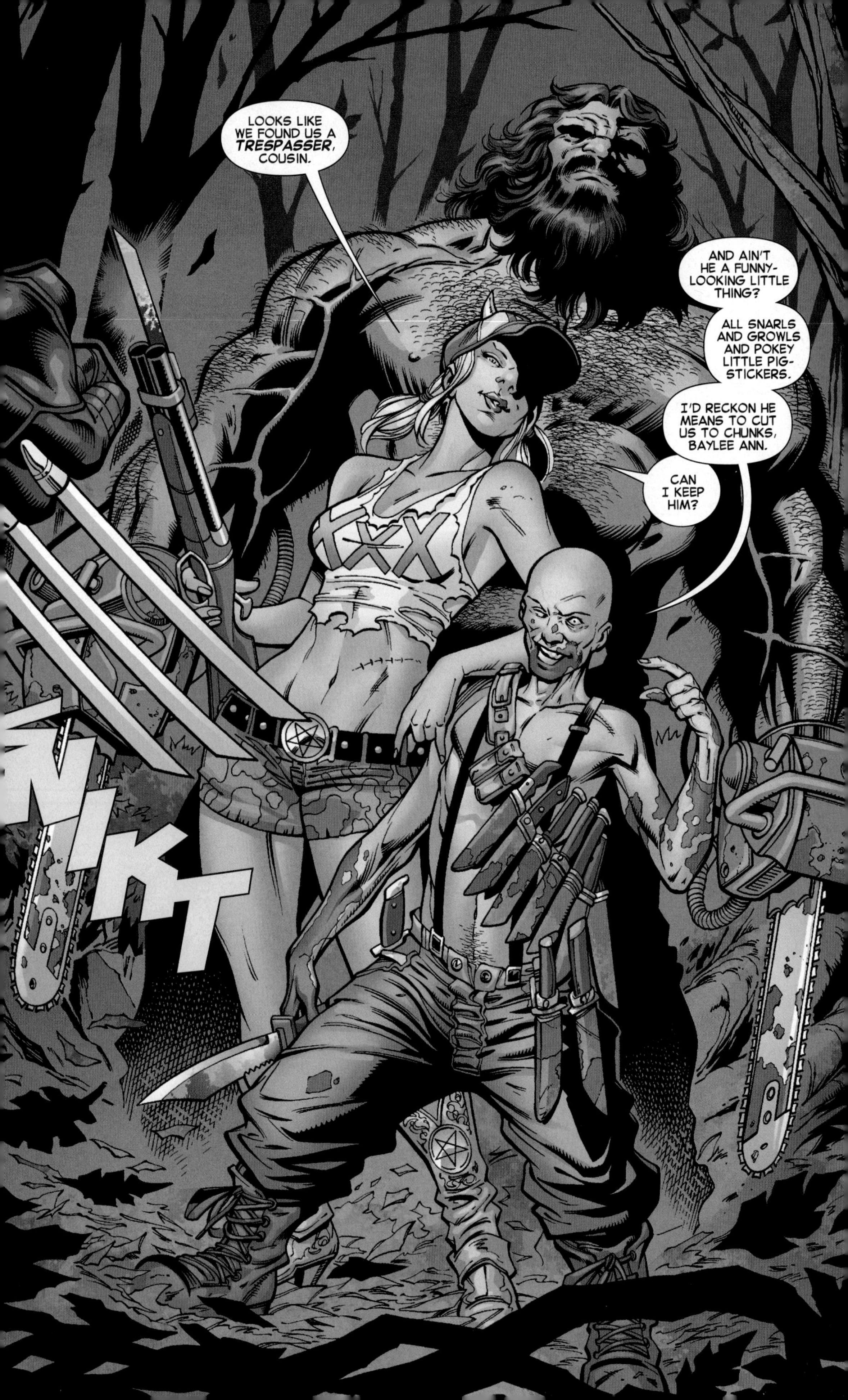

LOOKS LIKE WE FOUND US A *TRESPASSER*, COUSIN.
AND AIN'T HE A FUNNY-LOOKING LITTLE THING?
ALL SNARLS AND GROWLS AND POKEY LITTLE PIG-STICKERS.
I'D RECKON HE MEANS TO CUT US TO CHUNKS, BAYLEE ANN.
CAN I KEEP HIM?
NIKT

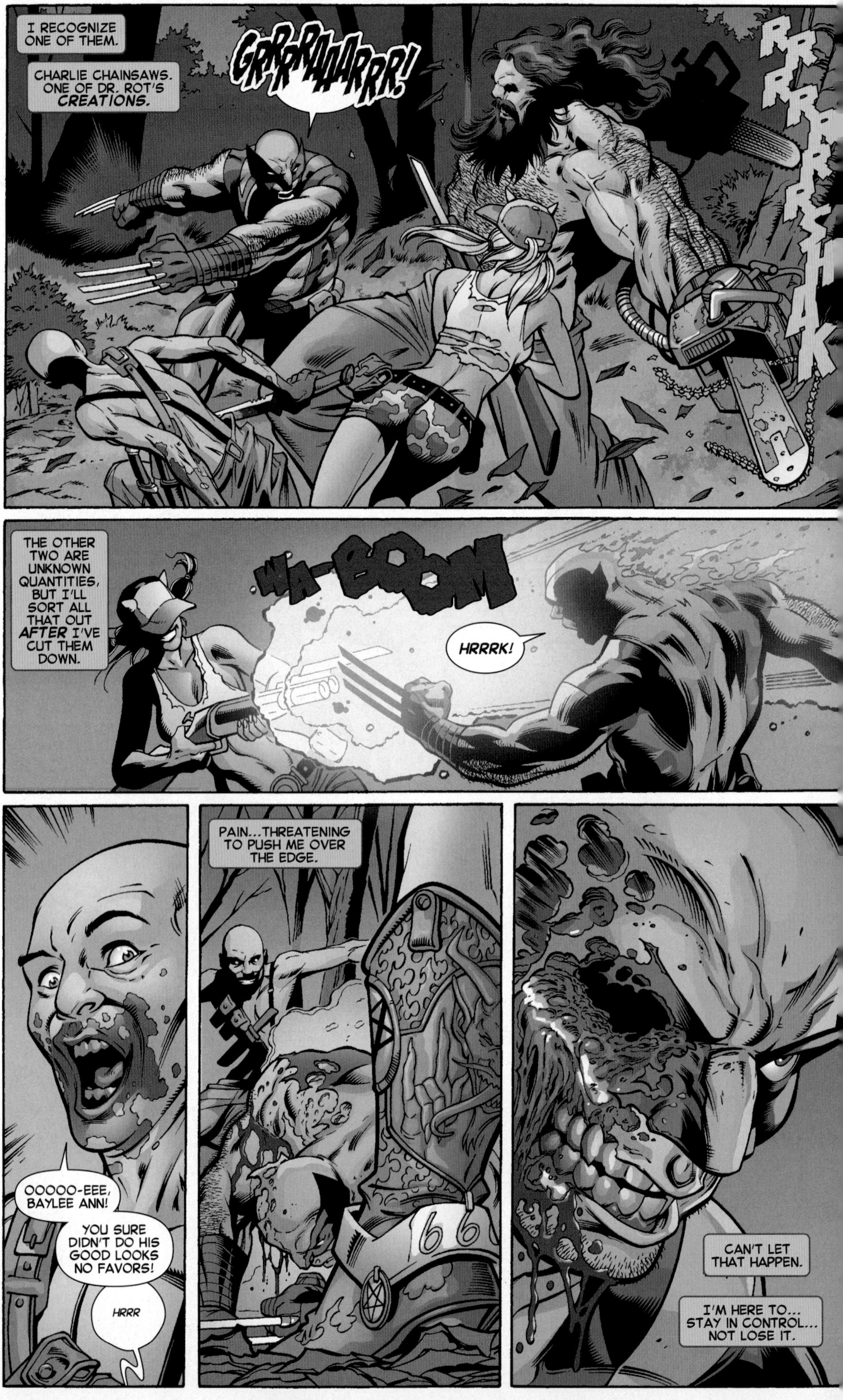
I RECOGNIZE ONE OF THEM.
CHARLIE CHAINSAWS. ONE OF DR. ROT'S CREATIONS.
GRRRRAAAARRR!
RRRRRRRRRSHAK
THE OTHER TWO ARE UNKNOWN QUANTITIES, BUT I'LL SORT ALL THAT OUT AFTER I'VE CUT THEM DOWN.
WA-BOOM
HRRRK!
OOOOO-EEE, BAYLEE ANN!
YOU SURE DIDN'T DO HIS GOOD LOOKS NO FAVORS!
HRRR
PAIN...THREATENING TO PUSH ME OVER THE EDGE.
CAN'T LET THAT HAPPEN.
I'M HERE TO... STAY IN CONTROL... NOT LOSE IT.

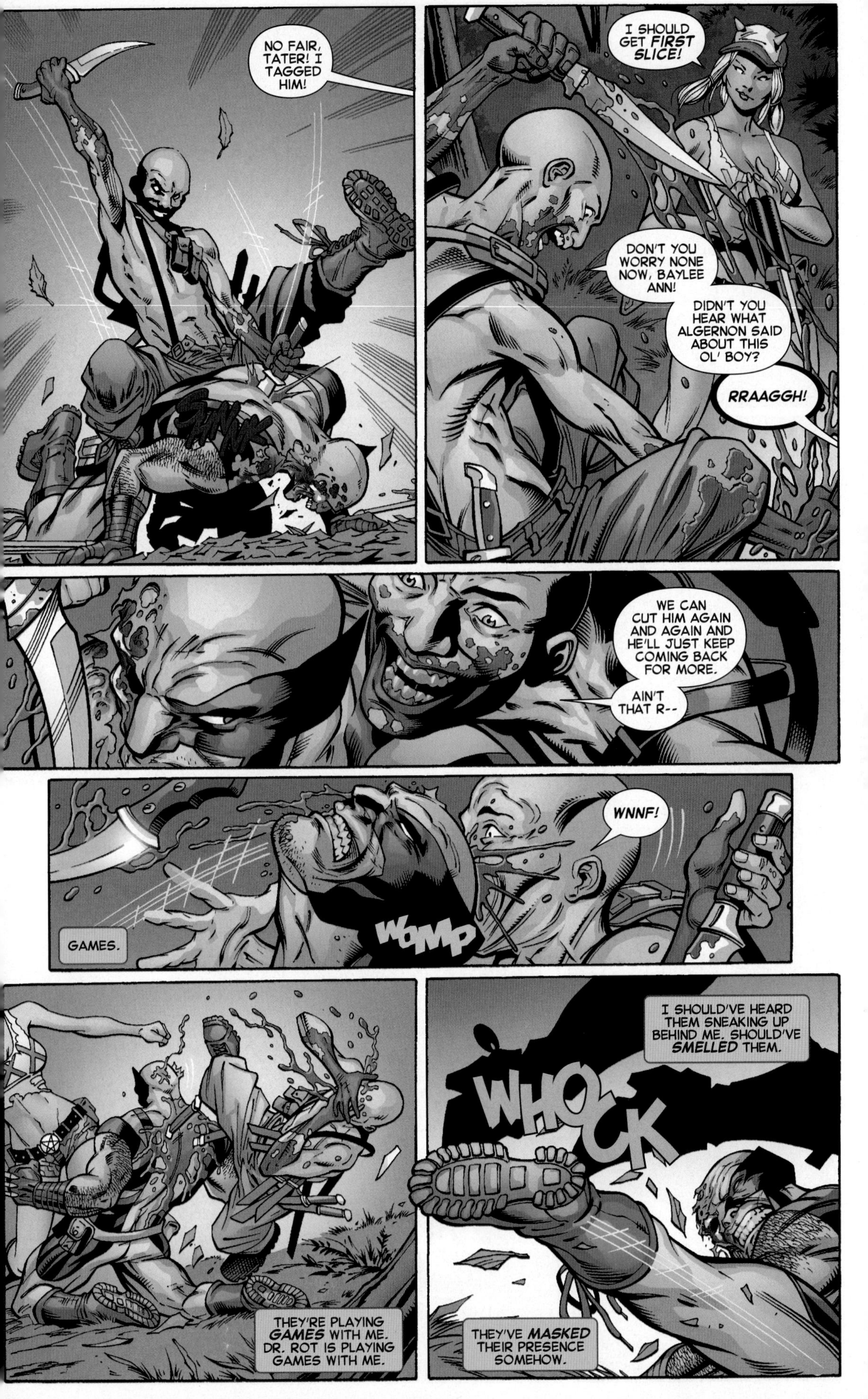
NO FAIR, TATER! I TAGGED HIM!
SHNK
I SHOULD GET FIRST SLICE!
DON'T YOU WORRY NONE NOW, BAYLEE ANN!
DIDN'T YOU HEAR WHAT ALGERNON SAID ABOUT THIS OL' BOY?
RRAAGGH!
WE CAN CUT HIM AGAIN AND AGAIN AND HE'LL JUST KEEP COMING BACK FOR MORE.
AIN'T THAT R--
WNNF!
GAMES.
WOMP
THEY'RE PLAYING GAMES WITH ME. DR. ROT IS PLAYING GAMES WITH ME.
I SHOULD'VE HEARD THEM SNEAKING UP BEHIND ME. SHOULD'VE SMELLED THEM.
WHOCK
THEY'VE MASKED THEIR PRESENCE SOMEHOW.

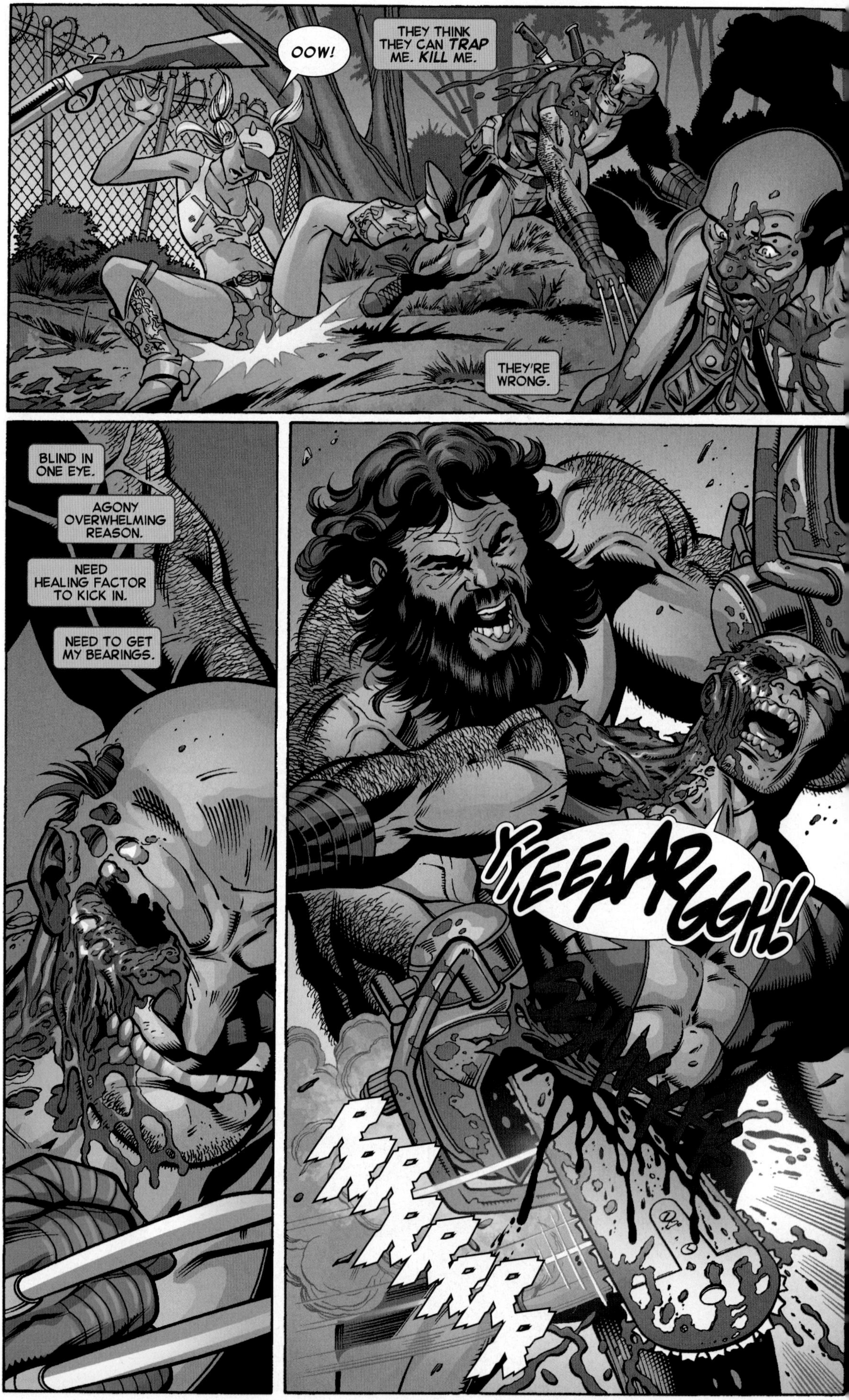
OOW!
THEY THINK THEY CAN TRAP ME. KILL ME.
THEY'RE WRONG.
BLIND IN ONE EYE.
AGONY OVERWHELMING REASON.
NEED HEALING FACTOR TO KICK IN.
NEED TO GET MY BEARINGS.
YYEEAARGGH!
RRRRRRRRR

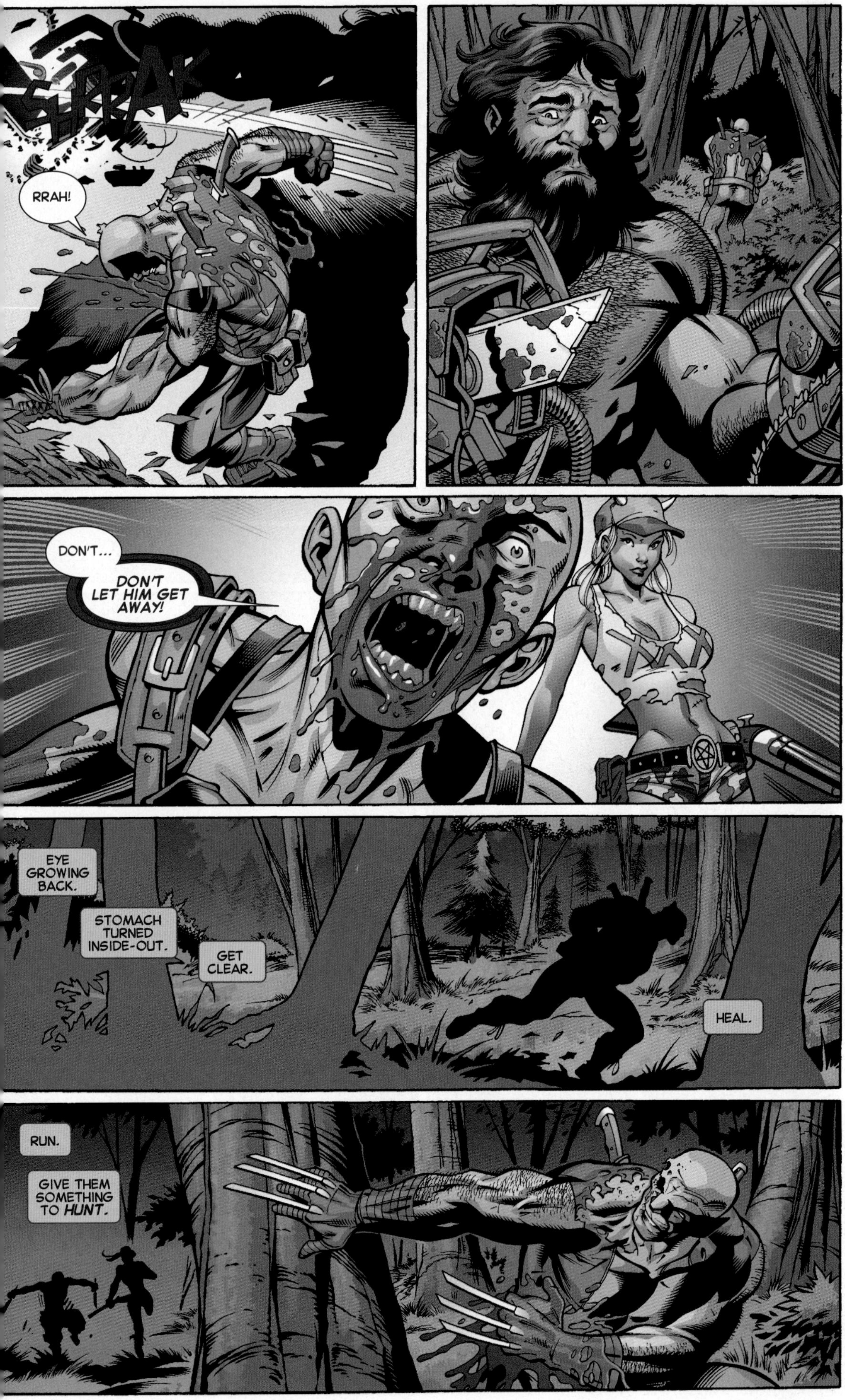
SHRRAK
RRAH!
DON'T...
DON'T LET HIM GET AWAY!
EYE GROWING BACK.
STOMACH TURNED INSIDE-OUT.
GET CLEAR.
HEAL.
RUN.
GIVE THEM SOMETHING TO HUNT.

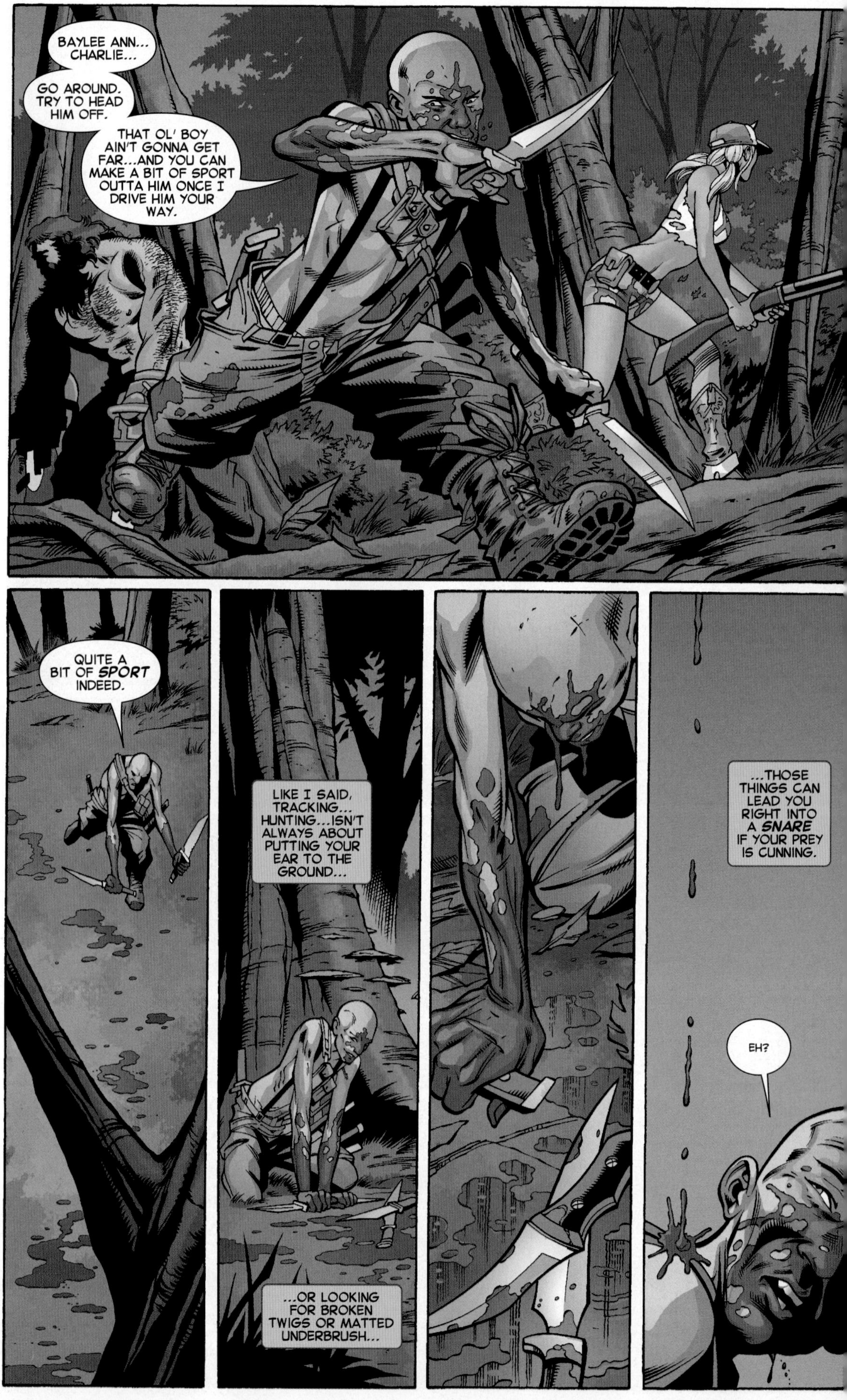
BAYLEE ANN... CHARLIE...
GO AROUND. TRY TO HEAD HIM OFF.
THAT OL' BOY AIN'T GONNA GET FAR...AND YOU CAN MAKE A BIT OF SPORT OUTTA HIM ONCE I DRIVE HIM YOUR WAY.
QUITE A BIT OF *SPORT* INDEED.
LIKE I SAID, TRACKING... HUNTING...ISN'T ALWAYS ABOUT PUTTING YOUR EAR TO THE GROUND...
...OR LOOKING FOR BROKEN TWIGS OR MATTED UNDERBRUSH...
...THOSE THINGS CAN LEAD YOU RIGHT INTO A *SNARE* IF YOUR PREY IS CUNNING.
EH?

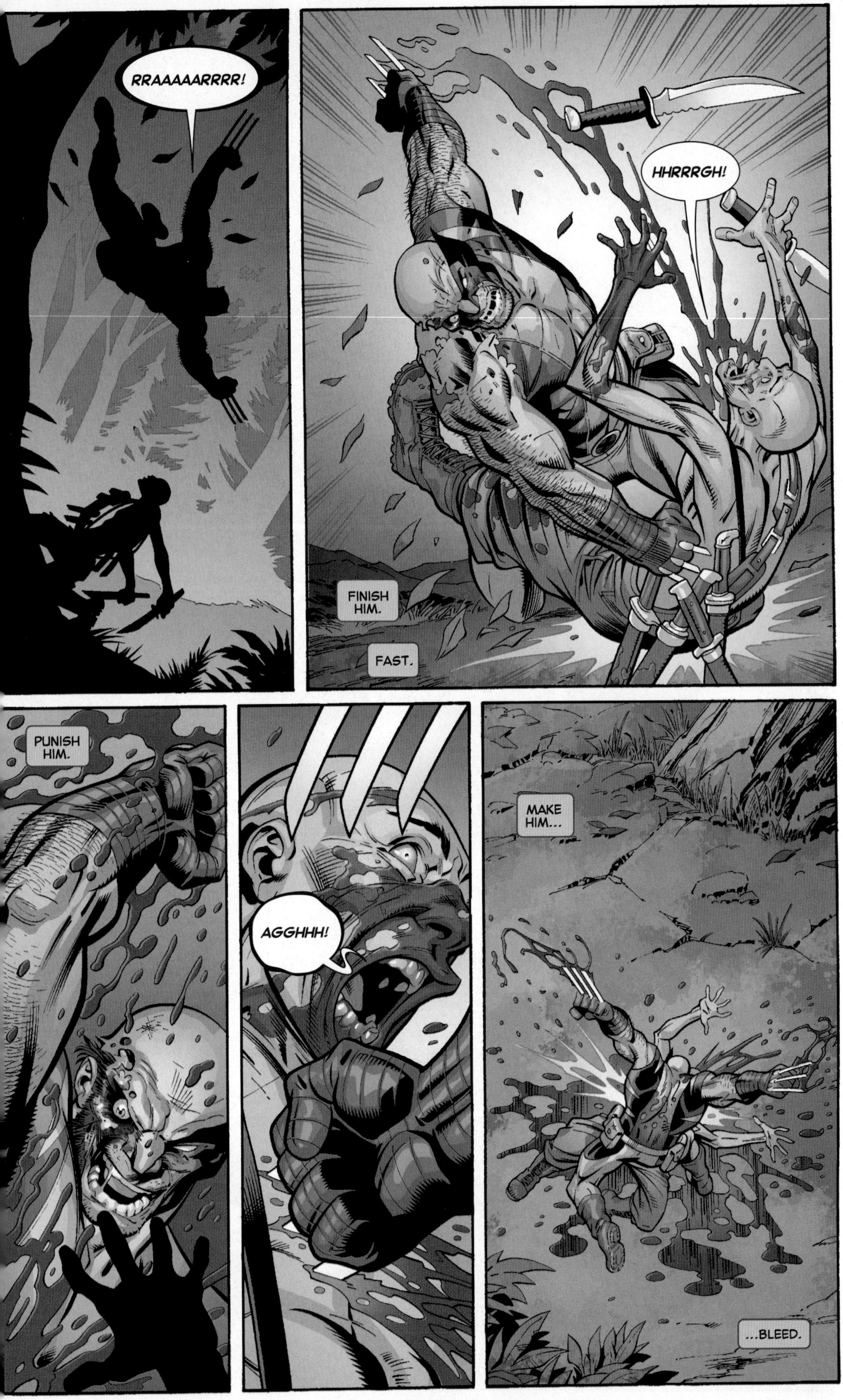
RRAAAAARRRR!
HHRRRGH!
FINISH HIM.
FAST.
PUNISH HIM.
AGGHHH!
MAKE HIM...
...BLEED.

SOME PEOPLE *DESERVE* TO DIE.

=HRRR=

=HRR=

BUT SOME DESERVE TO *LIVE*, TOO.

BECAUSE THE LONGER THEY LIVE, THE LONGER THEY CAN BE MADE TO--

--SUFFER.

GGGGGGG

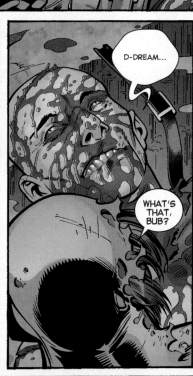

D-DREAM...

WHAT'S THAT, BUB?

FAMOUS LAST W--

DREAM A DREAM OF PRETTY PREY, AND BLOOD RED AS RAGE.

DREAM A DREAM OF P
PREY, AND BLOOD RED
EAM A DREAM OF PRET
ND BLOOD RED AS RAGE.
REAM OF PRETTY PREY, AND BL

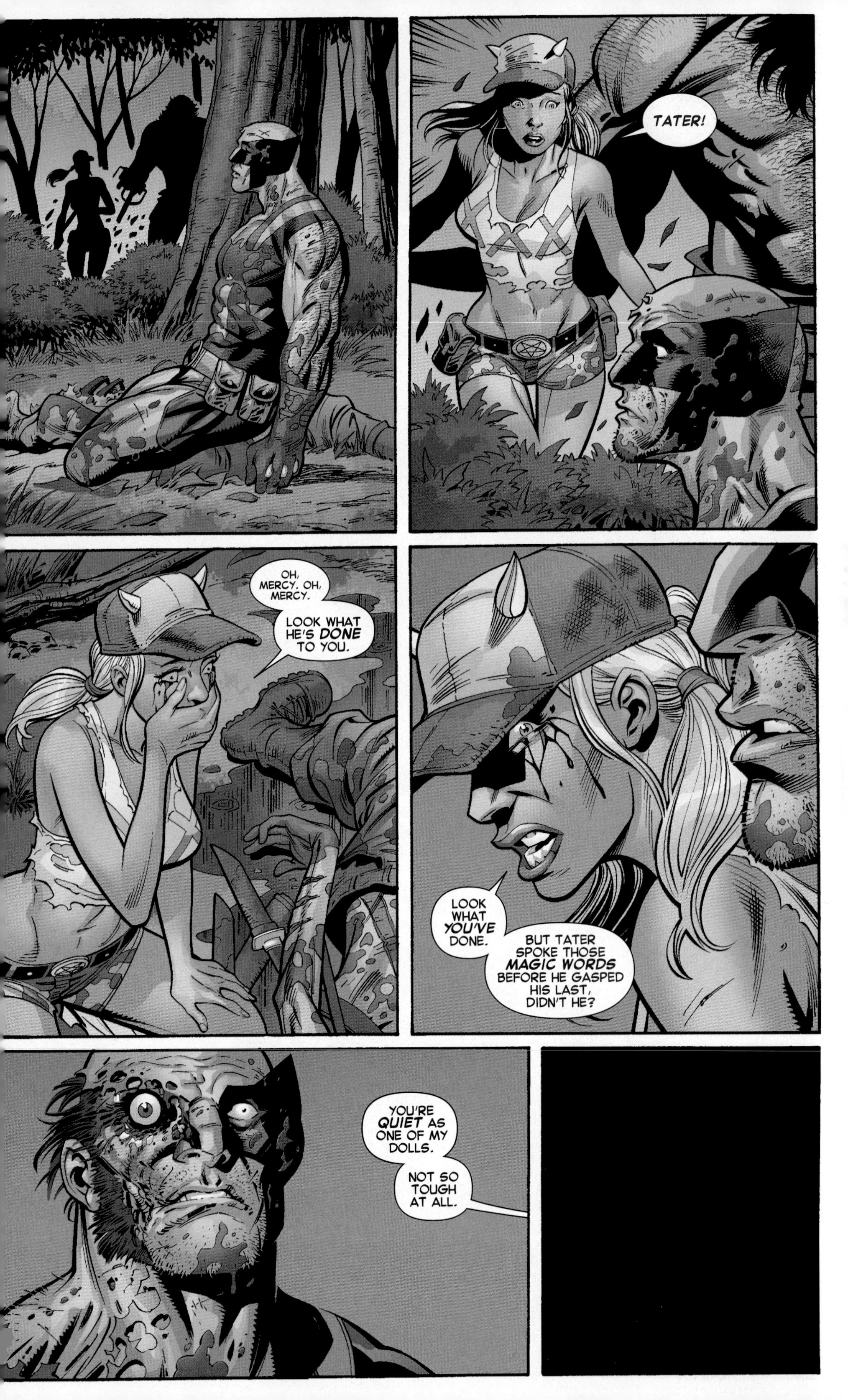
TATER!
OH, MERCY. OH, MERCY.
LOOK WHAT HE'S DONE TO YOU.
LOOK WHAT YOU'VE DONE.
BUT TATER SPOKE THOSE MAGIC WORDS BEFORE HE GASPED HIS LAST, DIDN'T HE?
YOU'RE QUIET AS ONE OF MY DOLLS.
NOT SO TOUGH AT ALL.

LOGAN, LOGAN, LOGAN.

OR IS IT JAMES?

WW ZZT?

OR WOLVERINE?

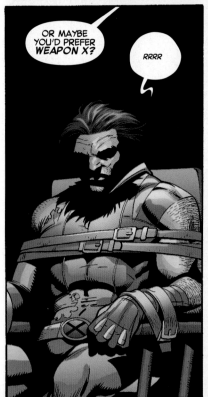
OR MAYBE YOU'D PREFER WEAPON X?

RRRR

YOU POOR CREATURE.

YOU HAVE NO IDEA WHO OR WHAT YOU ARE, DO YOU?

BUT DON'T YOU FRET.

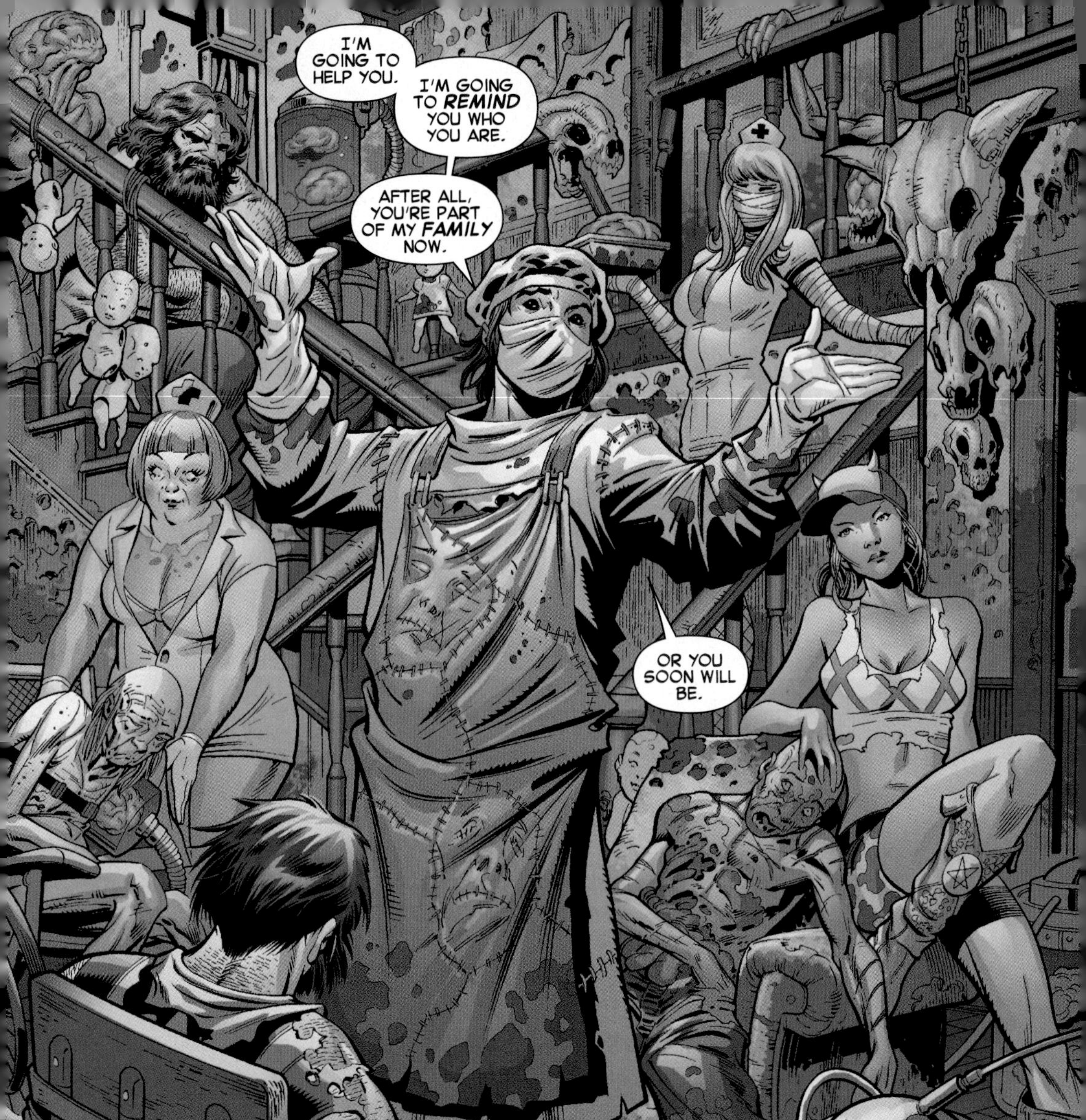
I'M GOING TO HELP YOU.
I'M GOING TO REMIND YOU WHO YOU ARE.
AFTER ALL, YOU'RE PART OF MY FAMILY NOW.
OR YOU SOON WILL BE.

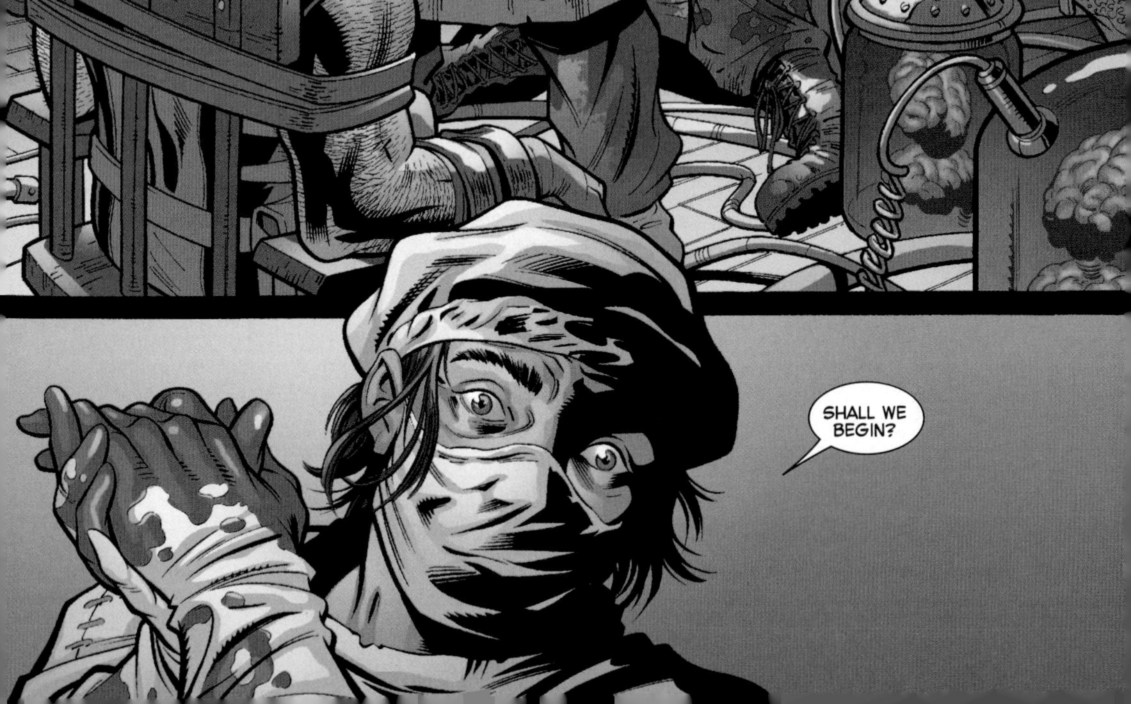
SHALL WE BEGIN?

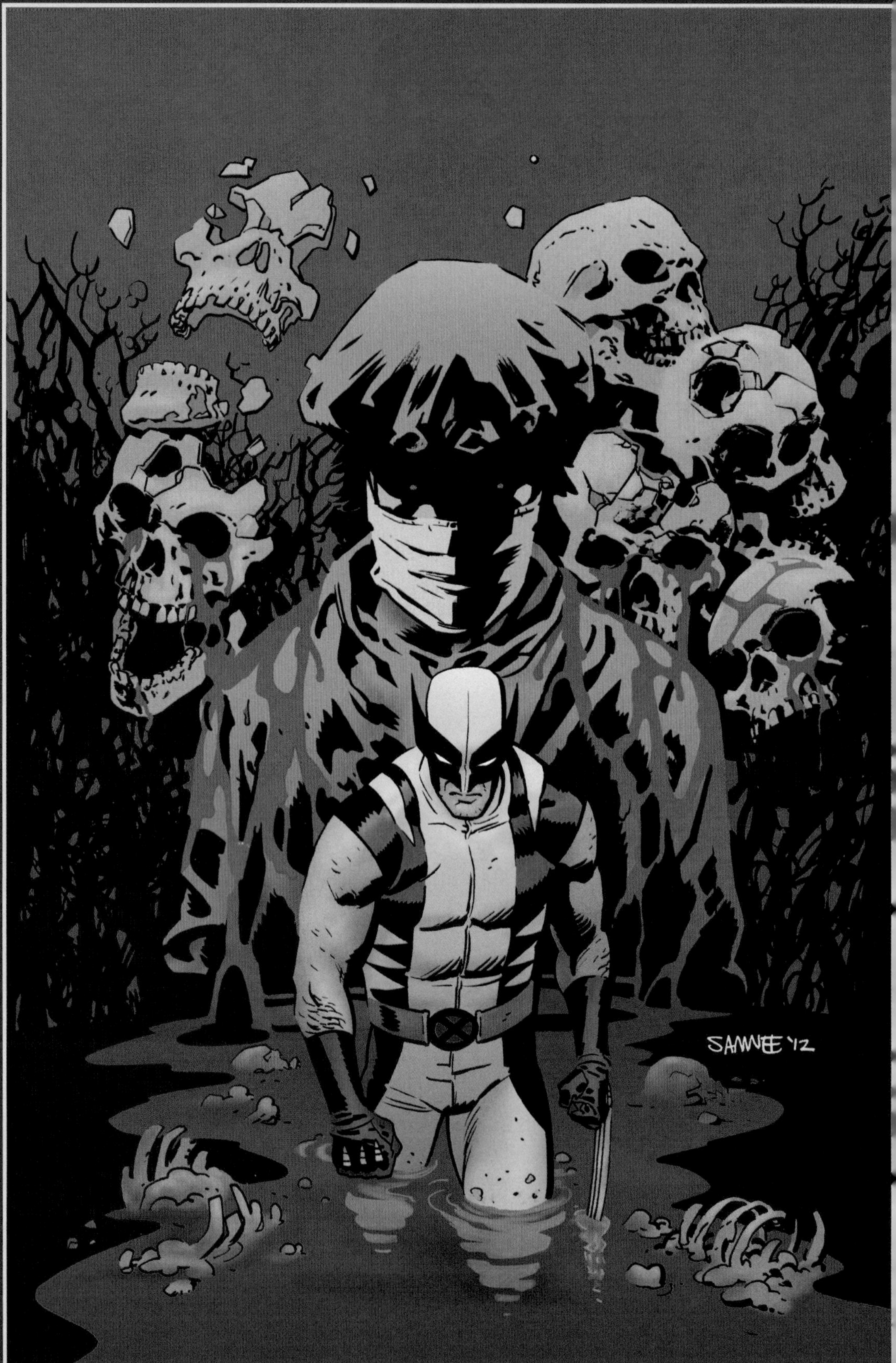
SAMNEE '12

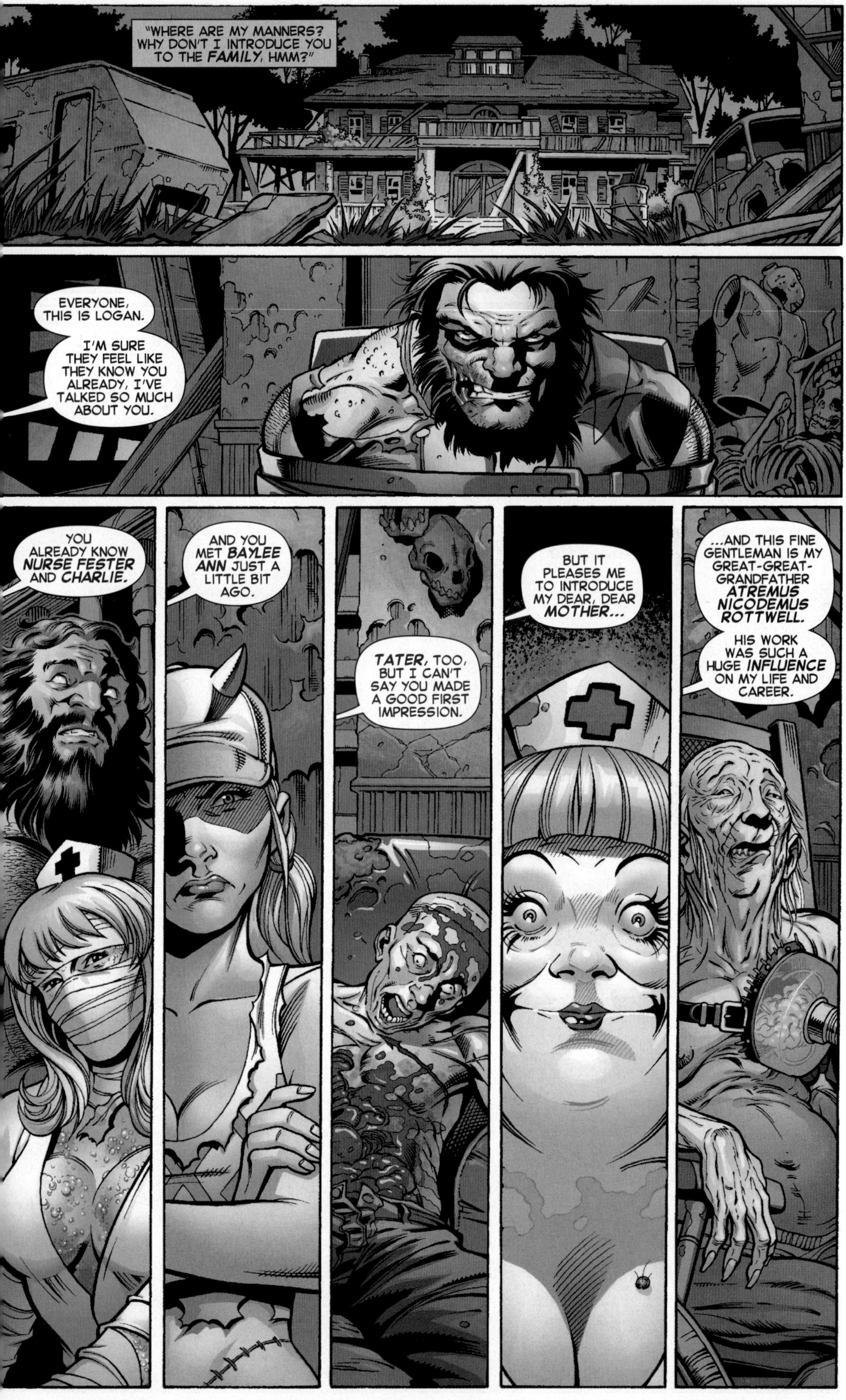
"WHERE ARE MY MANNERS? WHY DON'T I INTRODUCE YOU TO THE FAMILY, HMM?"
EVERYONE, THIS IS LOGAN.
I'M SURE THEY FEEL LIKE THEY KNOW YOU ALREADY, I'VE TALKED SO MUCH ABOUT YOU.
YOU ALREADY KNOW NURSE FESTER AND CHARLIE.
AND YOU MET BAYLEE ANN JUST A LITTLE BIT AGO.
TATER, TOO, BUT I CAN'T SAY YOU MADE A GOOD FIRST IMPRESSION.
BUT IT PLEASES ME TO INTRODUCE MY DEAR, DEAR MOTHER...
...AND THIS FINE GENTLEMAN IS MY GREAT-GREAT-GRANDFATHER ATREMUS NICODEMUS ROTTWELL.
HIS WORK WAS SUCH A HUGE INFLUENCE ON MY LIFE AND CAREER.

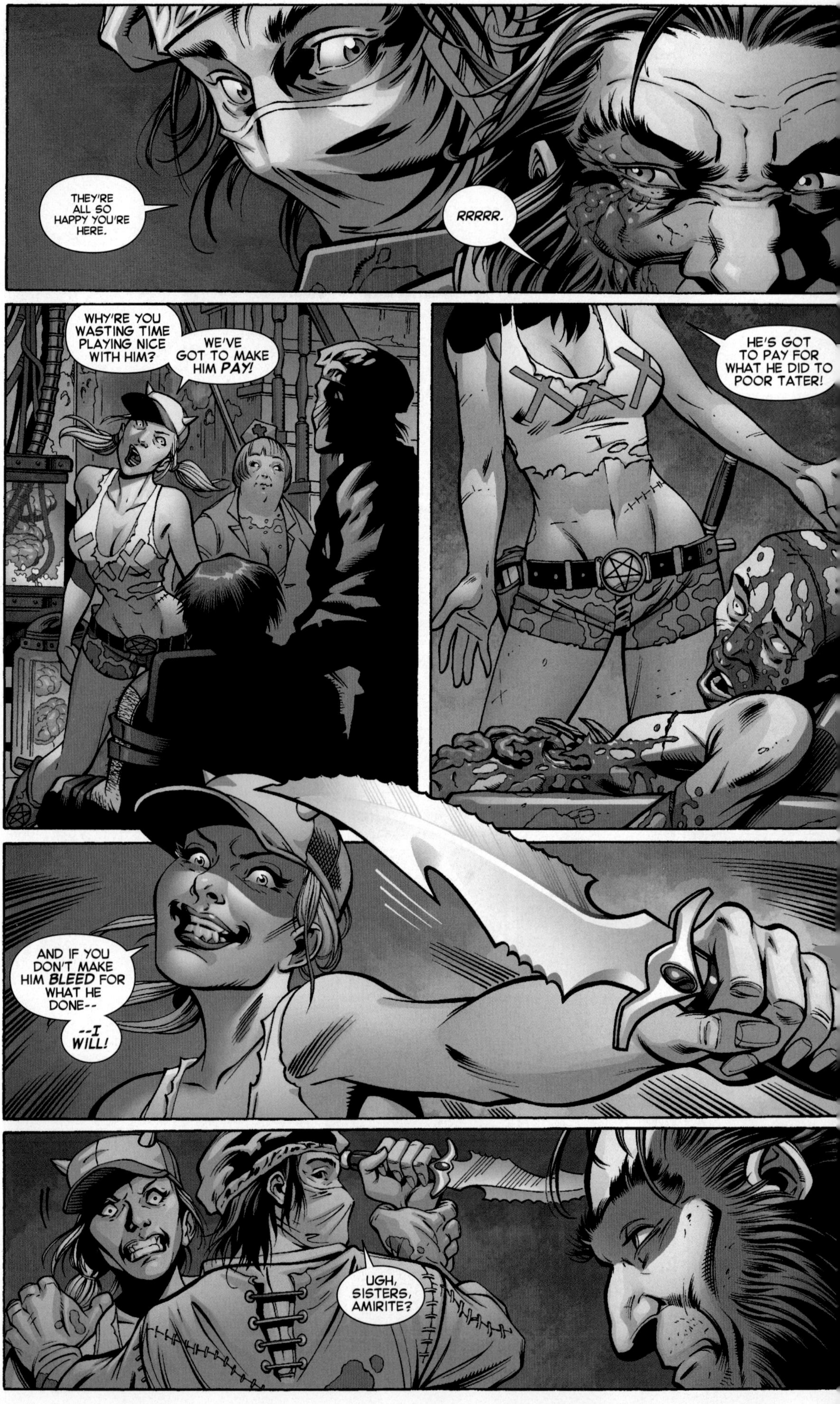
THEY'RE ALL SO HAPPY YOU'RE HERE.
RRRRR.
WHY'RE YOU WASTING TIME PLAYING NICE WITH HIM?
WE'VE GOT TO MAKE HIM *PAY!*
HE'S GOT TO PAY FOR WHAT HE DID TO POOR TATER!
AND IF YOU DON'T MAKE HIM *BLEED* FOR WHAT HE DONE--
--I WILL!
UGH, SISTERS, AMIRITE?

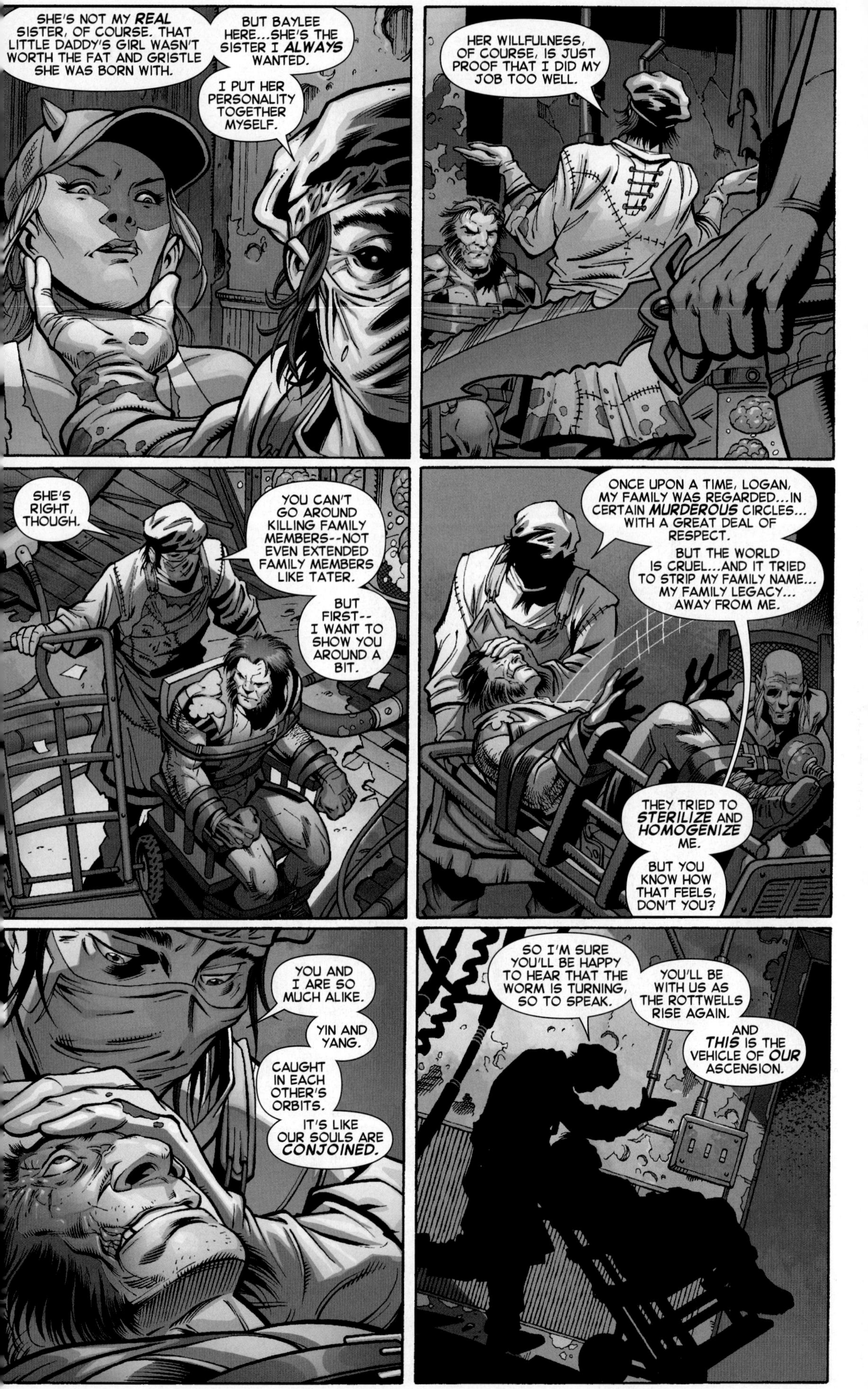

SHE'S NOT MY REAL SISTER, OF COURSE. THAT LITTLE DADDY'S GIRL WASN'T WORTH THE FAT AND GRISTLE SHE WAS BORN WITH.
BUT BAYLEE HERE...SHE'S THE SISTER I ALWAYS WANTED.
I PUT HER PERSONALITY TOGETHER MYSELF.
HER WILLFULNESS, OF COURSE, IS JUST PROOF THAT I DID MY JOB TOO WELL.
SHE'S RIGHT, THOUGH.
YOU CAN'T GO AROUND KILLING FAMILY MEMBERS--NOT EVEN EXTENDED FAMILY MEMBERS LIKE TATER.
BUT FIRST-- I WANT TO SHOW YOU AROUND A BIT.
ONCE UPON A TIME, LOGAN, MY FAMILY WAS REGARDED...IN CERTAIN MURDEROUS CIRCLES... WITH A GREAT DEAL OF RESPECT.
BUT THE WORLD IS CRUEL...AND IT TRIED TO STRIP MY FAMILY NAME... MY FAMILY LEGACY... AWAY FROM ME.
THEY TRIED TO STERILIZE AND HOMOGENIZE ME.
BUT YOU KNOW HOW THAT FEELS, DON'T YOU?
YOU AND I ARE SO MUCH ALIKE.
YIN AND YANG.
CAUGHT IN EACH OTHER'S ORBITS.
IT'S LIKE OUR SOULS ARE CONJOINED.
SO I'M SURE YOU'LL BE HAPPY TO HEAR THAT THE WORM IS TURNING, SO TO SPEAK.
YOU'LL BE WITH US AS THE ROTTWELLS RISE AGAIN.
AND THIS IS THE VEHICLE OF OUR ASCENSION.

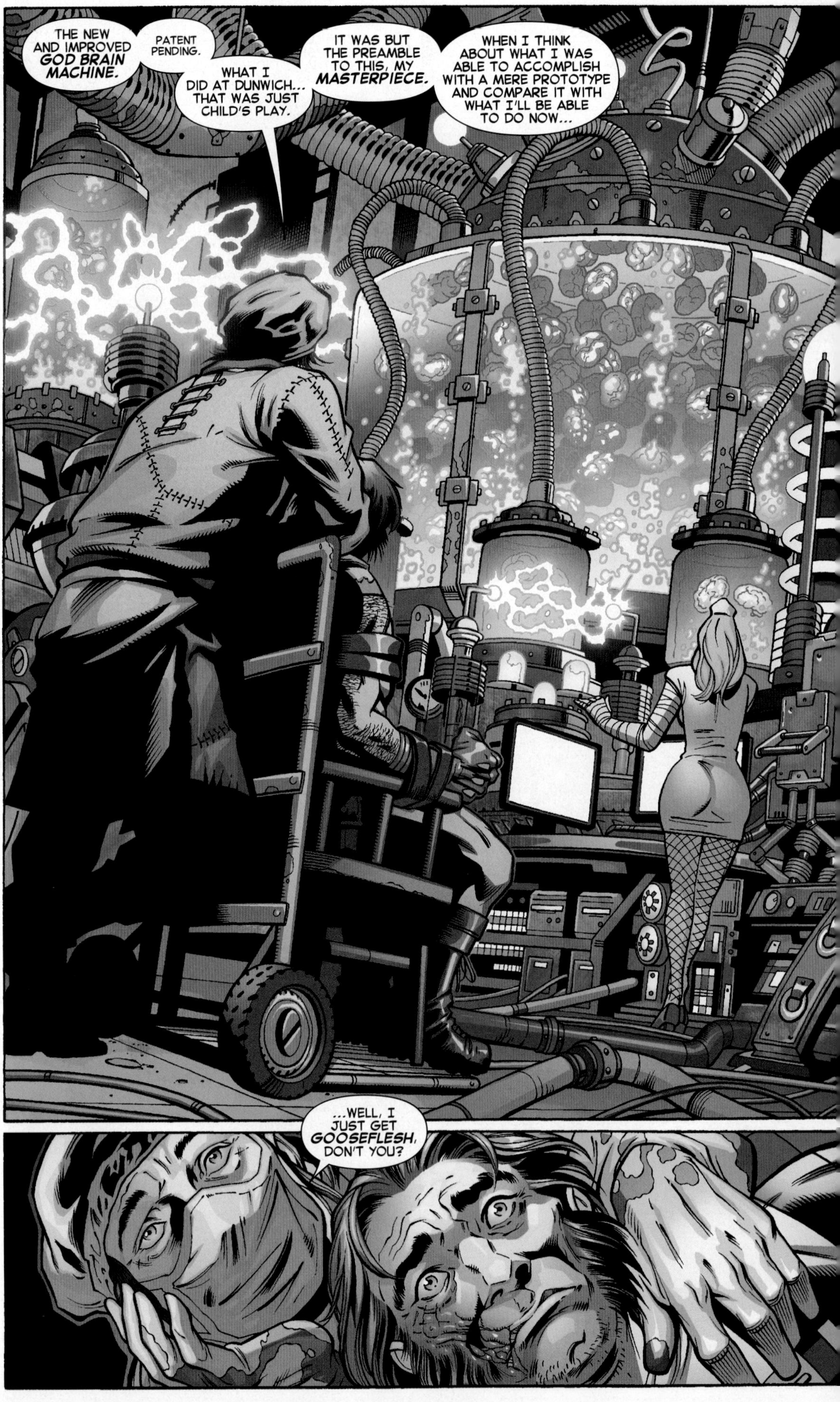
THE NEW AND IMPROVED GOD BRAIN MACHINE.
PATENT PENDING.
WHAT I DID AT DUNWICH... THAT WAS JUST CHILD'S PLAY.
IT WAS BUT THE PREAMBLE TO THIS, MY MASTERPIECE.
WHEN I THINK ABOUT WHAT I WAS ABLE TO ACCOMPLISH WITH A MERE PROTOTYPE AND COMPARE IT WITH WHAT I'LL BE ABLE TO DO NOW...
...WELL, I JUST GET GOOSEFLESH, DON'T YOU?

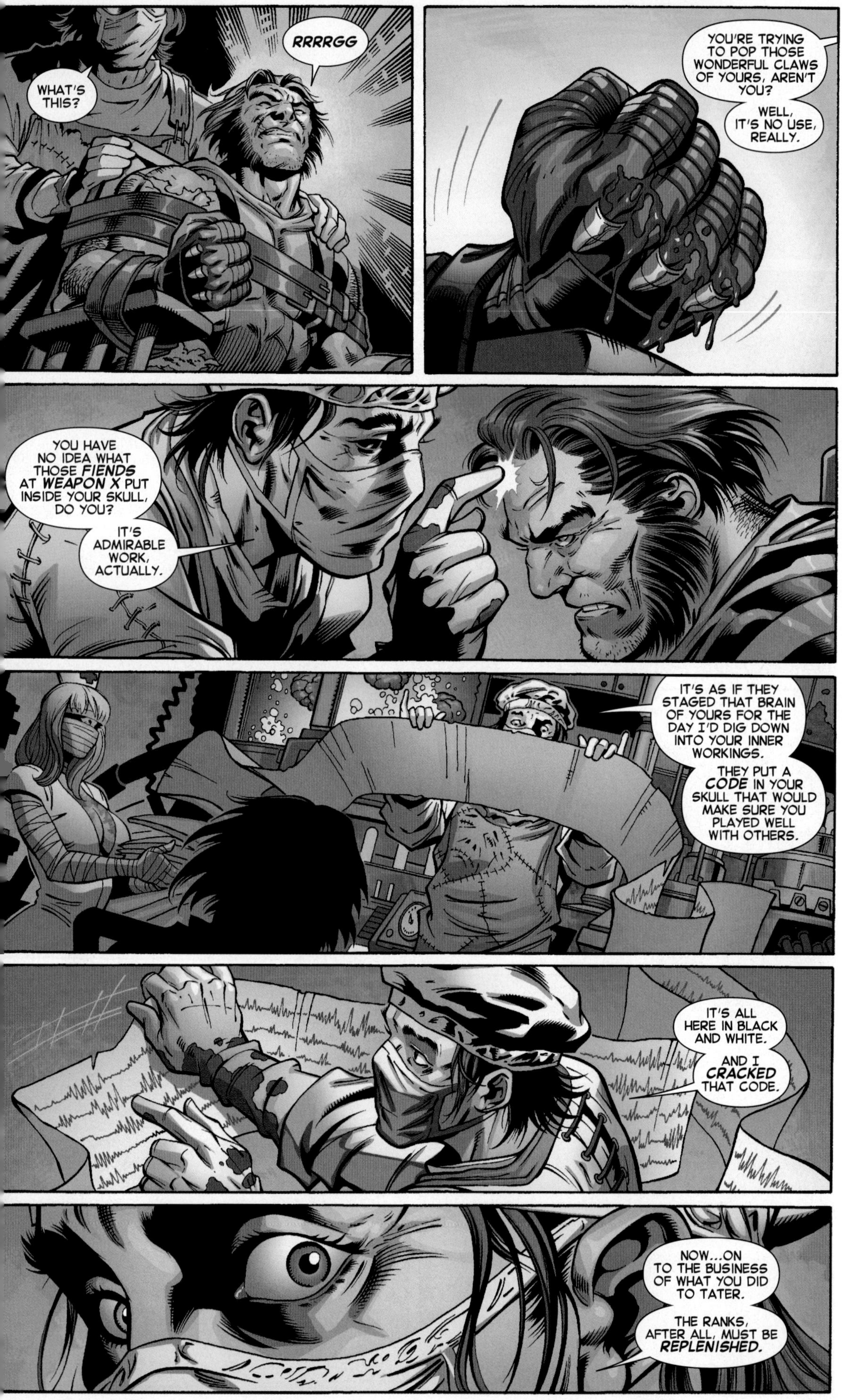
WHAT'S THIS?
RRRRGG
YOU'RE TRYING TO POP THOSE WONDERFUL CLAWS OF YOURS, AREN'T YOU?
WELL, IT'S NO USE, REALLY.
YOU HAVE NO IDEA WHAT THOSE FIENDS AT WEAPON X PUT INSIDE YOUR SKULL, DO YOU?
IT'S ADMIRABLE WORK, ACTUALLY.
IT'S AS IF THEY STAGED THAT BRAIN OF YOURS FOR THE DAY I'D DIG DOWN INTO YOUR INNER WORKINGS.
THEY PUT A CODE IN YOUR SKULL THAT WOULD MAKE SURE YOU PLAYED WELL WITH OTHERS.
IT'S ALL HERE IN BLACK AND WHITE.
AND I CRACKED THAT CODE.
NOW...ON TO THE BUSINESS OF WHAT YOU DID TO TATER.
THE RANKS, AFTER ALL, MUST BE REPLENISHED.

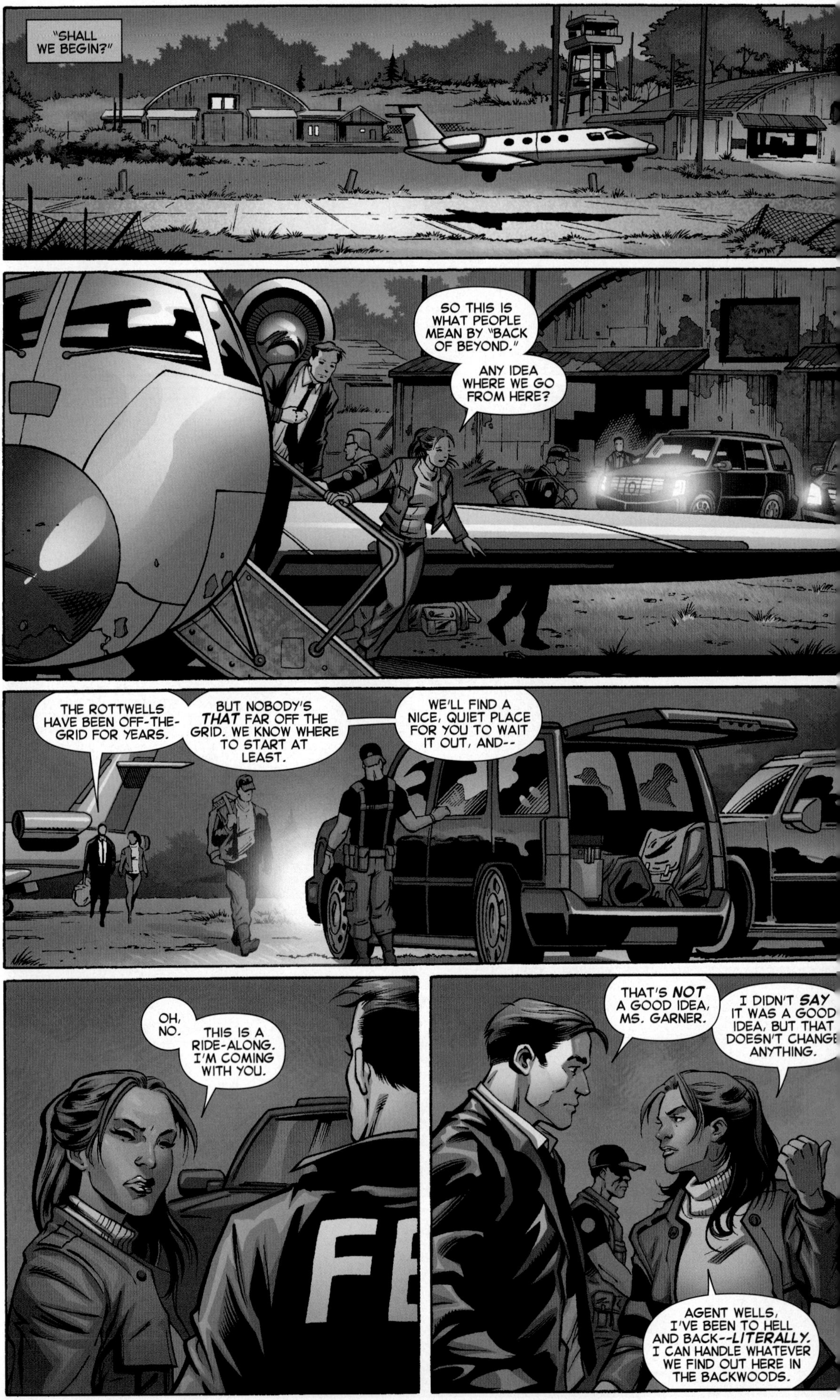
"SHALL WE BEGIN?"
SO THIS IS WHAT PEOPLE MEAN BY "BACK OF BEYOND."
ANY IDEA WHERE WE GO FROM HERE?
THE ROTTWELLS HAVE BEEN OFF-THE-GRID FOR YEARS.
BUT NOBODY'S *THAT* FAR OFF THE GRID. WE KNOW WHERE TO START AT LEAST.
WE'LL FIND A NICE, QUIET PLACE FOR YOU TO WAIT IT OUT, AND--
OH, NO.
THIS IS A RIDE-ALONG. I'M COMING WITH YOU.
FB
THAT'S *NOT* A GOOD IDEA, MS. GARNER.
I DIDN'T *SAY* IT WAS A GOOD IDEA, BUT THAT DOESN'T CHANGE ANYTHING.
AGENT WELLS, I'VE BEEN TO HELL AND BACK--*LITERALLY.* I CAN HANDLE WHATEVER WE FIND OUT HERE IN THE BACKWOODS.

ALL RIGHT, ALL RIGHT. BUT DON'T MAKE ME REGRET THIS.

MY GUESS IS GPS ISN'T GOING TO DO US MUCH GOOD OUT HERE.

LET'S SEE ABOUT ASKING THE LOCALS FOR DIRECTIONS.

EXCUSE ME. WE'RE LOOKING FOR THE ROTTWELL ESTATE.

I WONDERED IF YOU MIGHT--

YOU LOOKING FOR THEM ROTTWELLS, ALL YOU GOTTA DO IS FOLLOW YOUR NOSE.

FOLLOW OUR--

PLACE STINKS LIKE AN OPEN GRAVE.

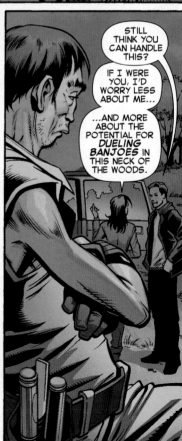

STILL THINK YOU CAN HANDLE THIS?

IF I WERE YOU, I'D WORRY LESS ABOUT ME...

...AND MORE ABOUT THE POTENTIAL FOR DUELING BANJOES IN THIS NECK OF THE WOODS.

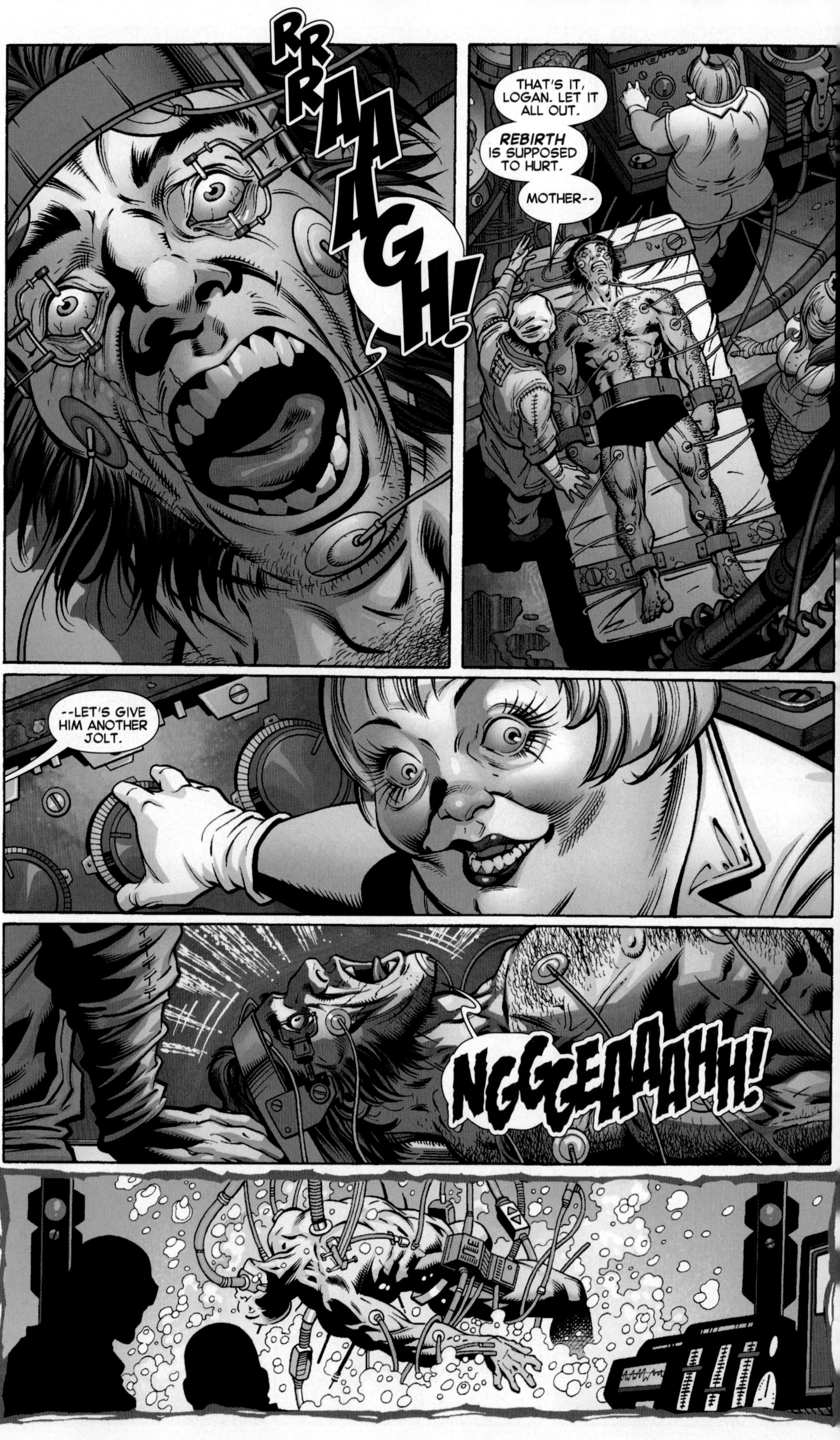
RRRAAAGH!
THAT'S IT, LOGAN. LET IT ALL OUT.
REBIRTH IS SUPPOSED TO HURT.
MOTHER--
--LET'S GIVE HIM ANOTHER JOLT.
NGGGEAAAHHH!

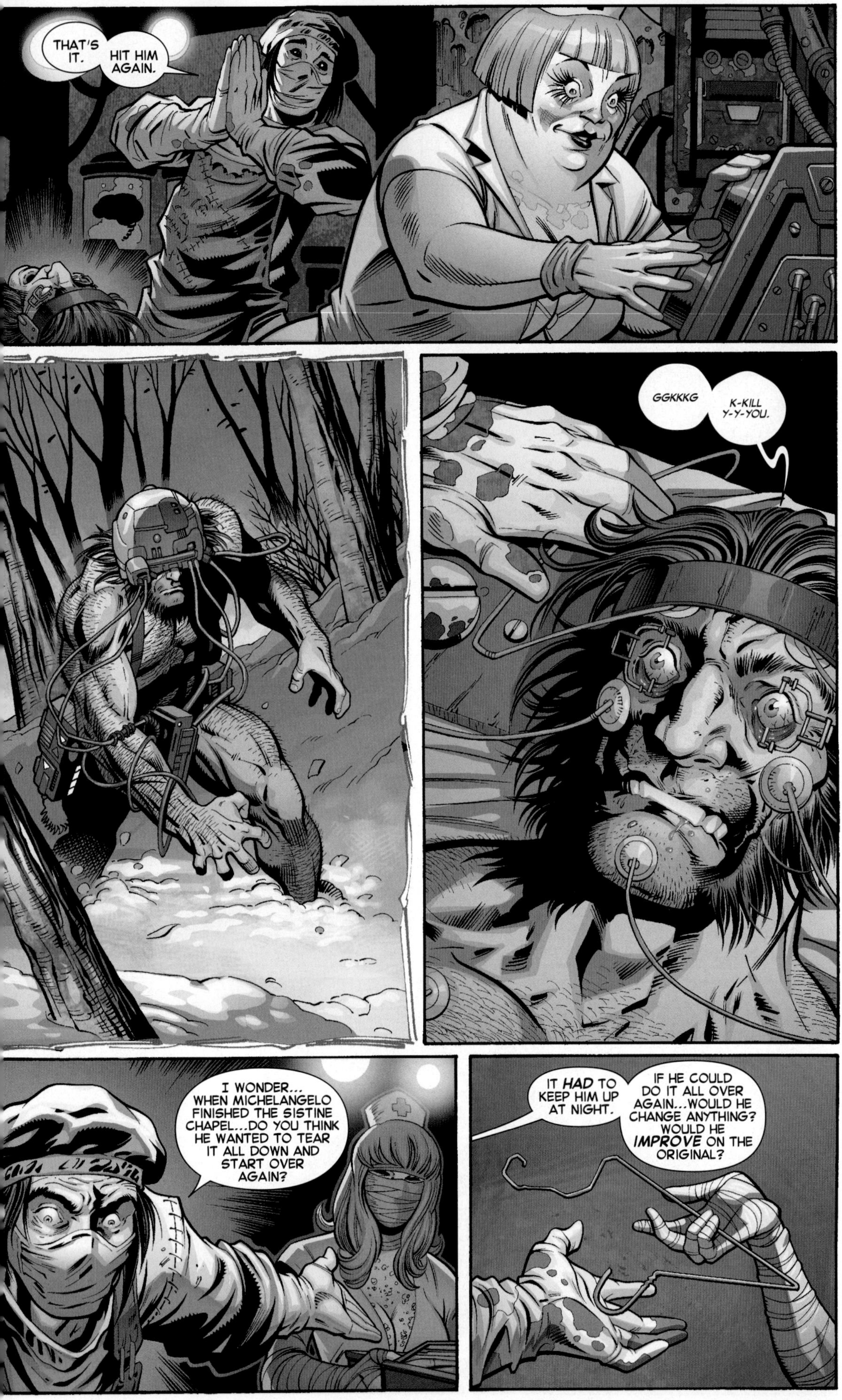
THAT'S IT.
HIT HIM AGAIN.
GGKKKG
K-KILL Y-Y-YOU.
I WONDER... WHEN MICHELANGELO FINISHED THE SISTINE CHAPEL...DO YOU THINK HE WANTED TO TEAR IT ALL DOWN AND START OVER AGAIN?
IT HAD TO KEEP HIM UP AT NIGHT.
IF HE COULD DO IT ALL OVER AGAIN...WOULD HE CHANGE ANYTHING? WOULD HE IMPROVE ON THE ORIGINAL?

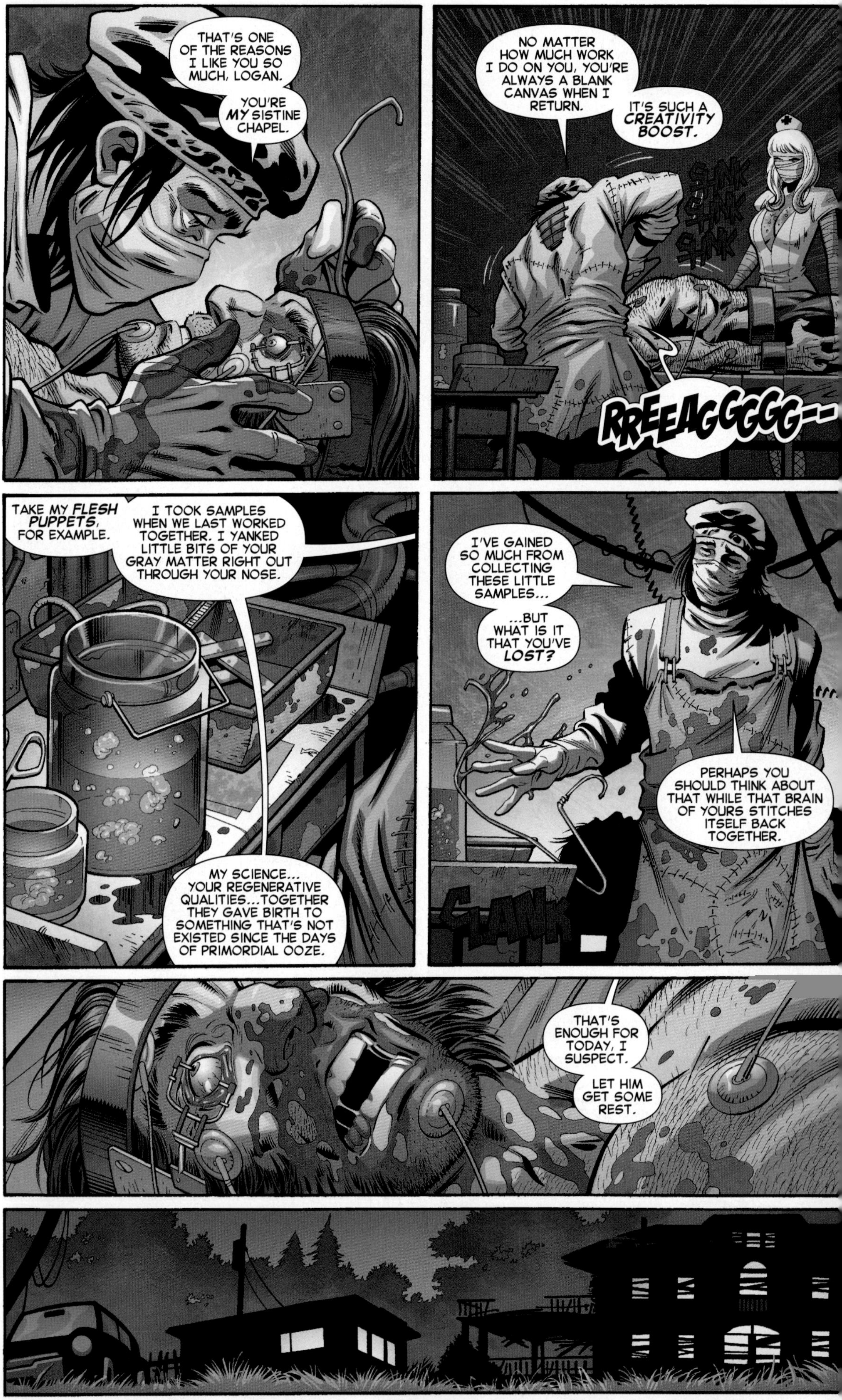
THAT'S ONE OF THE REASONS I LIKE YOU SO MUCH, LOGAN.
YOU'RE *MY* SISTINE CHAPEL.
NO MATTER HOW MUCH WORK I DO ON YOU, YOU'RE ALWAYS A BLANK CANVAS WHEN I RETURN.
IT'S SUCH A *CREATIVITY BOOST.*
SHINK SHINK SHINK SHINK
RREEAGGGGG--
TAKE MY *FLESH PUPPETS,* FOR EXAMPLE.
I TOOK SAMPLES WHEN WE LAST WORKED TOGETHER. I YANKED LITTLE BITS OF YOUR GRAY MATTER RIGHT OUT THROUGH YOUR NOSE.
MY SCIENCE... YOUR REGENERATIVE QUALITIES...TOGETHER THEY GAVE BIRTH TO SOMETHING THAT'S NOT EXISTED SINCE THE DAYS OF PRIMORDIAL OOZE.
I'VE GAINED SO MUCH FROM COLLECTING THESE LITTLE SAMPLES...
...BUT WHAT IS IT THAT YOU'VE *LOST?*
PERHAPS YOU SHOULD THINK ABOUT THAT WHILE THAT BRAIN OF YOURS STITCHES ITSELF BACK TOGETHER.
CLANK
THAT'S ENOUGH FOR TODAY, I SUSPECT.
LET HIM GET SOME REST.

NNNNN--

WHATEVER THEY DID TO ME... IT'S STARTING TO WEAR OFF.

HEAD CLEARING.

MUSCLES WORKING.

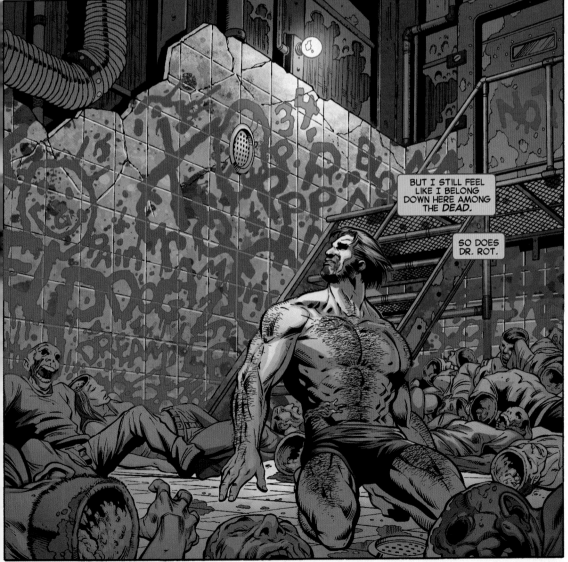

BUT I STILL FEEL LIKE I BELONG DOWN HERE AMONG THE DEAD.

SO DOES DR. ROT.

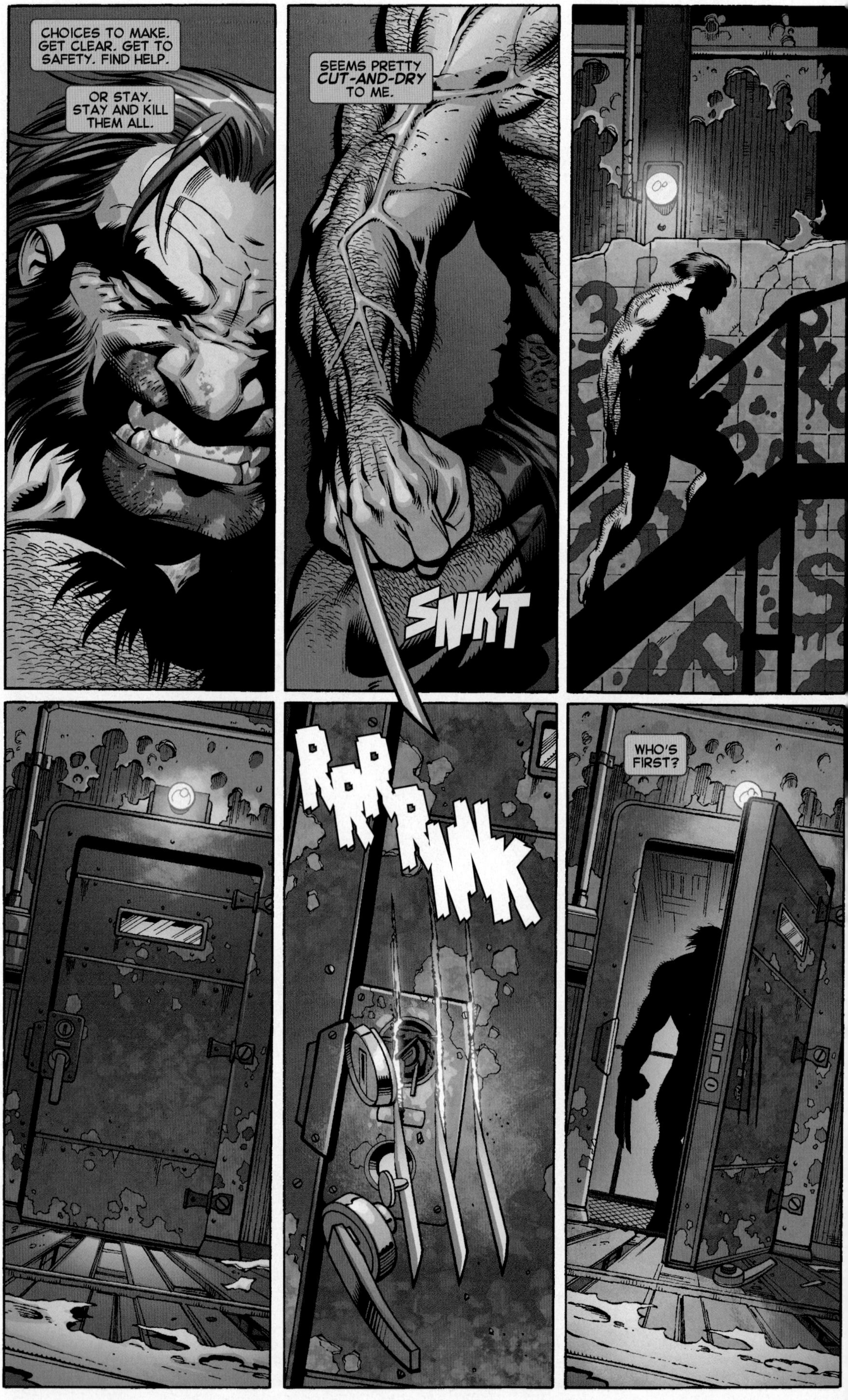
CHOICES TO MAKE. GET CLEAR. GET TO SAFETY. FIND HELP.
OR STAY. STAY AND KILL THEM ALL.
SEEMS PRETTY CUT-AND-DRY TO ME.
SNIKT
RRRRNNK
WHO'S FIRST?

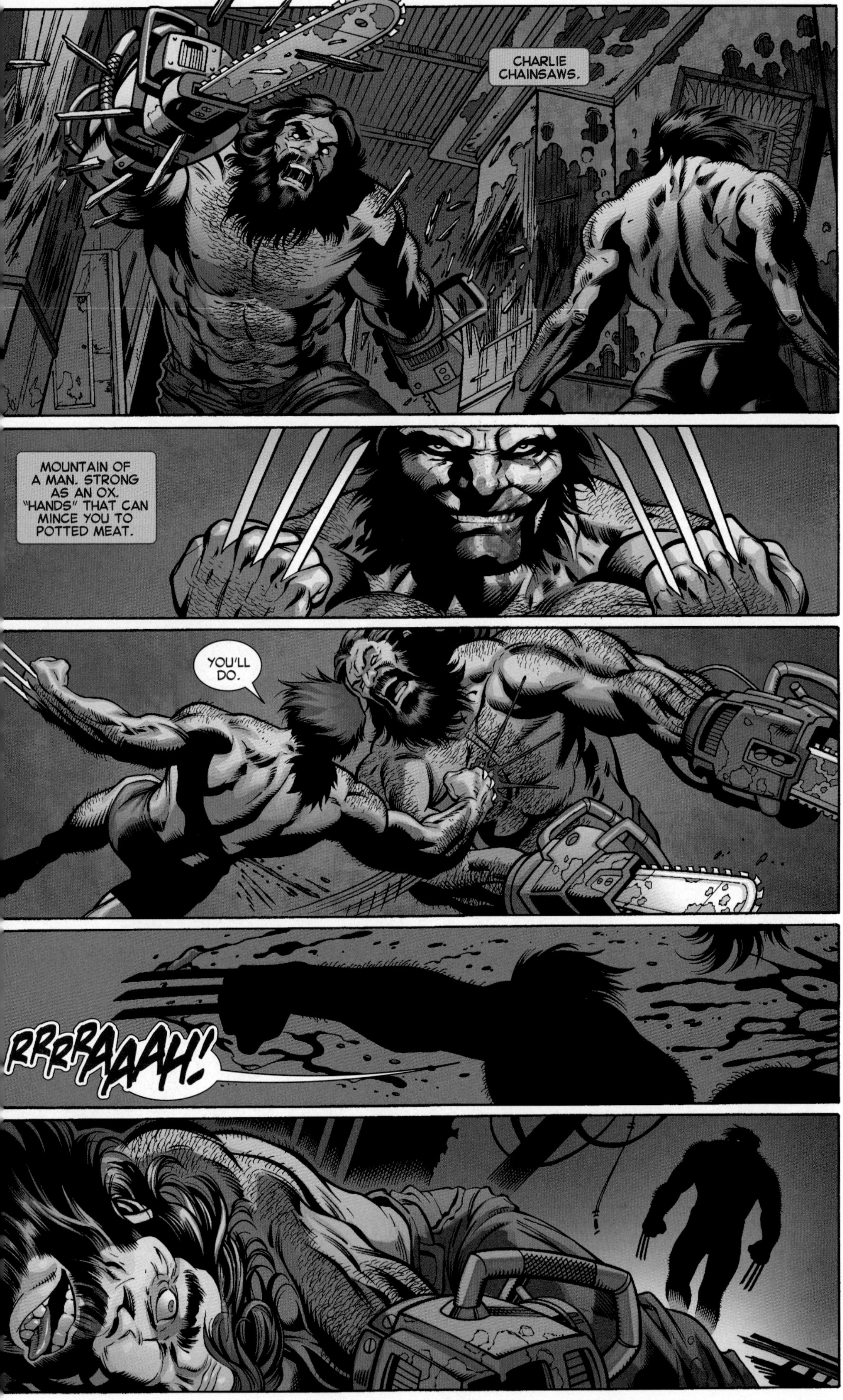

CHARLIE CHAINSAWS.
MOUNTAIN OF A MAN. STRONG AS AN OX. "HANDS" THAT CAN MINCE YOU TO POTTED MEAT.
YOU'LL DO.
RRRRAAAH!

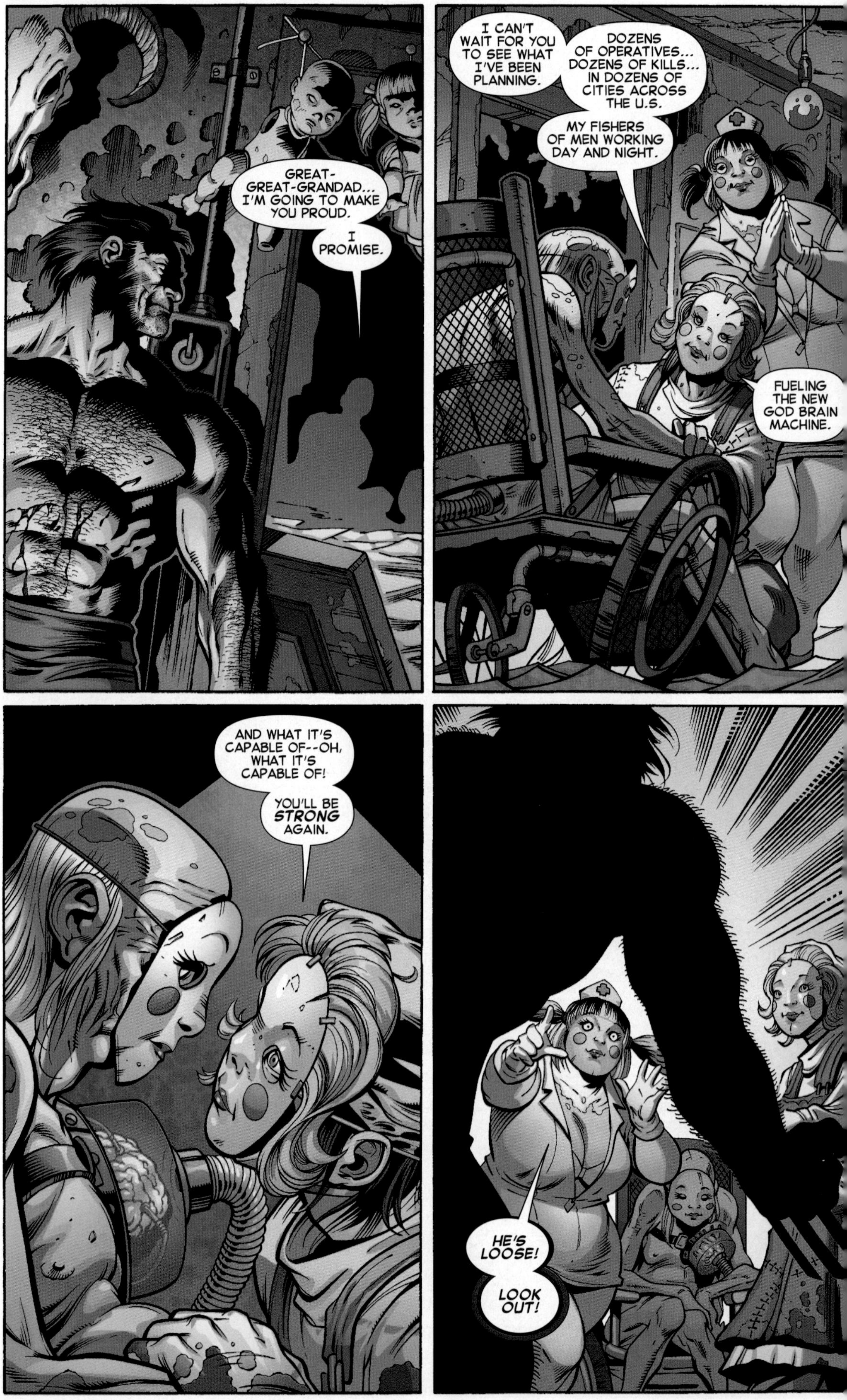
GREAT-GREAT-GRANDAD... I'M GOING TO MAKE YOU PROUD.
I PROMISE.
I CAN'T WAIT FOR YOU TO SEE WHAT I'VE BEEN PLANNING.
DOZENS OF OPERATIVES... DOZENS OF KILLS... IN DOZENS OF CITIES ACROSS THE U.S.
MY FISHERS OF MEN WORKING DAY AND NIGHT.
FUELING THE NEW GOD BRAIN MACHINE.
AND WHAT IT'S CAPABLE OF--OH, WHAT IT'S CAPABLE OF!
YOU'LL BE STRONG AGAIN.
HE'S LOOSE!
LOOK OUT!

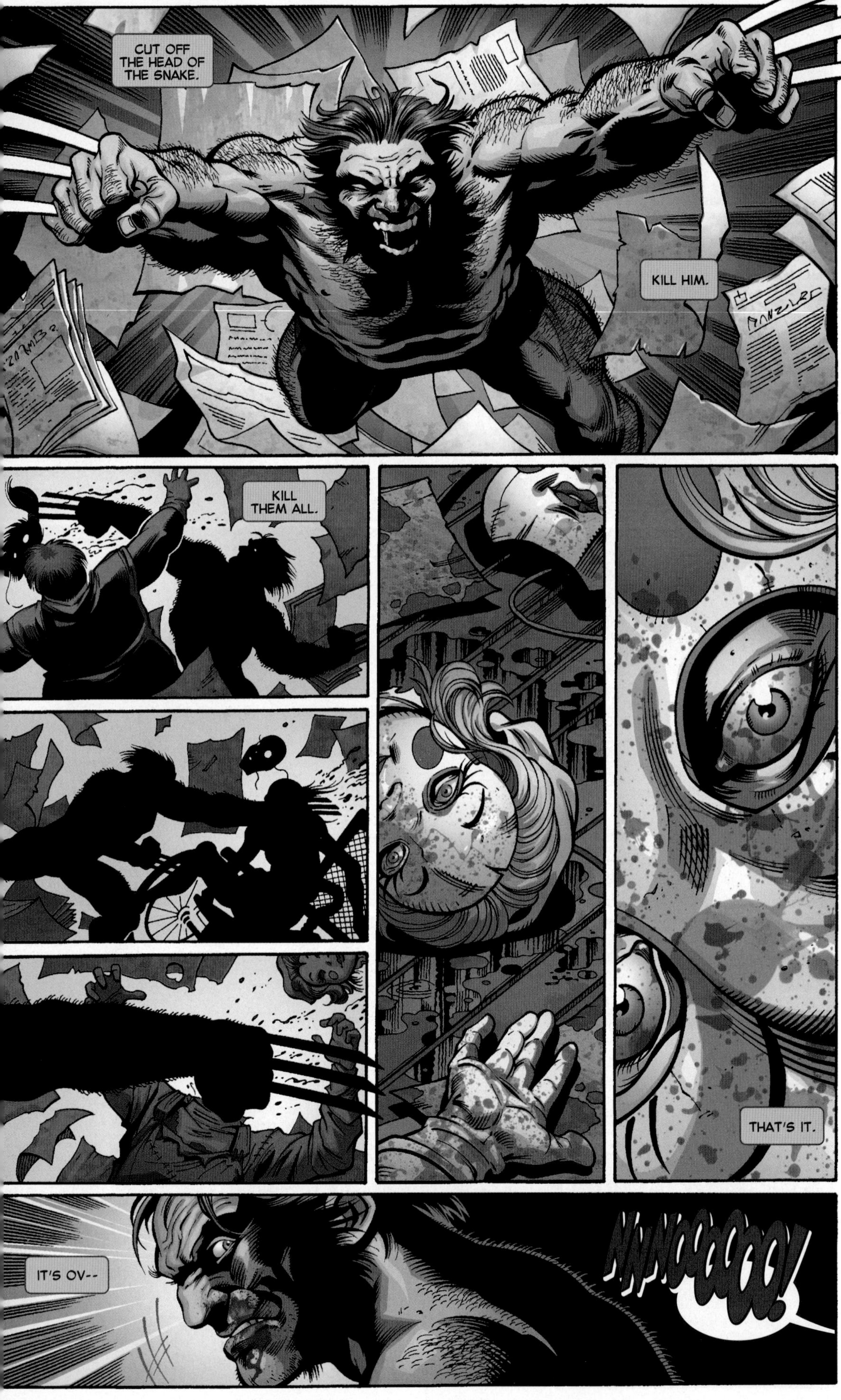
CUT OFF THE HEAD OF THE SNAKE.
KILL HIM.
KILL THEM ALL.
THAT'S IT.
IT'S OV--
NNNOOOOOO!

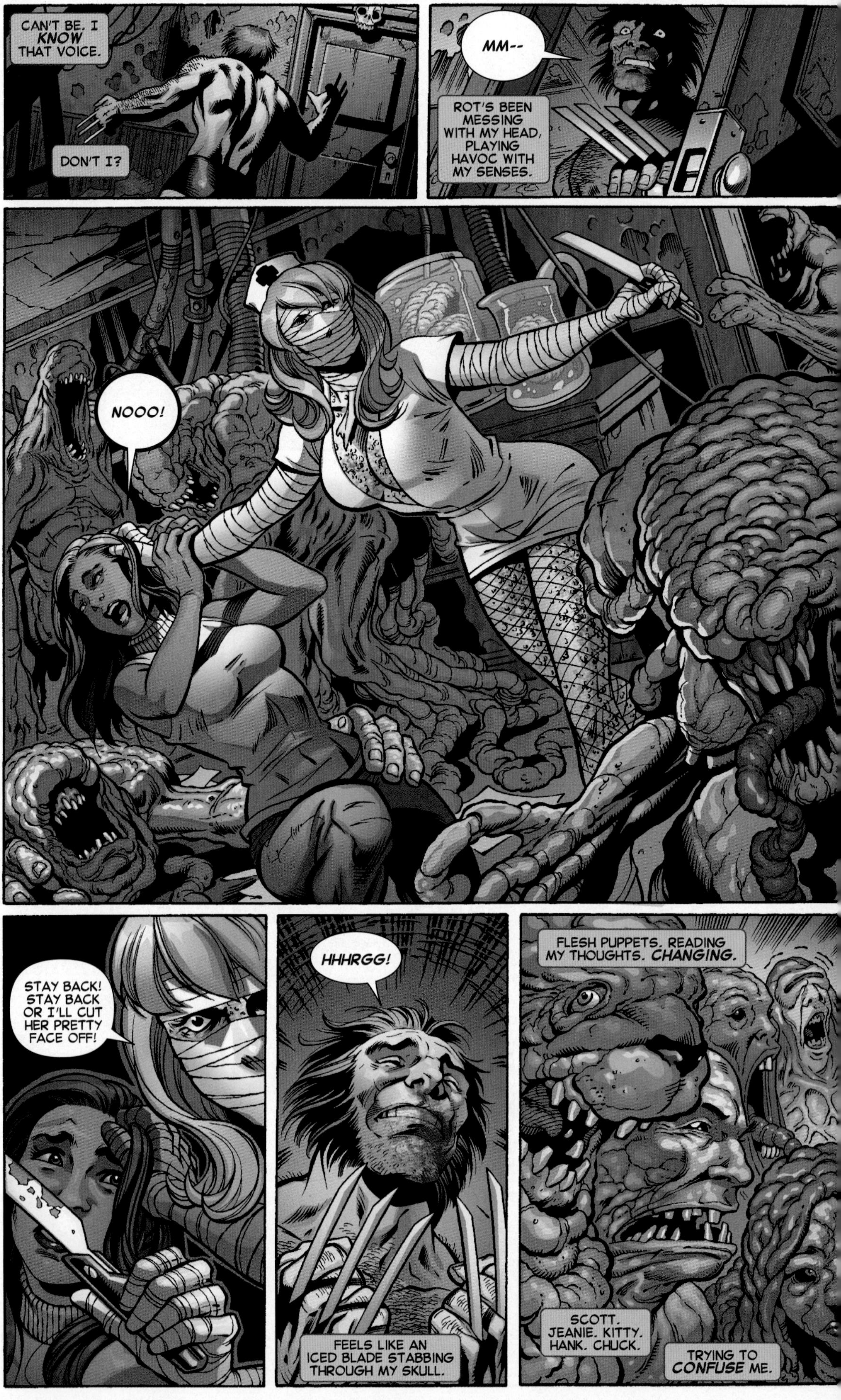
CAN'T BE. I KNOW THAT VOICE.
DON'T I?
MM--
ROT'S BEEN MESSING WITH MY HEAD, PLAYING HAVOC WITH MY SENSES.
NOOO!
STAY BACK! STAY BACK OR I'LL CUT HER PRETTY FACE OFF!
HHHRGG!
FEELS LIKE AN ICED BLADE STABBING THROUGH MY SKULL.
FLESH PUPPETS. READING MY THOUGHTS. CHANGING.
SCOTT. JEANIE. KITTY. HANK. CHUCK.
TRYING TO CONFUSE ME.

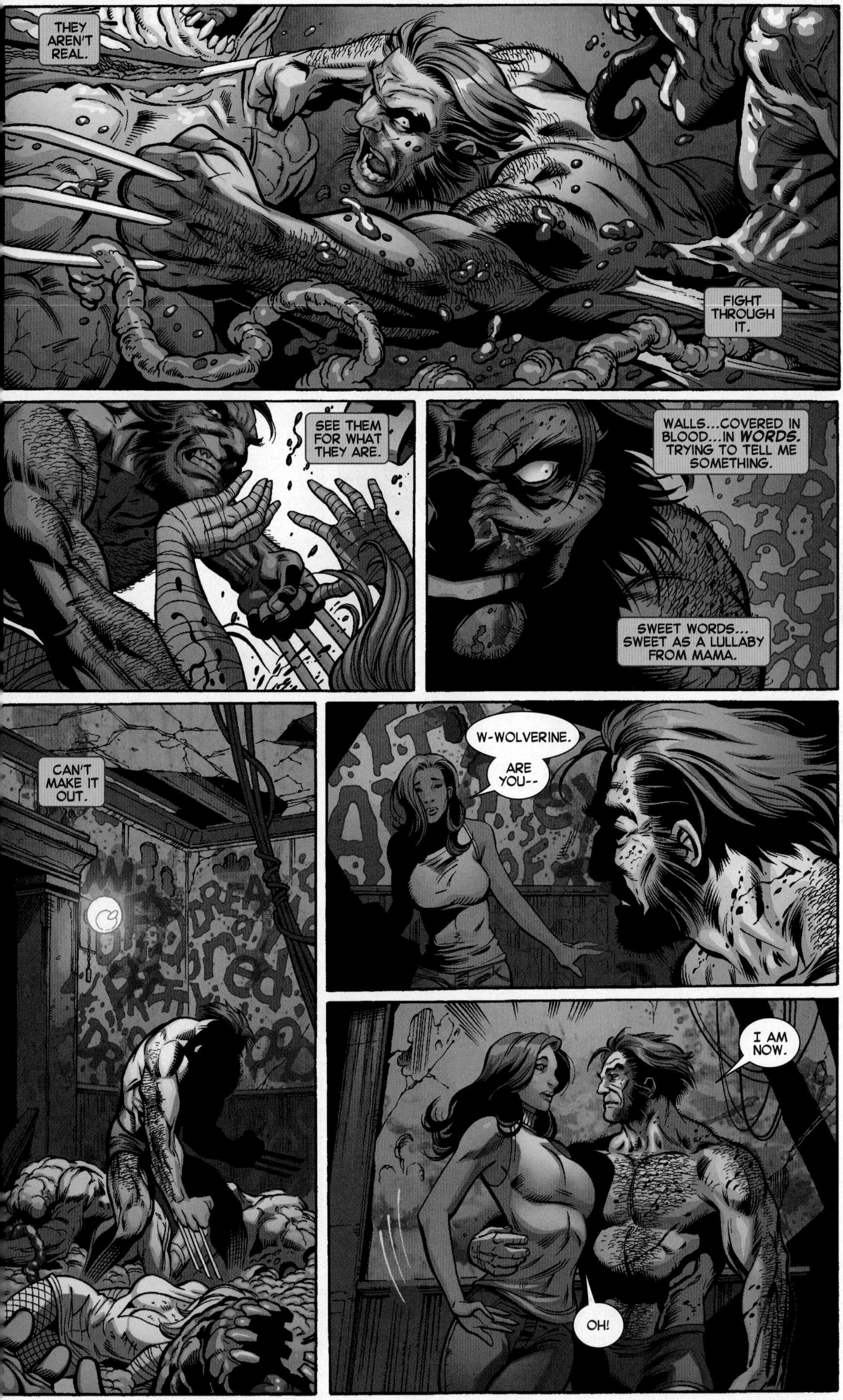
THEY AREN'T REAL.
FIGHT THROUGH IT.
SEE THEM FOR WHAT THEY ARE.
WALLS...COVERED IN BLOOD...IN WORDS. TRYING TO TELL ME SOMETHING.
SWEET WORDS... SWEET AS A LULLABY FROM MAMA.
CAN'T MAKE IT OUT.
W-WOLVERINE.
ARE YOU--
I AM NOW.
OH!

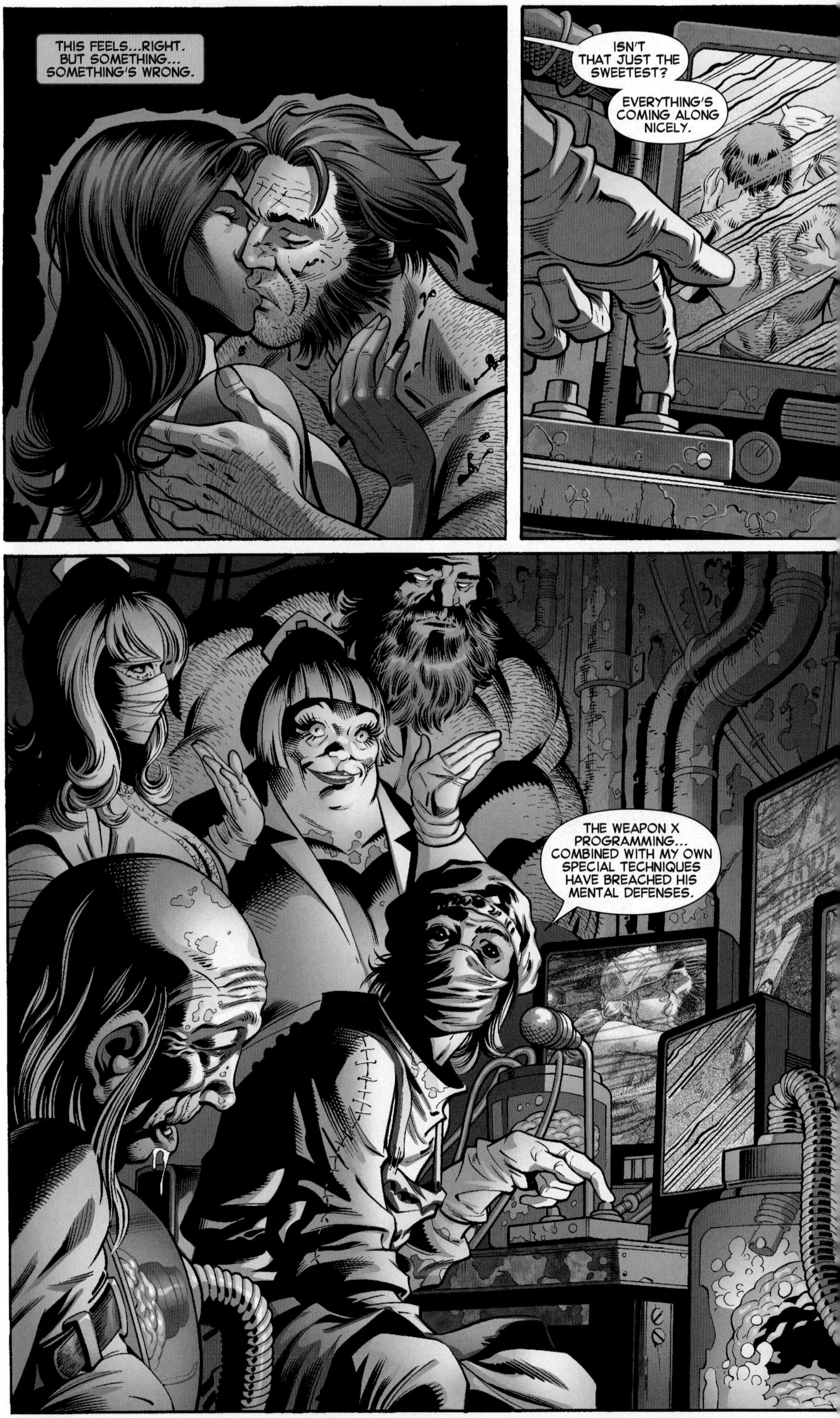
THIS FEELS...RIGHT. BUT SOMETHING... SOMETHING'S WRONG.
ISN'T THAT JUST THE SWEETEST?
EVERYTHING'S COMING ALONG NICELY.
THE WEAPON X PROGRAMMING... COMBINED WITH MY OWN SPECIAL TECHNIQUES HAVE BREACHED HIS MENTAL DEFENSES.

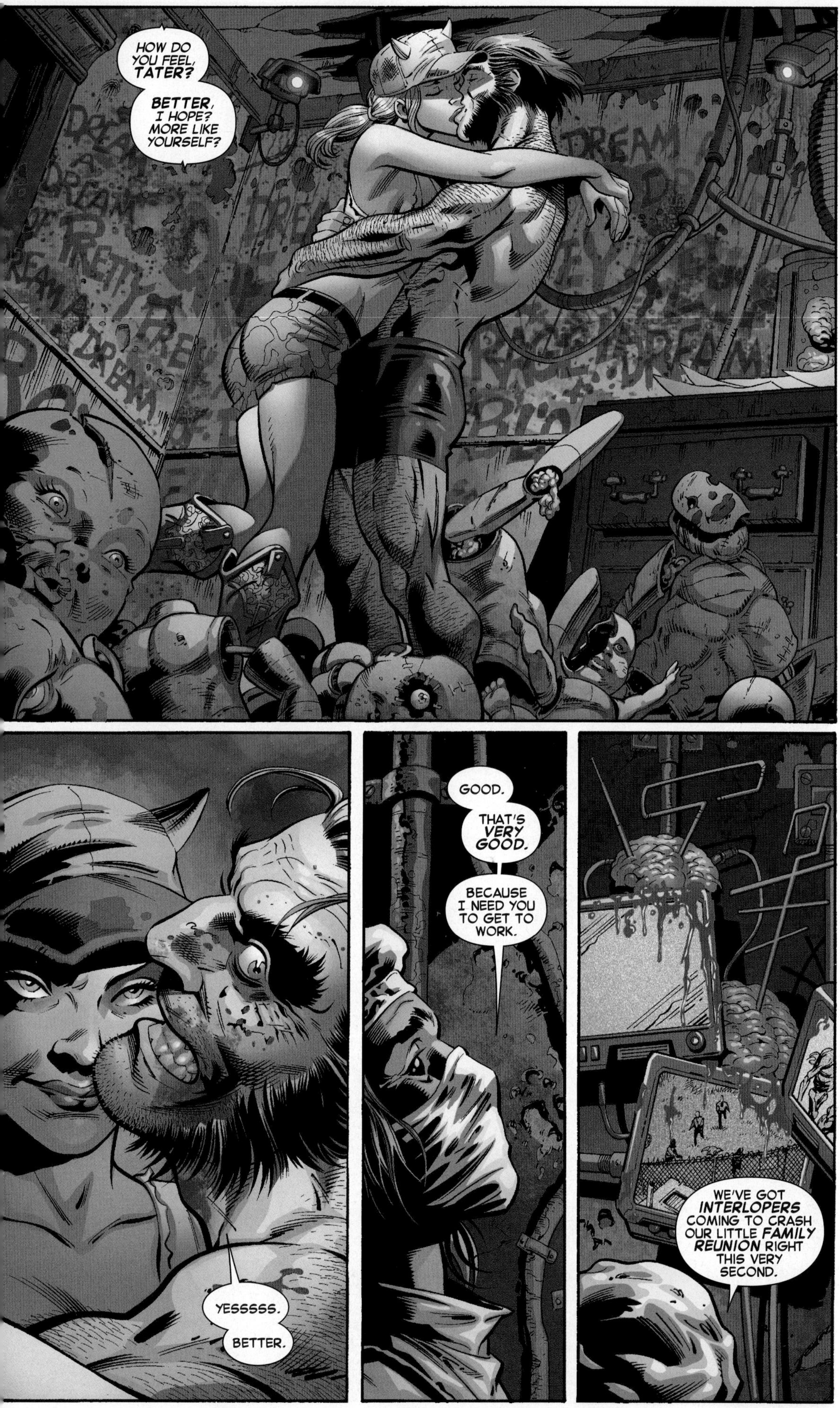
HOW DO YOU FEEL, TATER?
BETTER, I HOPE? MORE LIKE YOURSELF?
YESSSSS.
BETTER.
GOOD.
THAT'S VERY GOOD.
BECAUSE I NEED YOU TO GET TO WORK.
WE'VE GOT INTERLOPERS COMING TO CRASH OUR LITTLE FAMILY REUNION RIGHT THIS VERY SECOND.

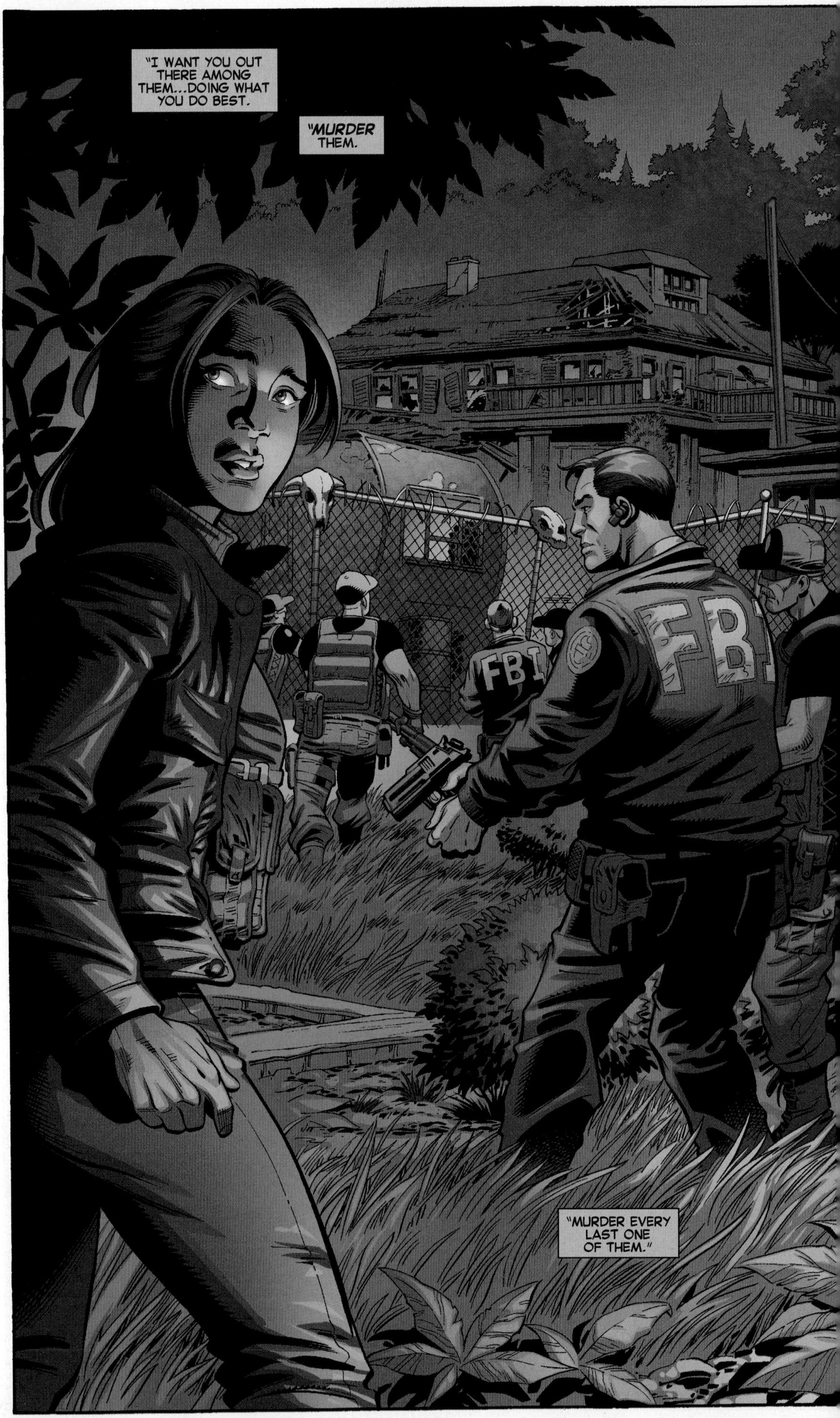
"I WANT YOU OUT THERE AMONG THEM...DOING WHAT YOU DO BEST.
"MURDER THEM.
FBI
FBI
"MURDER EVERY LAST ONE OF THEM."

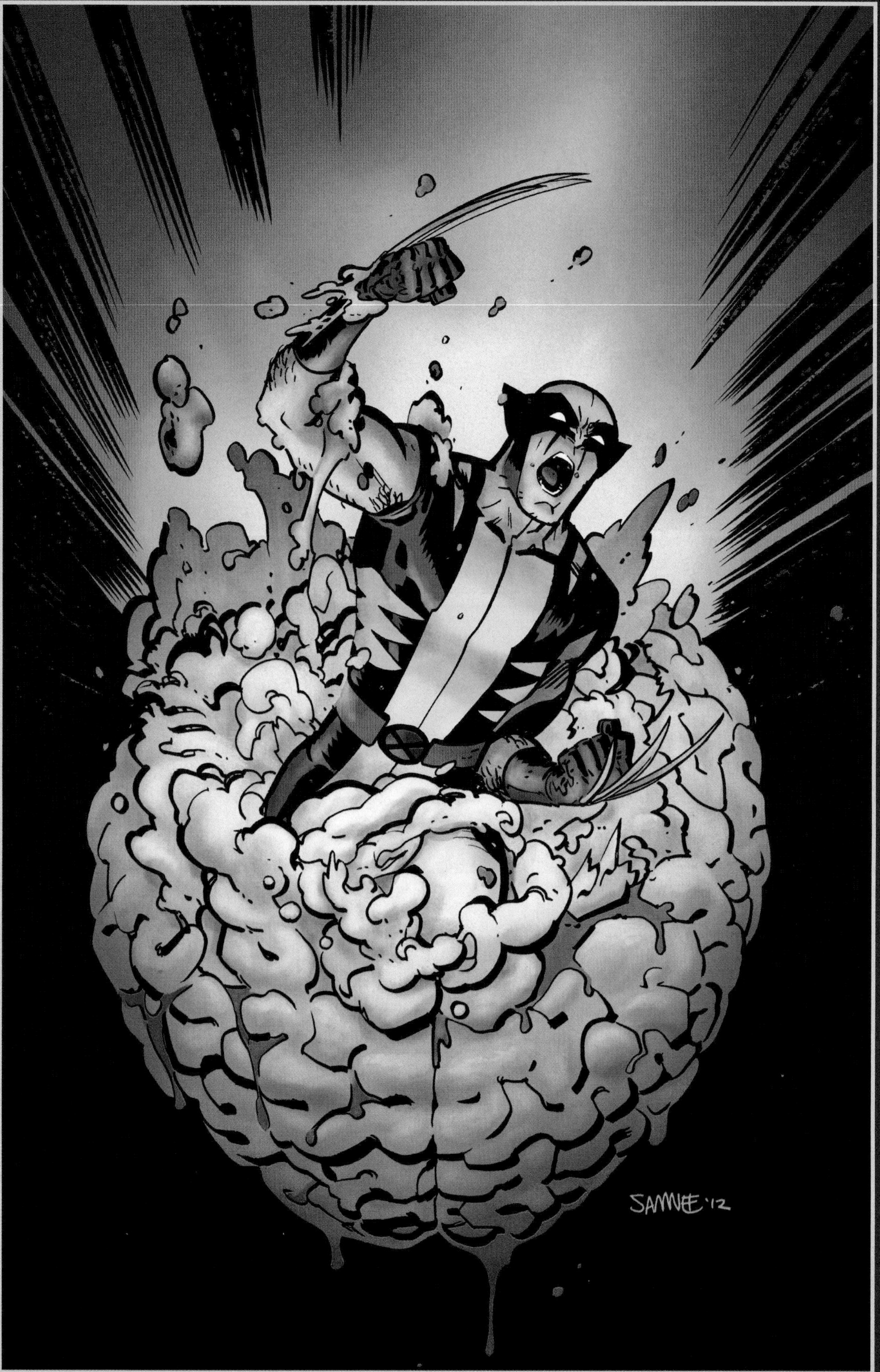
SAMNEE '12

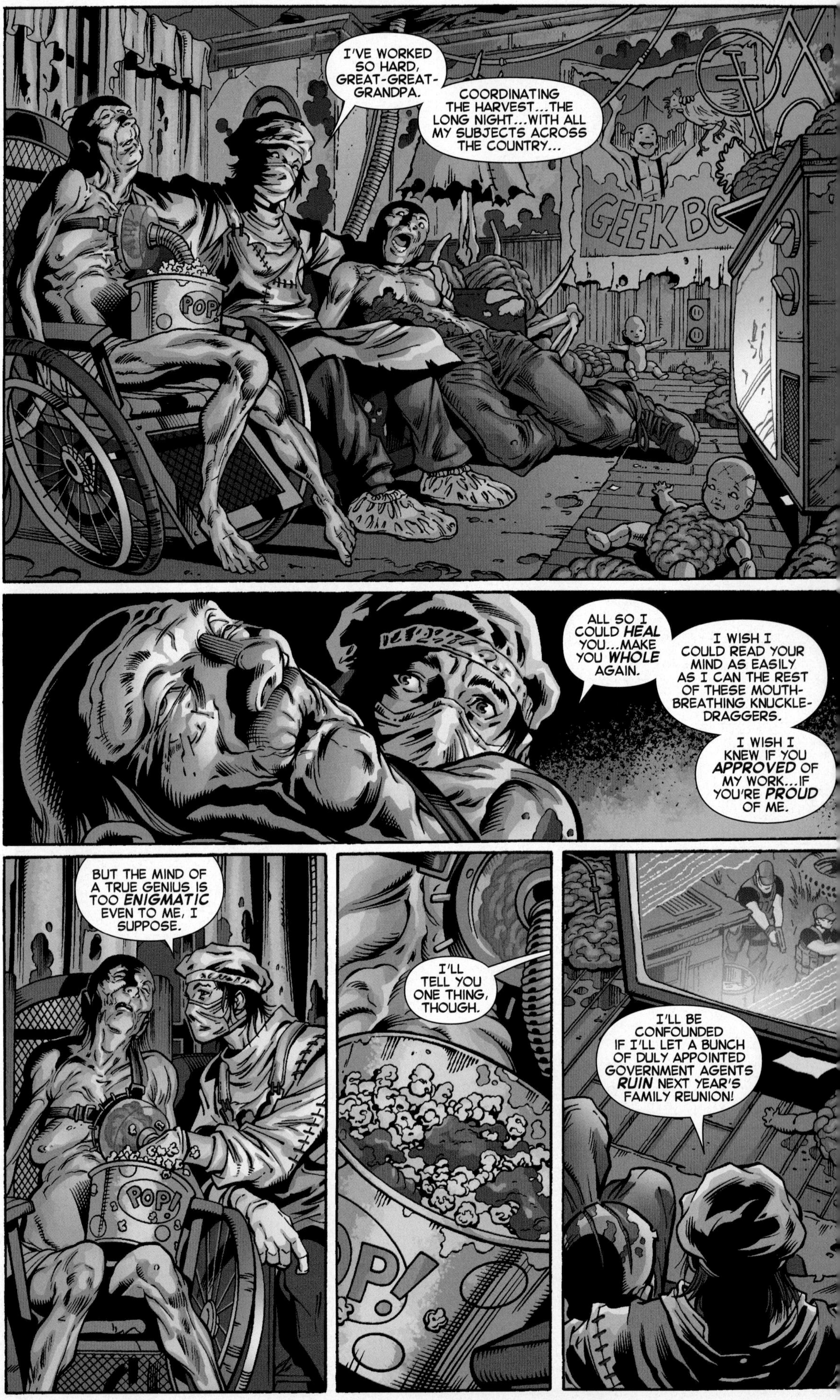
I'VE WORKED SO HARD, GREAT-GREAT-GRANDPA.
COORDINATING THE HARVEST...THE LONG NIGHT...WITH ALL MY SUBJECTS ACROSS THE COUNTRY...
GEEK BO
POP!
ALL SO I COULD HEAL YOU...MAKE YOU WHOLE AGAIN.
I WISH I COULD READ YOUR MIND AS EASILY AS I CAN THE REST OF THESE MOUTH-BREATHING KNUCKLE-DRAGGERS.
I WISH I KNEW IF YOU APPROVED OF MY WORK...IF YOU'RE PROUD OF ME.
BUT THE MIND OF A TRUE GENIUS IS TOO ENIGMATIC EVEN TO ME, I SUPPOSE.
POP!
I'LL TELL YOU ONE THING, THOUGH.
I'LL BE CONFOUNDED IF I'LL LET A BUNCH OF DULY APPOINTED GOVERNMENT AGENTS RUIN NEXT YEAR'S FAMILY REUNION!

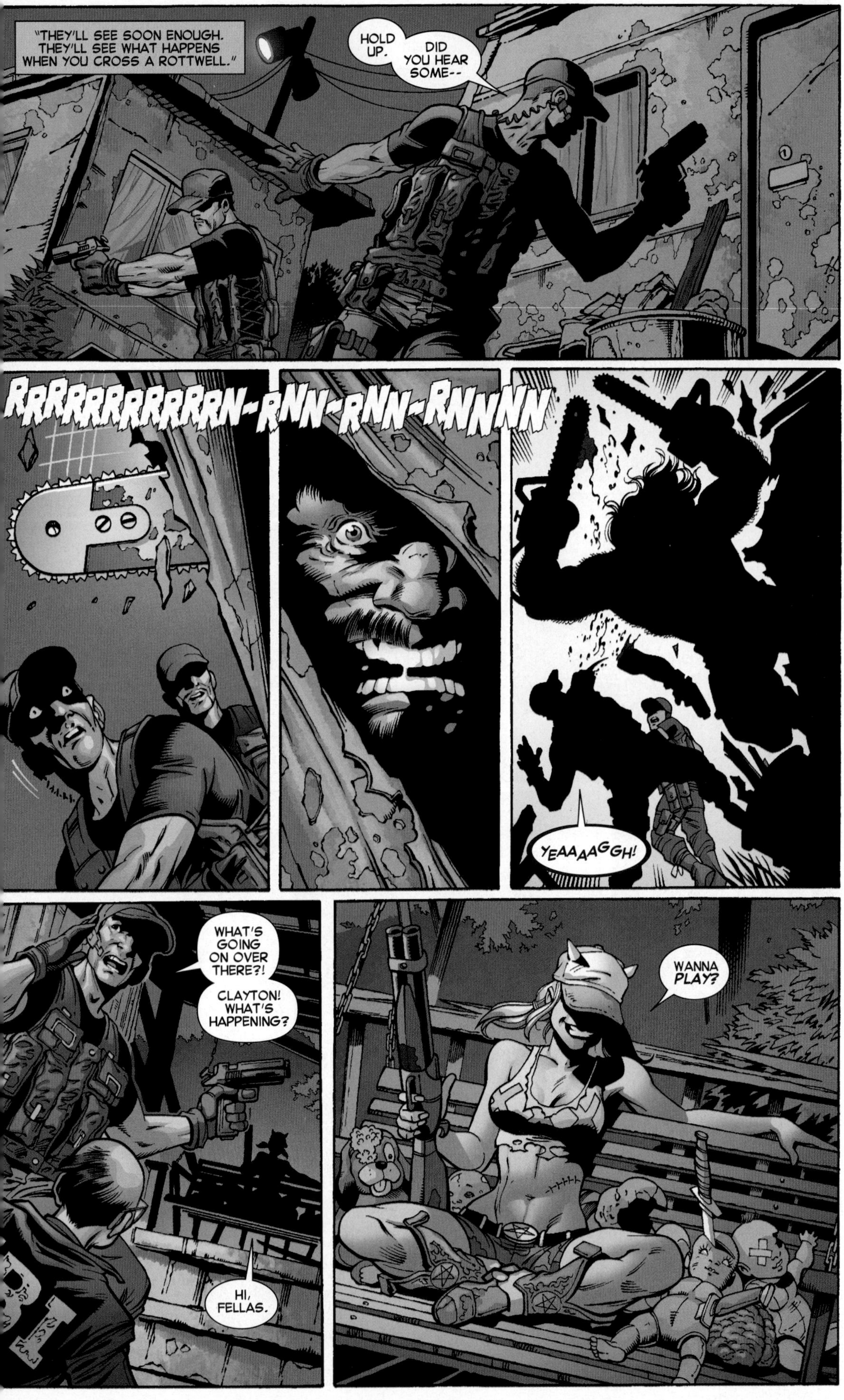
"THEY'LL SEE SOON ENOUGH. THEY'LL SEE WHAT HAPPENS WHEN YOU CROSS A ROTTWELL."
HOLD UP.
DID YOU HEAR SOME--
RRRRRRRRRRRRN-RNN-RNN-RNNNN
YEAAAAGGH!
WHAT'S GOING ON OVER THERE?!
CLAYTON! WHAT'S HAPPENING?
HI, FELLAS.
WANNA PLAY?

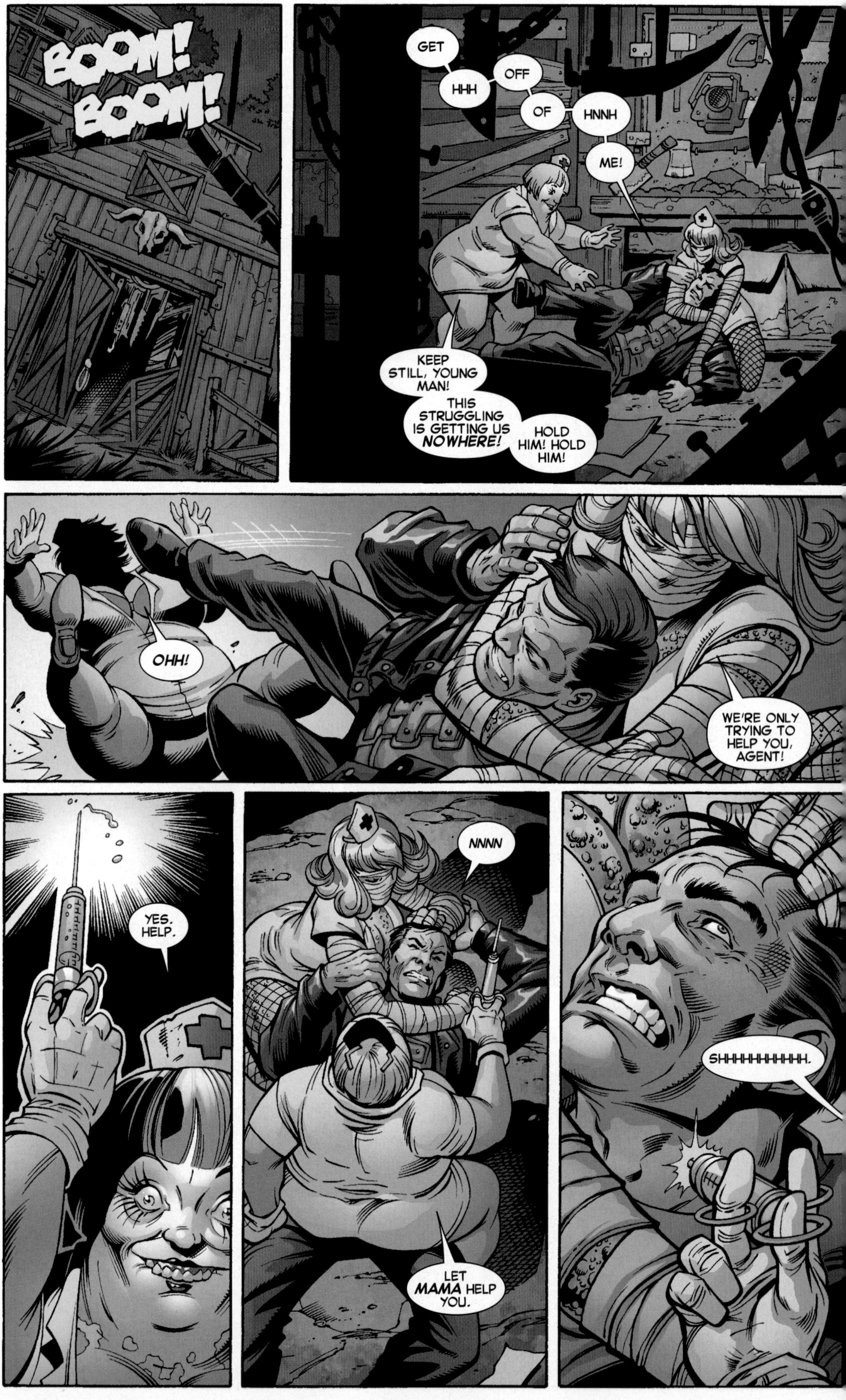
BOOM! BOOM!
GET
HHH
OFF
OF
HNNH
ME!
KEEP STILL, YOUNG MAN!
THIS STRUGGLING IS GETTING US NOWHERE!
HOLD HIM! HOLD HIM!
OHH!
WE'RE ONLY TRYING TO HELP YOU, AGENT!
YES. HELP.
NNNN
LET MAMA HELP YOU.
SHHHHHHHHHH.

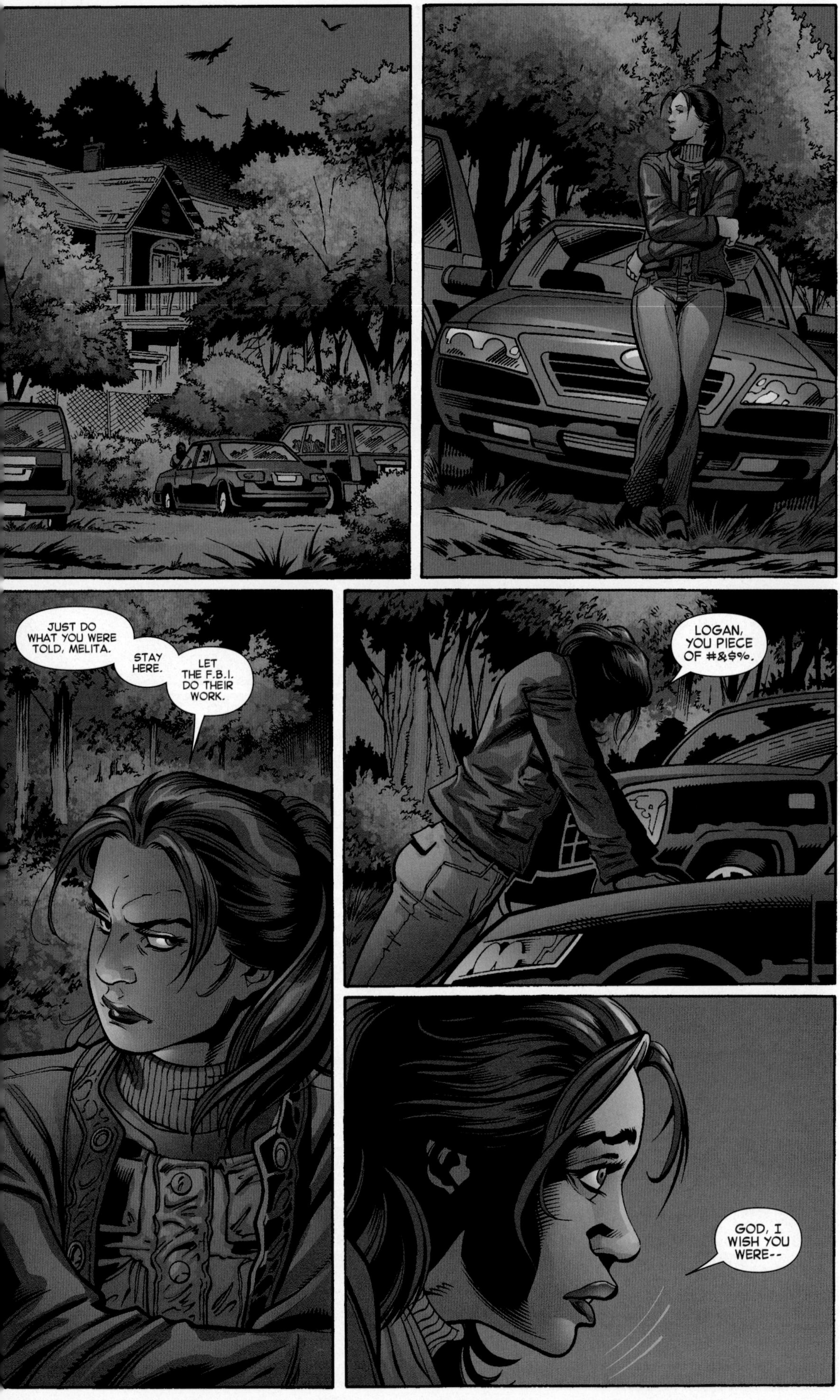
JUST DO WHAT YOU WERE TOLD, MELITA.
STAY HERE.
LET THE F.B.I. DO THEIR WORK.
LOGAN, YOU PIECE OF #&$%.
GOD, I WISH YOU WERE--

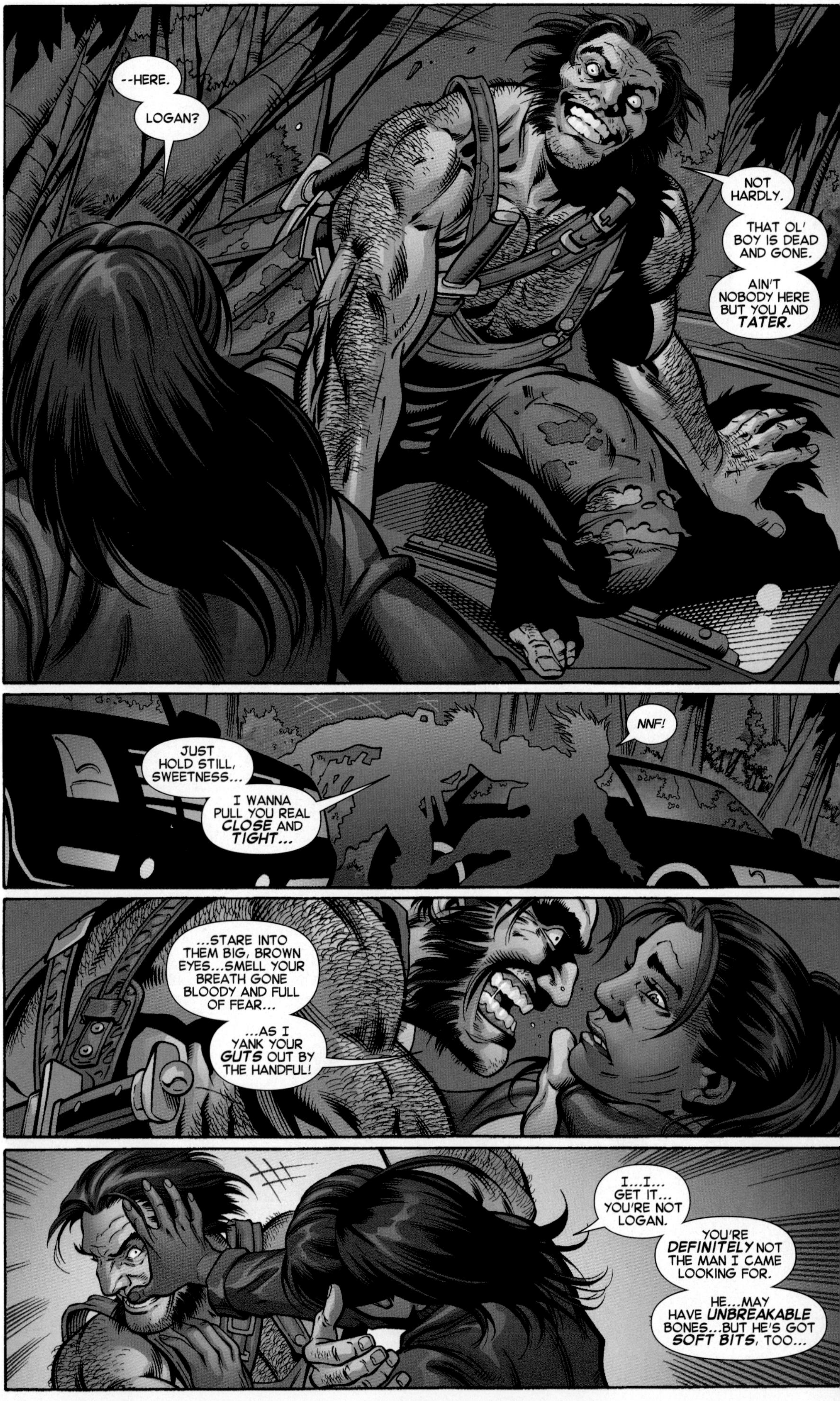
--HERE.
LOGAN?
NOT HARDLY.
THAT OL' BOY IS DEAD AND GONE.
AIN'T NOBODY HERE BUT YOU AND TATER.
JUST HOLD STILL, SWEETNESS...
I WANNA PULL YOU REAL CLOSE AND TIGHT...
NNF!
...STARE INTO THEM BIG, BROWN EYES...SMELL YOUR BREATH GONE BLOODY AND FULL OF FEAR...
...AS I YANK YOUR GUTS OUT BY THE HANDFUL!
I...I... GET IT... YOU'RE NOT LOGAN.
YOU'RE DEFINITELY NOT THE MAN I CAME LOOKING FOR.
HE...MAY HAVE UNBREAKABLE BONES...BUT HE'S GOT SOFT BITS, TOO...

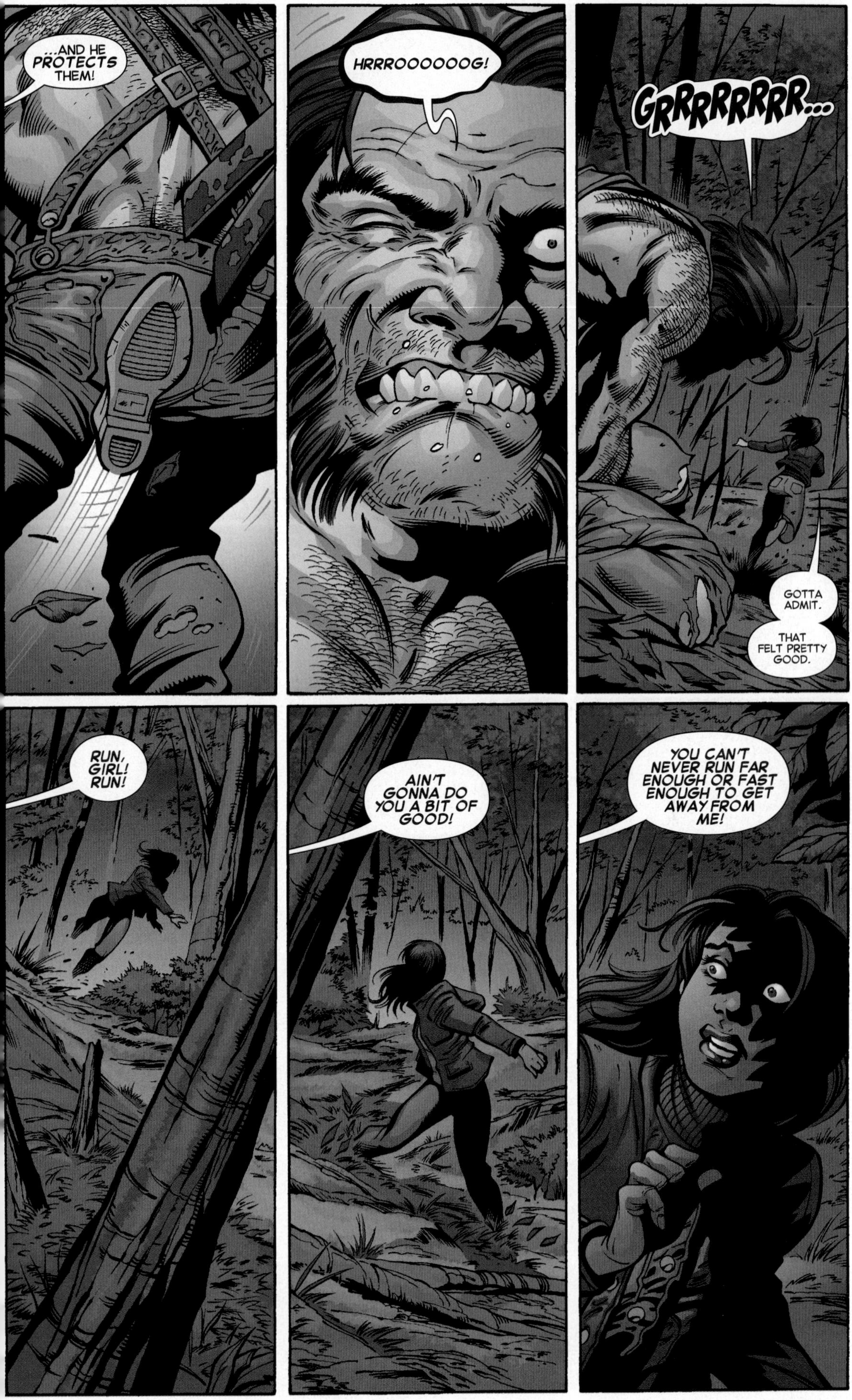
...AND HE PROTECTS THEM!
HRRROOOOOOG!
GRRRRRRRR...
GOTTA ADMIT.
THAT FELT PRETTY GOOD.
RUN, GIRL! RUN!
AIN'T GONNA DO YOU A BIT OF GOOD!
YOU CAN'T NEVER RUN FAR ENOUGH OR FAST ENOUGH TO GET AWAY FROM ME!

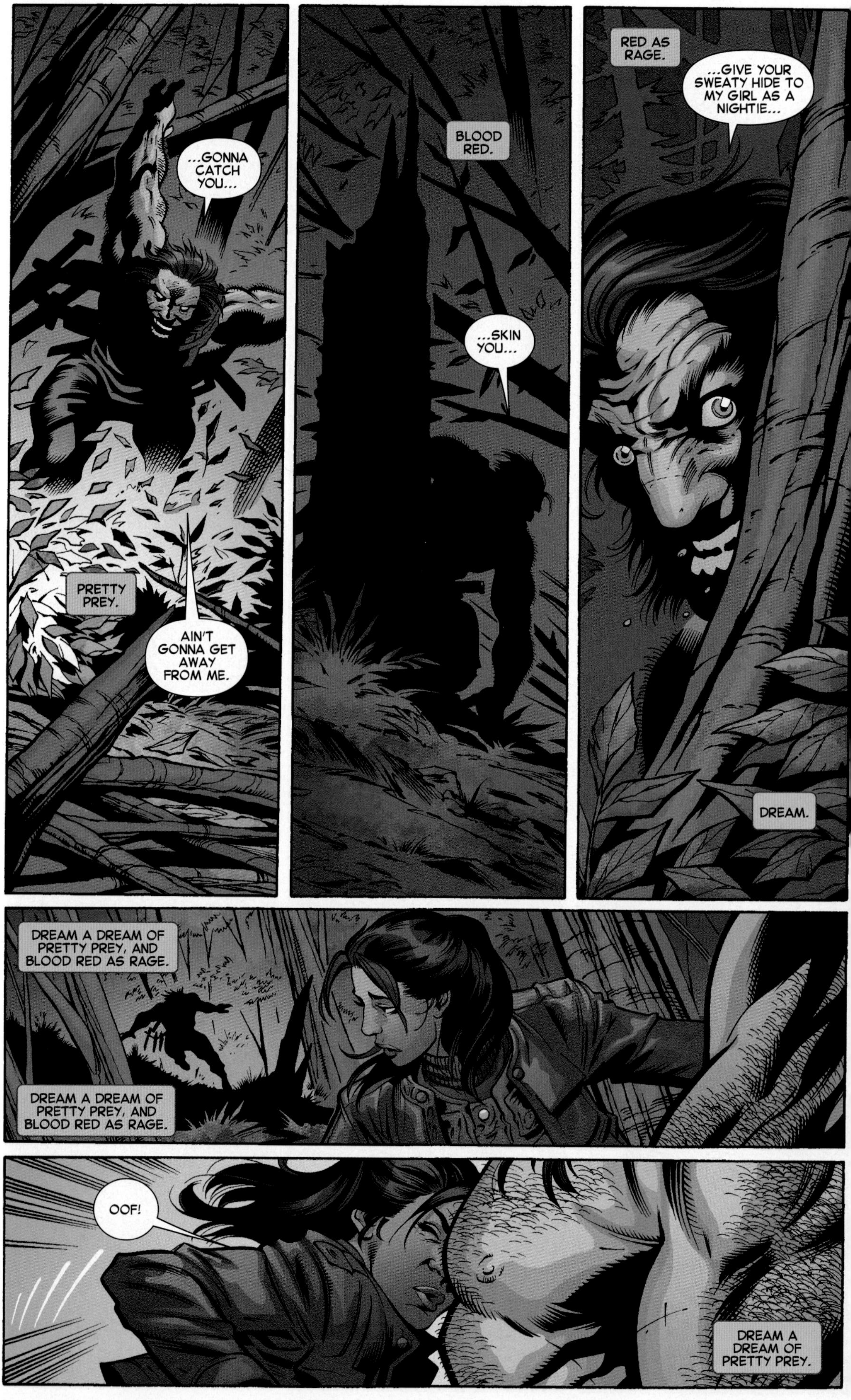
...GONNA CATCH YOU...
PRETTY PREY.
AIN'T GONNA GET AWAY FROM ME.
BLOOD RED.
...SKIN YOU...
RED AS RAGE.
...GIVE YOUR SWEATY HIDE TO MY GIRL AS A NIGHTIE...
DREAM.
DREAM A DREAM OF PRETTY PREY, AND BLOOD RED AS RAGE.
DREAM A DREAM OF PRETTY PREY, AND BLOOD RED AS RAGE.
OOF!
DREAM A DREAM OF PRETTY PREY.

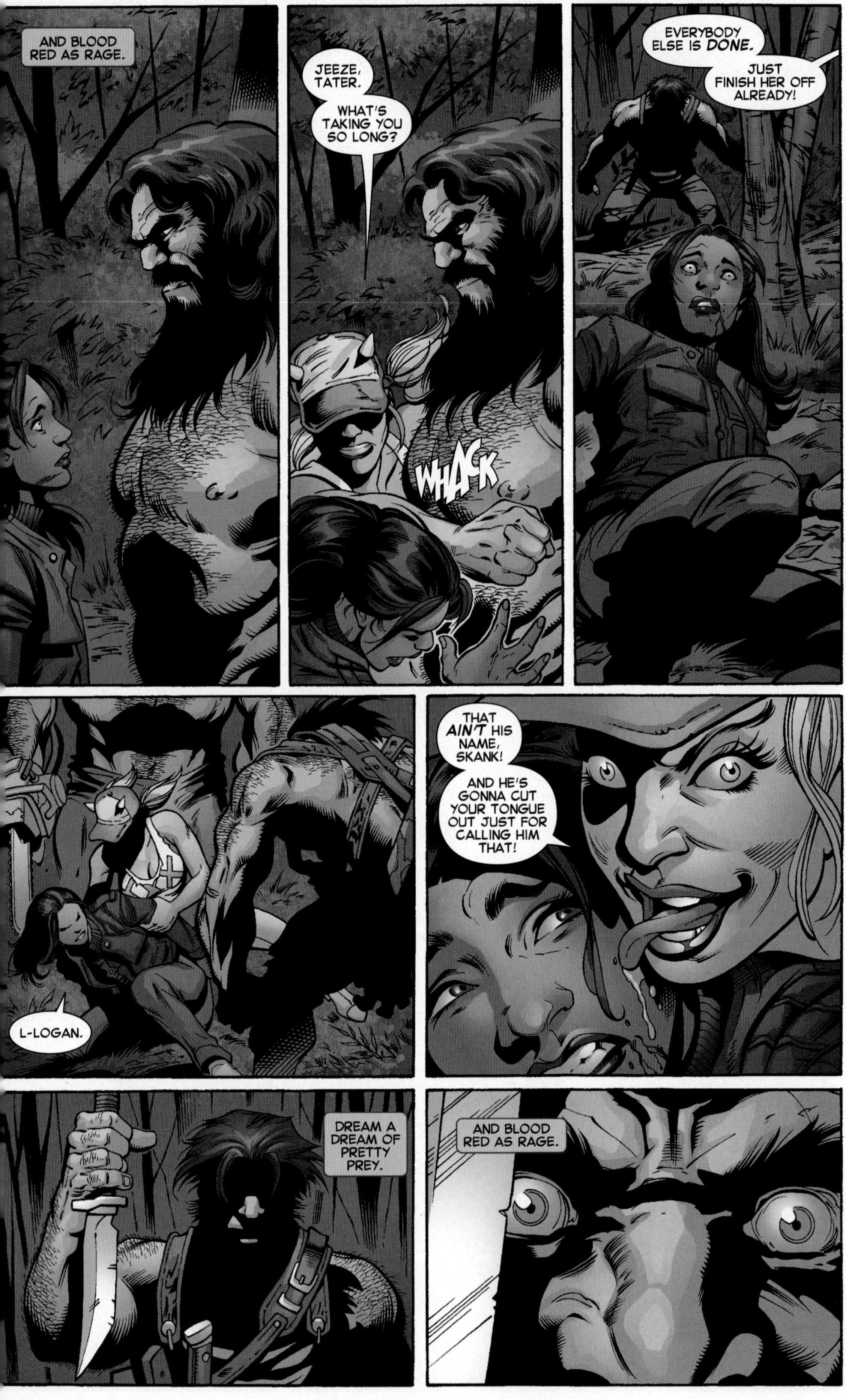
AND BLOOD RED AS RAGE.
JEEZE, TATER.
WHAT'S TAKING YOU SO LONG?
WHACK
EVERYBODY ELSE IS DONE.
JUST FINISH HER OFF ALREADY!
L-LOGAN.
THAT AIN'T HIS NAME, SKANK!
AND HE'S GONNA CUT YOUR TONGUE OUT JUST FOR CALLING HIM THAT!
DREAM A DREAM OF PRETTY PREY.
AND BLOOD RED AS RAGE.

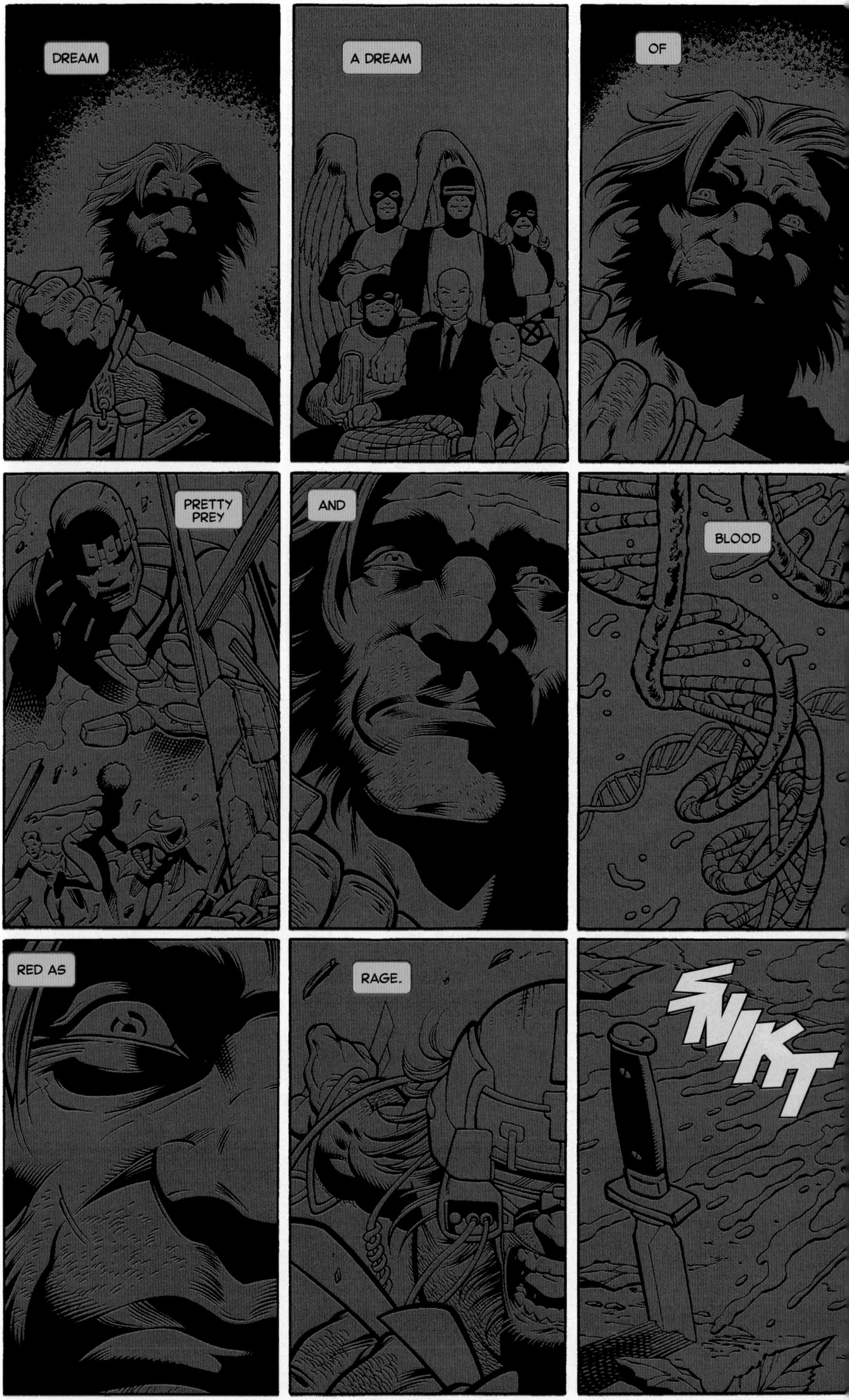
DREAM
A DREAM
OF
PRETTY PREY
AND
BLOOD
RED AS
RAGE.
SNIKT

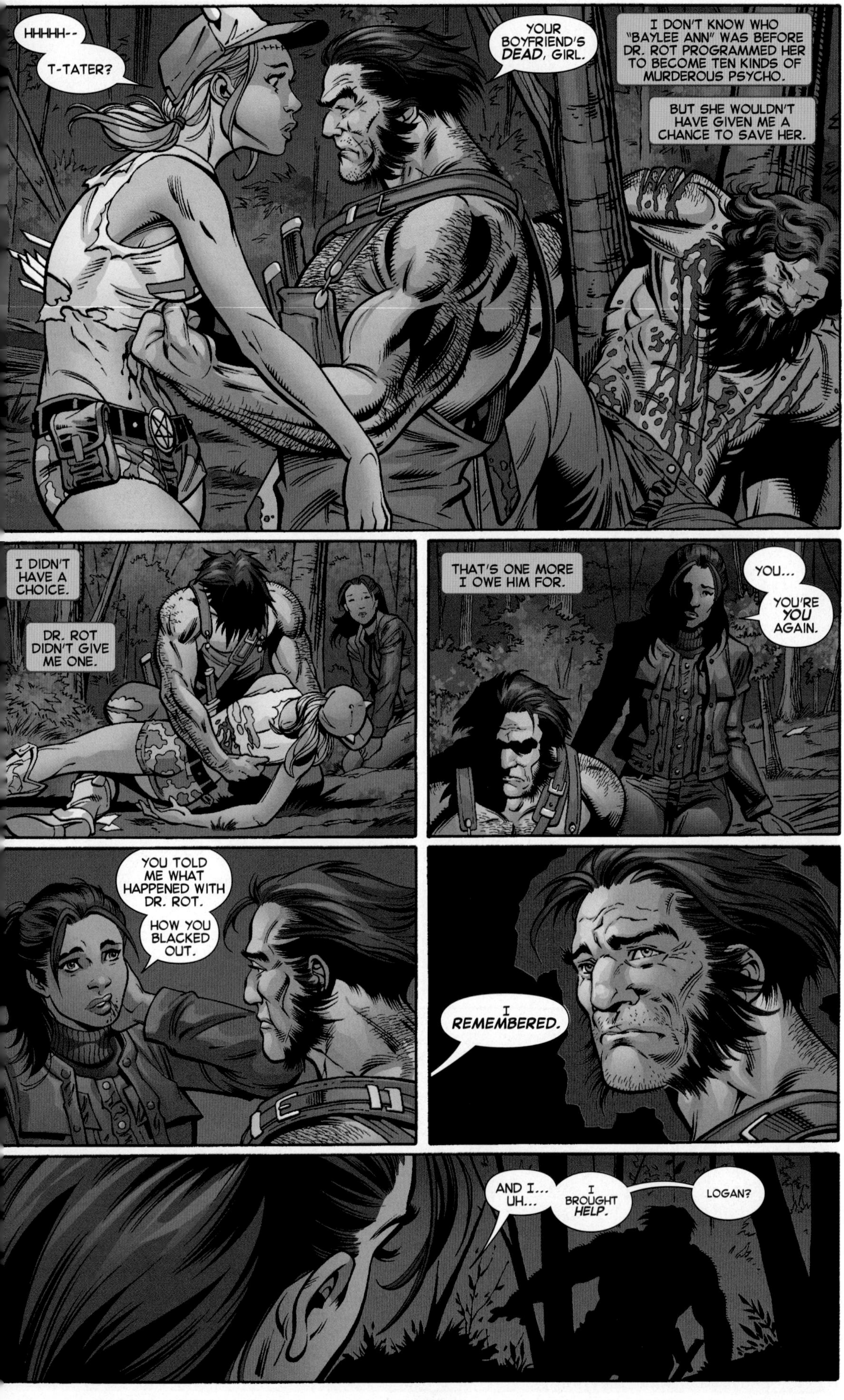
HHHHH--
T-TATER?
YOUR BOYFRIEND'S DEAD, GIRL.
I DON'T KNOW WHO "BAYLEE ANN" WAS BEFORE DR. ROT PROGRAMMED HER TO BECOME TEN KINDS OF MURDEROUS PSYCHO.
BUT SHE WOULDN'T HAVE GIVEN ME A CHANCE TO SAVE HER.
I DIDN'T HAVE A CHOICE.
DR. ROT DIDN'T GIVE ME ONE.
THAT'S ONE MORE I OWE HIM FOR.
YOU...
YOU'RE YOU AGAIN.
YOU TOLD ME WHAT HAPPENED WITH DR. ROT.
HOW YOU BLACKED OUT.
I REMEMBERED.
AND I... UH...
I BROUGHT HELP.
LOGAN?

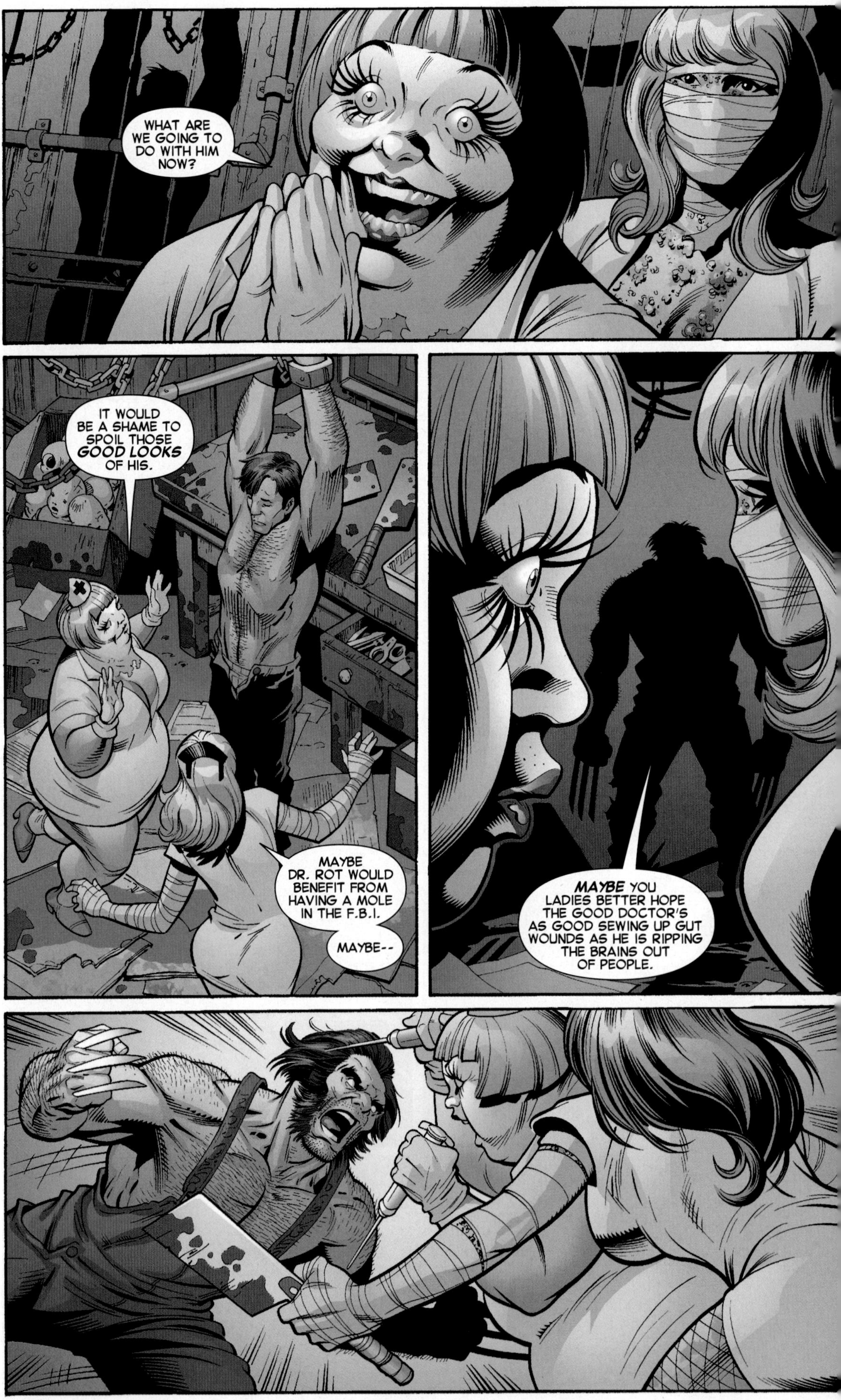
WHAT ARE WE GOING TO DO WITH HIM NOW?
IT WOULD BE A SHAME TO SPOIL THOSE GOOD LOOKS OF HIS.
MAYBE DR. ROT WOULD BENEFIT FROM HAVING A MOLE IN THE F.B.I.
MAYBE--
MAYBE YOU LADIES BETTER HOPE THE GOOD DOCTOR'S AS GOOD SEWING UP GUT WOUNDS AS HE IS RIPPING THE BRAINS OUT OF PEOPLE.

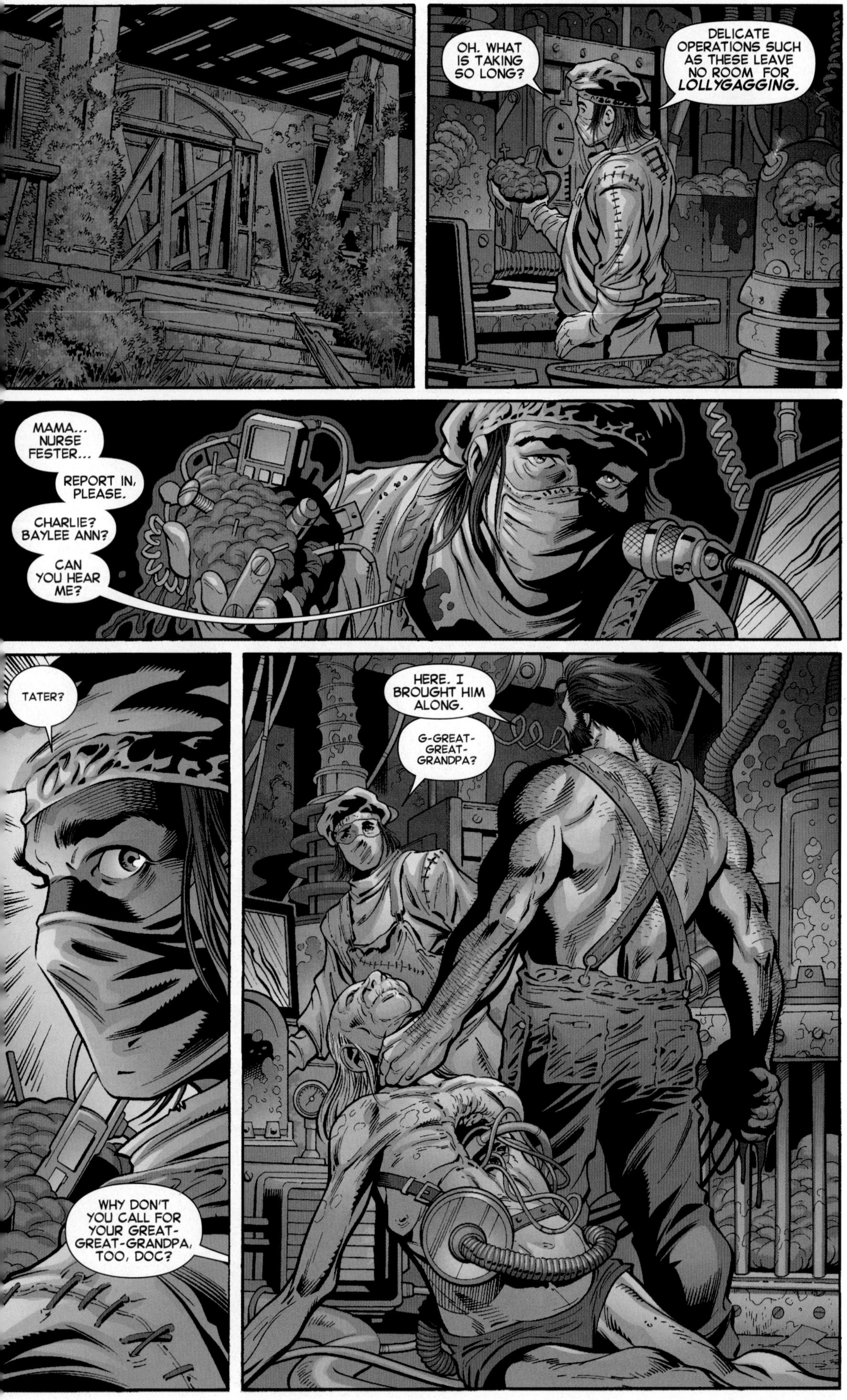
OH. WHAT IS TAKING SO LONG?
DELICATE OPERATIONS SUCH AS THESE LEAVE NO ROOM FOR LOLLYGAGGING.
MAMA... NURSE FESTER...
REPORT IN, PLEASE.
CHARLIE? BAYLEE ANN?
CAN YOU HEAR ME?
TATER?
WHY DON'T YOU CALL FOR YOUR GREAT-GREAT-GRANDPA, TOO, DOC?
HERE. I BROUGHT HIM ALONG.
G-GREAT-GREAT-GRANDPA?

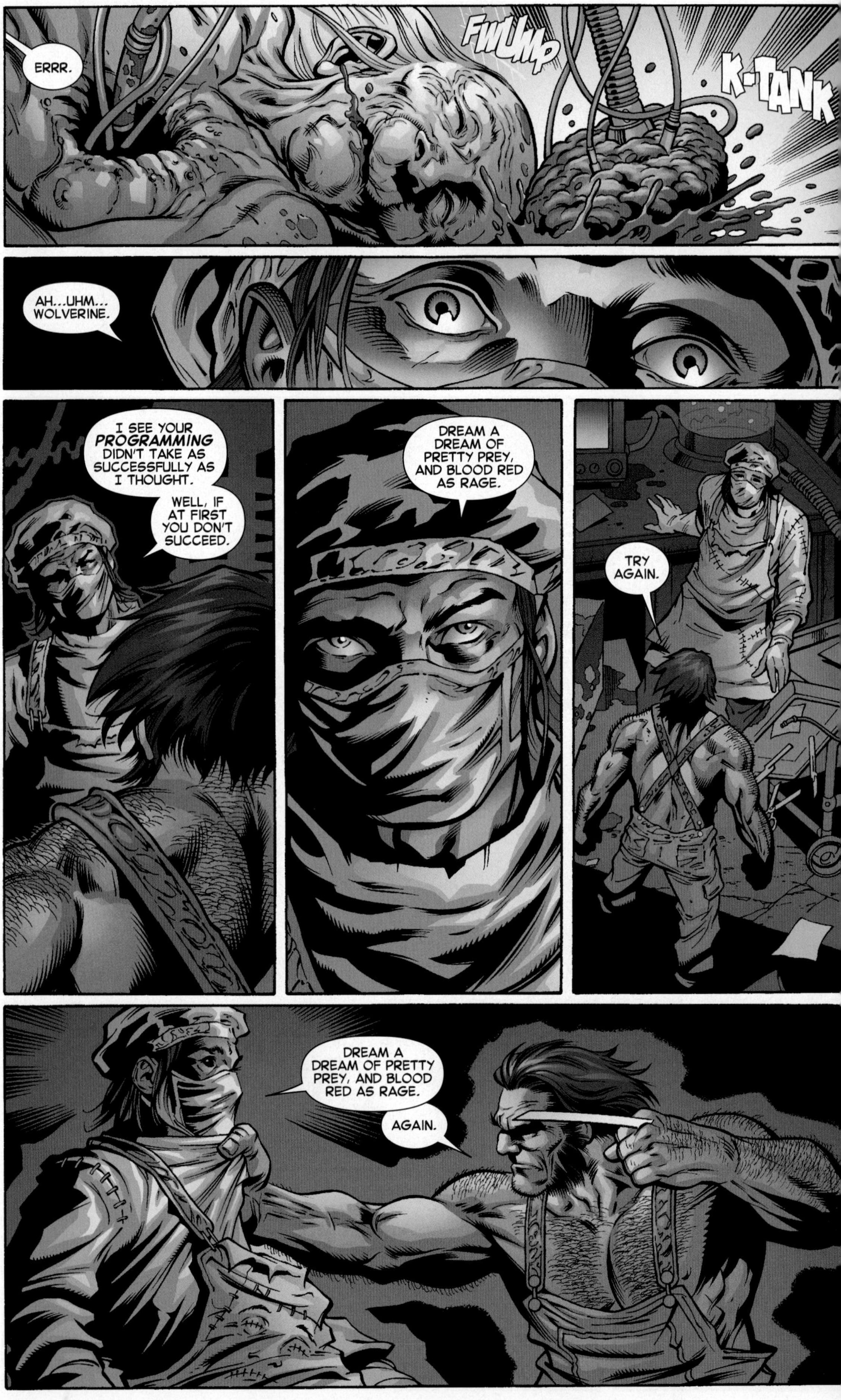
ERRR.
FWUMP
K-TANK
AH...UHM... WOLVERINE.
I SEE YOUR PROGRAMMING DIDN'T TAKE AS SUCCESSFULLY AS I THOUGHT.
WELL, IF AT FIRST YOU DON'T SUCCEED.
DREAM A DREAM OF PRETTY PREY, AND BLOOD RED AS RAGE.
TRY AGAIN.
DREAM A DREAM OF PRETTY PREY, AND BLOOD RED AS RAGE.
AGAIN.

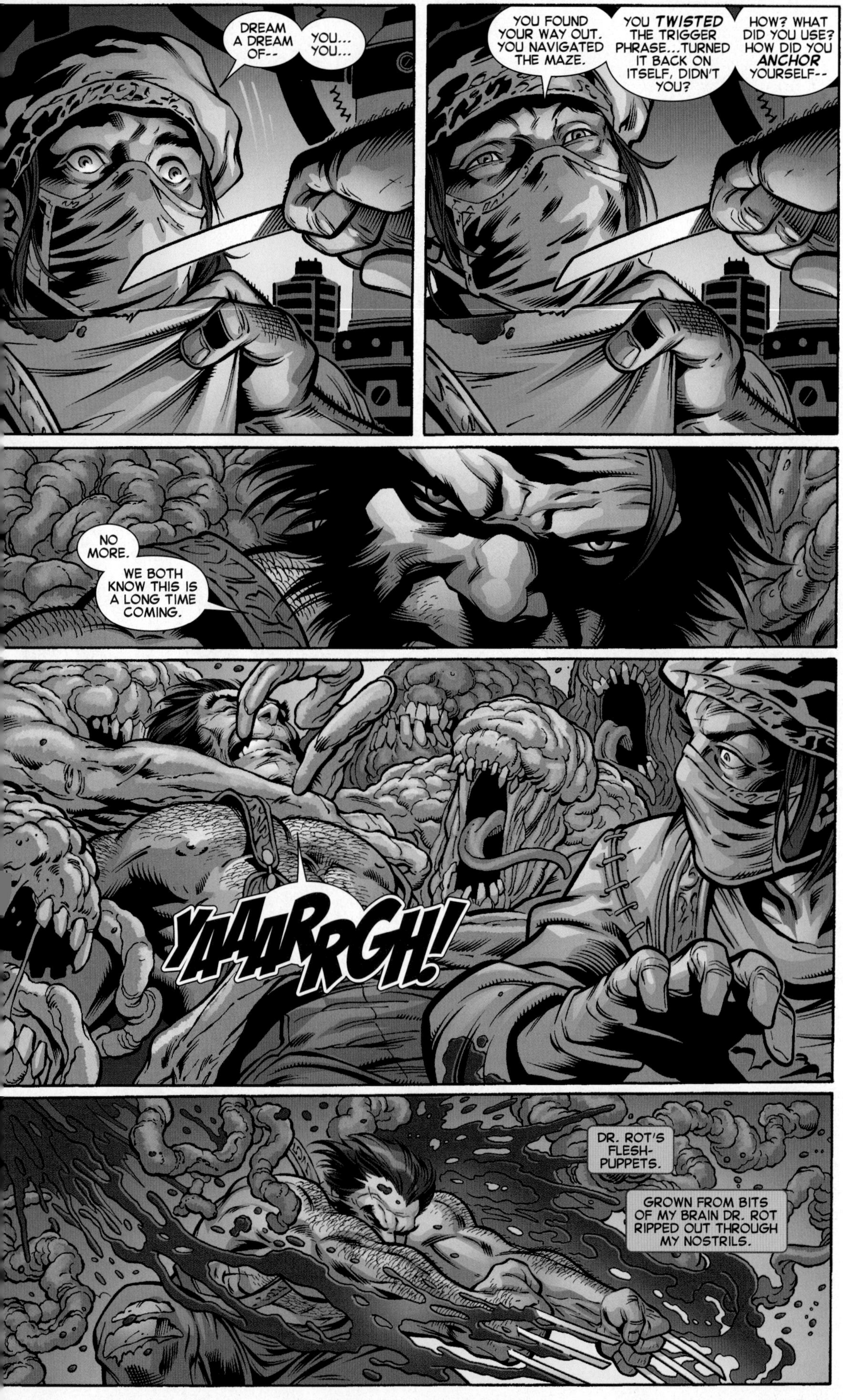
DREAM A DREAM OF--
YOU... YOU...
YOU FOUND YOUR WAY OUT. YOU NAVIGATED THE MAZE.
YOU *TWISTED* THE TRIGGER PHRASE...TURNED IT BACK ON ITSELF, DIDN'T YOU?
HOW? WHAT DID YOU USE? HOW DID YOU *ANCHOR* YOURSELF--
NO MORE.
WE BOTH KNOW THIS IS A LONG TIME COMING.
YAAARRGH!
DR. ROT'S FLESH-PUPPETS.
GROWN FROM BITS OF MY BRAIN DR. ROT RIPPED OUT THROUGH MY NOSTRILS.

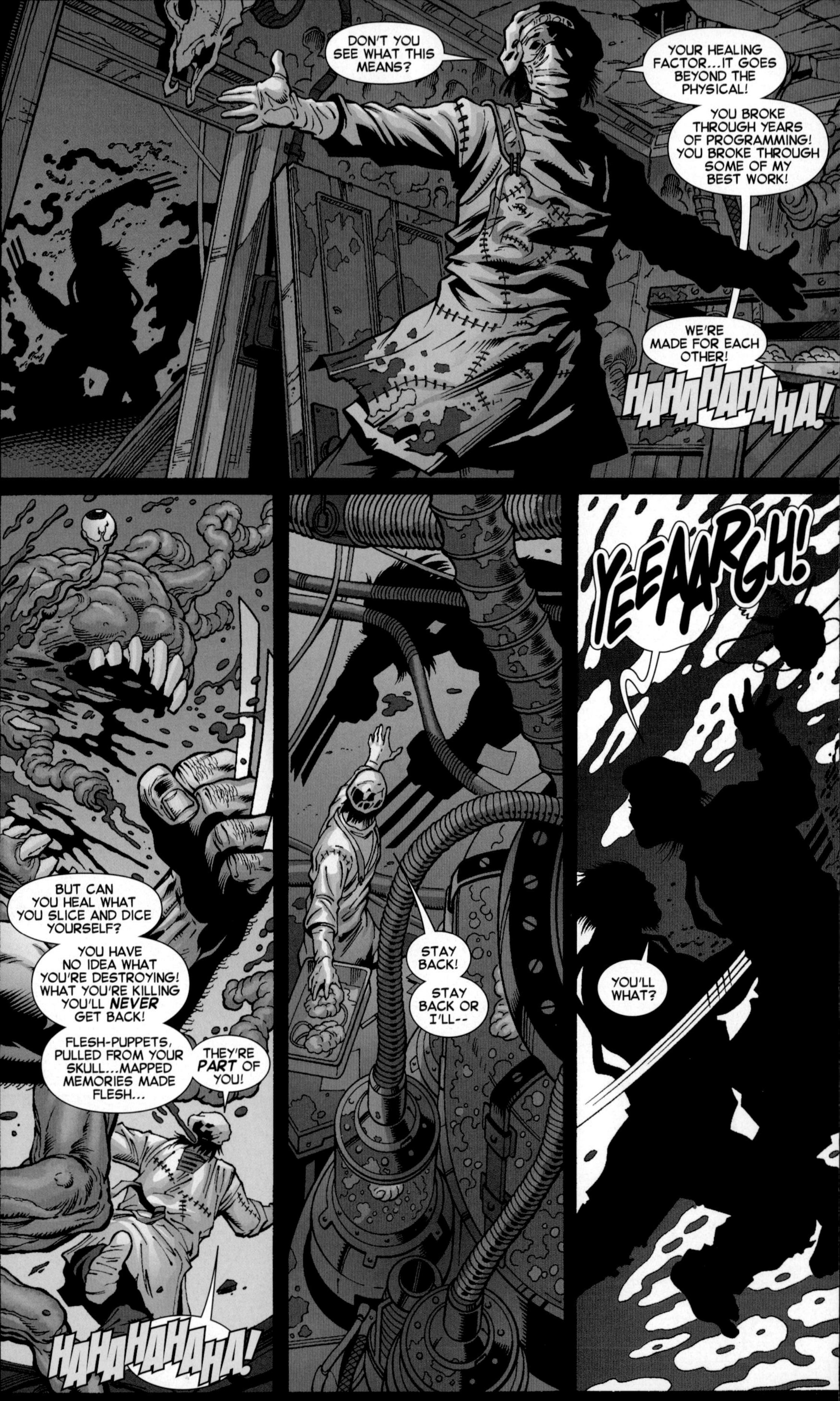
DON'T YOU SEE WHAT THIS MEANS?
YOUR HEALING FACTOR...IT GOES BEYOND THE PHYSICAL!
YOU BROKE THROUGH YEARS OF PROGRAMMING! YOU BROKE THROUGH SOME OF MY BEST WORK!
WE'RE MADE FOR EACH OTHER!
HAHAHAHAHAHA!
BUT CAN YOU HEAL WHAT YOU SLICE AND DICE YOURSELF?
YOU HAVE NO IDEA WHAT YOU'RE DESTROYING! WHAT YOU'RE KILLING YOU'LL NEVER GET BACK!
FLESH-PUPPETS, PULLED FROM YOUR SKULL...MAPPED MEMORIES MADE FLESH...
THEY'RE PART OF YOU!
HAHAHAHAHAHA!
STAY BACK!
STAY BACK OR I'LL--
YEEAARGH!
YOU'LL WHAT?

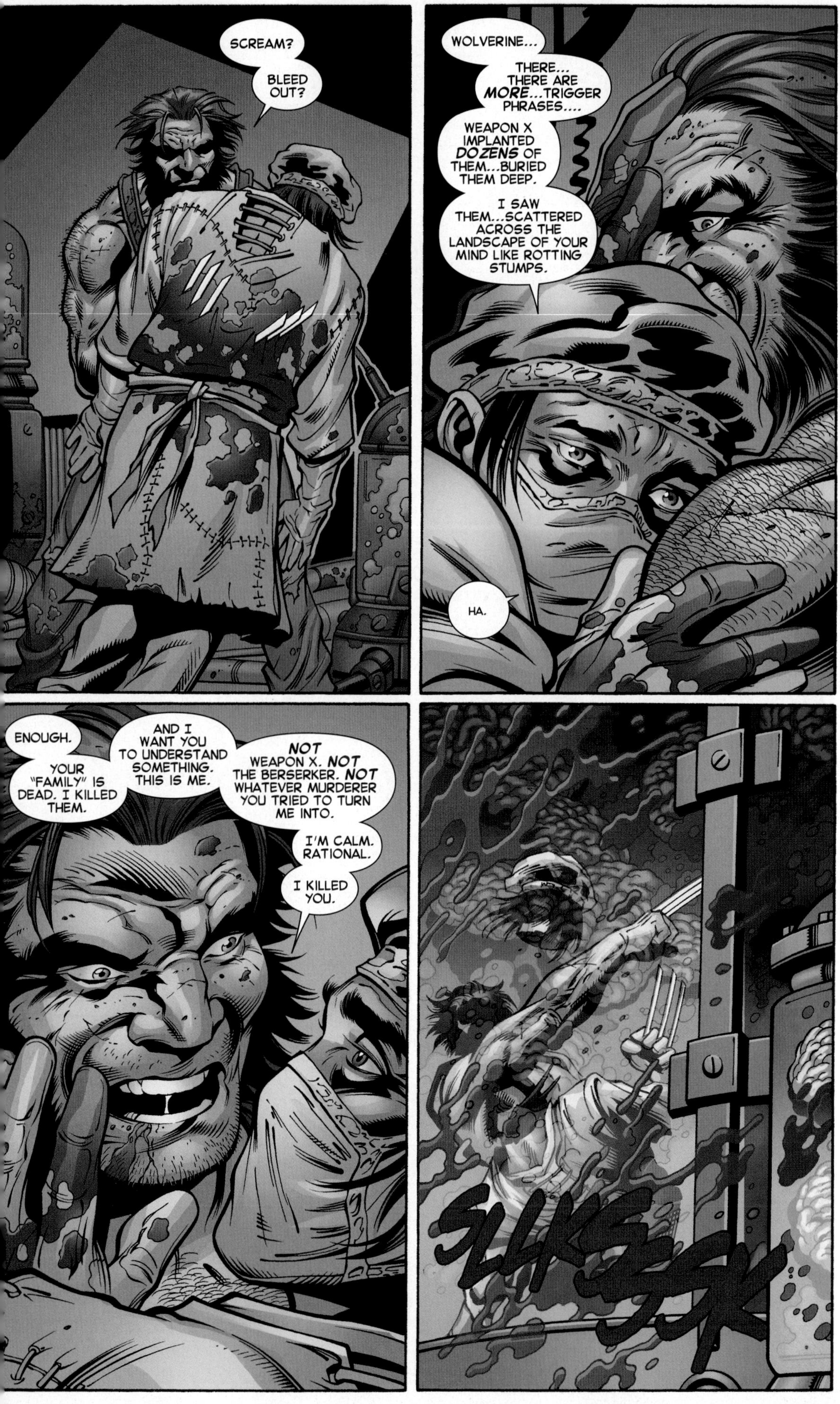
SCREAM?
BLEED OUT?
WOLVERINE...
THERE... THERE ARE MORE...TRIGGER PHRASES....
WEAPON X IMPLANTED DOZENS OF THEM...BURIED THEM DEEP.
I SAW THEM...SCATTERED ACROSS THE LANDSCAPE OF YOUR MIND LIKE ROTTING STUMPS.
HA.
ENOUGH.
YOUR "FAMILY" IS DEAD. I KILLED THEM.
AND I WANT YOU TO UNDERSTAND SOMETHING. THIS IS ME.
NOT WEAPON X. NOT THE BERSERKER. NOT WHATEVER MURDERER YOU TRIED TO TURN ME INTO.
I'M CALM. RATIONAL.
I KILLED YOU.

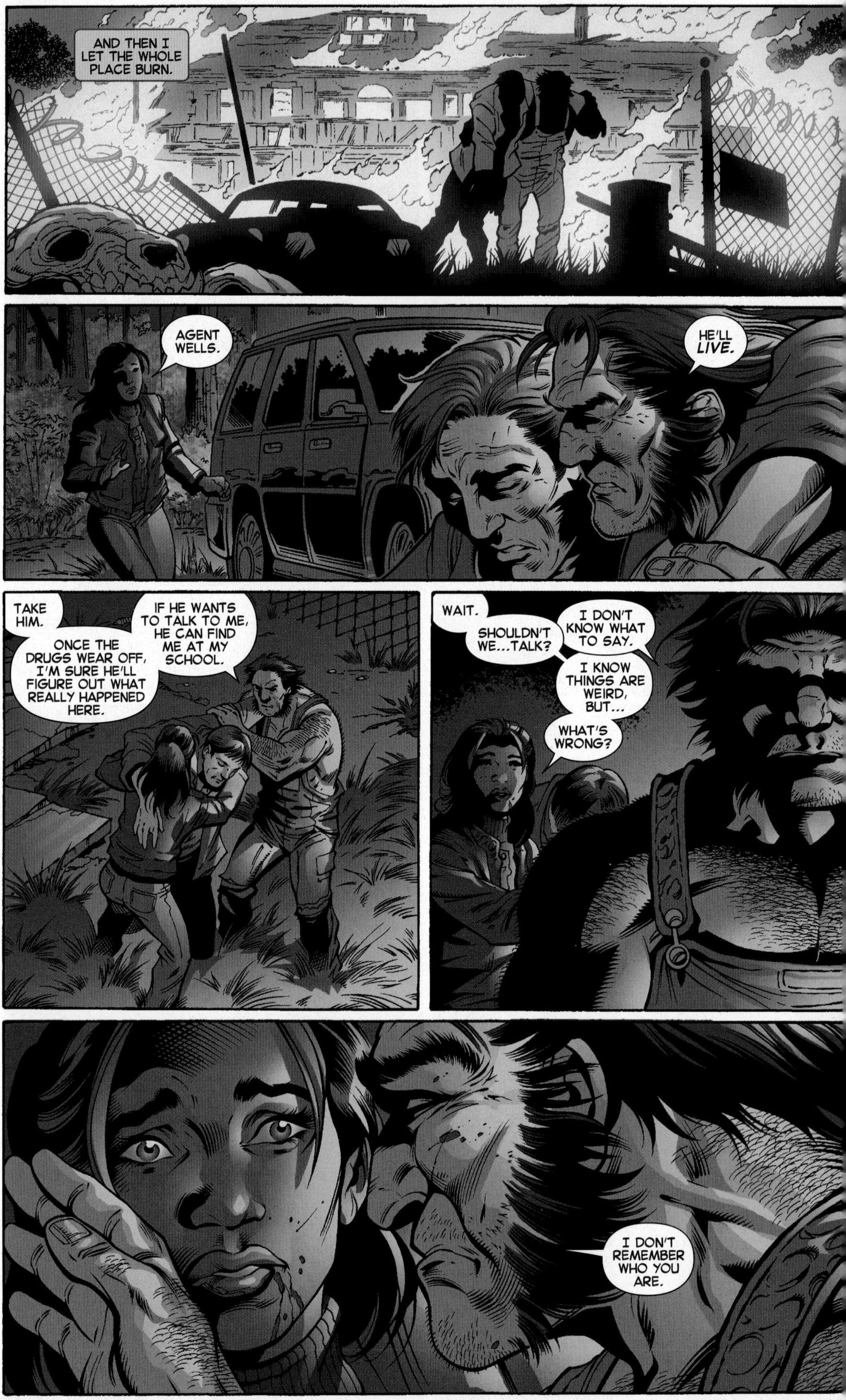
AND THEN I LET THE WHOLE PLACE BURN.
AGENT WELLS.
HE'LL *LIVE.*
TAKE HIM.
ONCE THE DRUGS WEAR OFF, I'M SURE HE'LL FIGURE OUT WHAT REALLY HAPPENED HERE.
IF HE WANTS TO TALK TO ME, HE CAN FIND ME AT MY SCHOOL.
WAIT.
SHOULDN'T WE...TALK?
I DON'T KNOW WHAT TO SAY.
I KNOW THINGS ARE WEIRD, BUT...
WHAT'S WRONG?
I DON'T REMEMBER WHO YOU ARE.

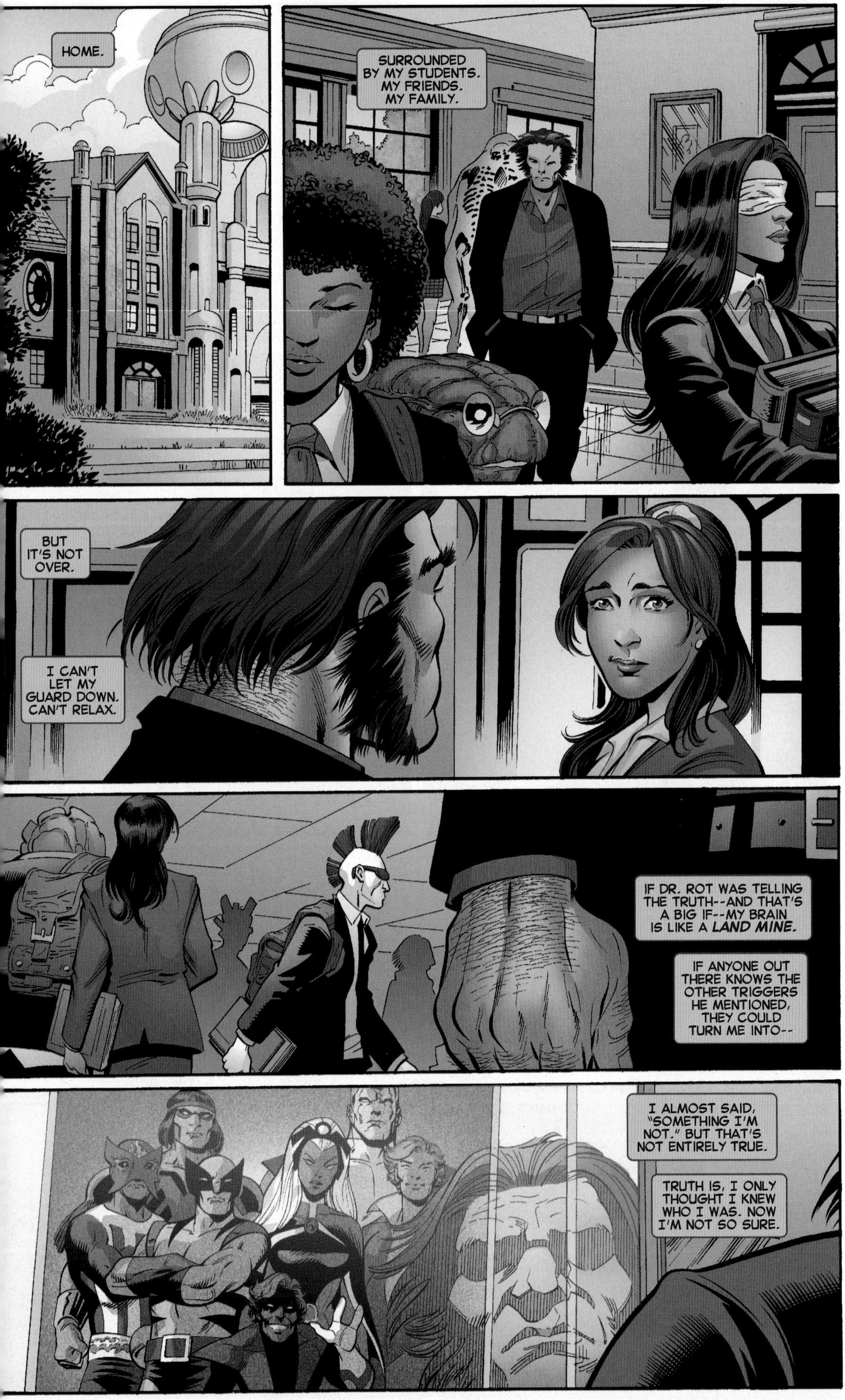

HOME.
SURROUNDED BY MY STUDENTS. MY FRIENDS. MY FAMILY.
BUT IT'S NOT OVER.
I CAN'T LET MY GUARD DOWN. CAN'T RELAX.
IF DR. ROT WAS TELLING THE TRUTH--AND THAT'S A BIG IF--MY BRAIN IS LIKE A *LAND MINE.*
IF ANYONE OUT THERE KNOWS THE OTHER TRIGGERS HE MENTIONED, THEY COULD TURN ME INTO--
I ALMOST SAID, "SOMETHING I'M NOT." BUT THAT'S NOT ENTIRELY TRUE.
TRUTH IS, I ONLY THOUGHT I KNEW WHO I WAS. NOW I'M NOT SO SURE.

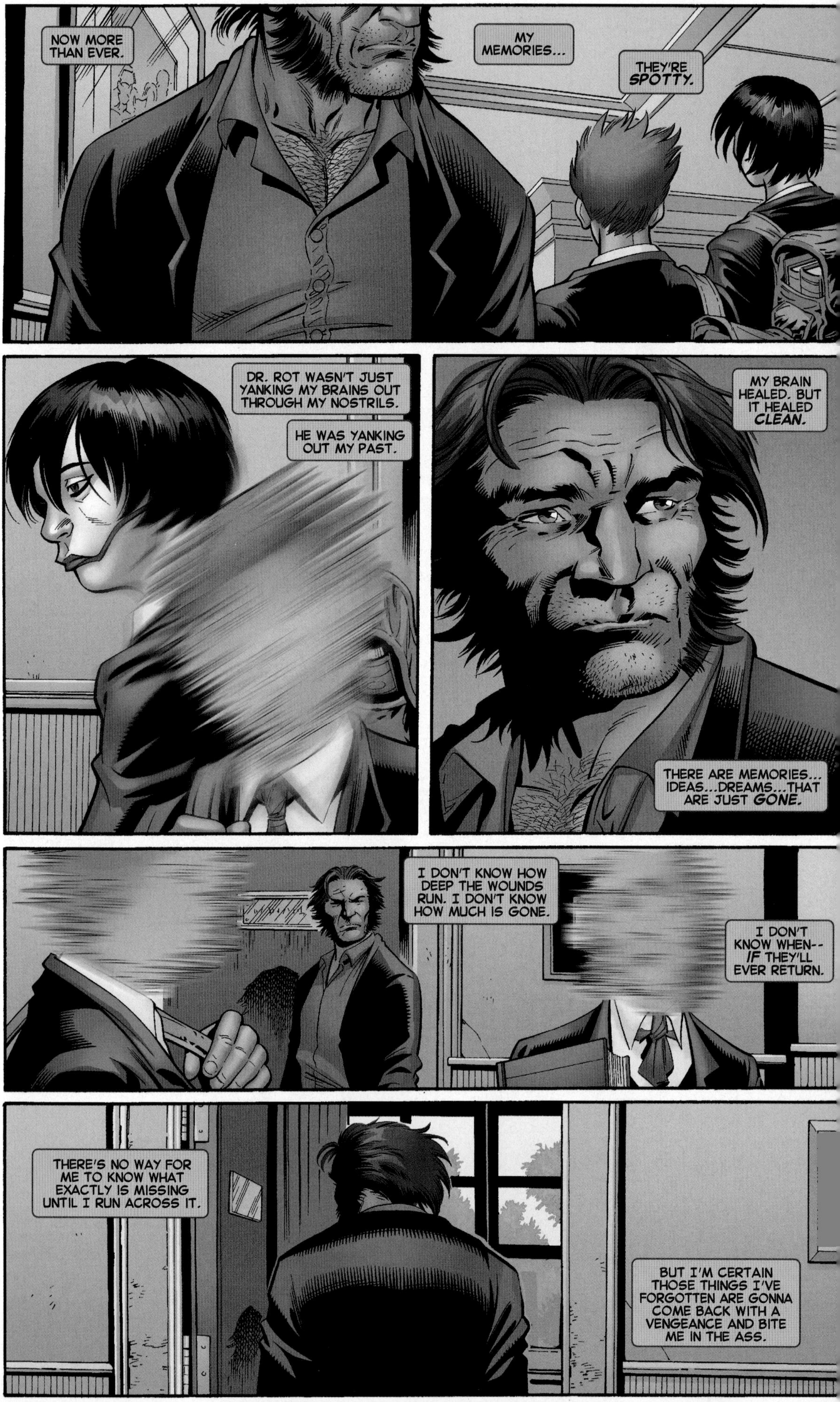
NOW MORE THAN EVER.
MY MEMORIES...
THEY'RE SPOTTY.
DR. ROT WASN'T JUST YANKING MY BRAINS OUT THROUGH MY NOSTRILS.
HE WAS YANKING OUT MY PAST.
MY BRAIN HEALED. BUT IT HEALED CLEAN.
THERE ARE MEMORIES... IDEAS...DREAMS...THAT ARE JUST GONE.
I DON'T KNOW HOW DEEP THE WOUNDS RUN. I DON'T KNOW HOW MUCH IS GONE.
I DON'T KNOW WHEN--IF THEY'LL EVER RETURN.
THERE'S NO WAY FOR ME TO KNOW WHAT EXACTLY IS MISSING UNTIL I RUN ACROSS IT.
BUT I'M CERTAIN THOSE THINGS I'VE FORGOTTEN ARE GONNA COME BACK WITH A VENGEANCE AND BITE ME IN THE ASS.

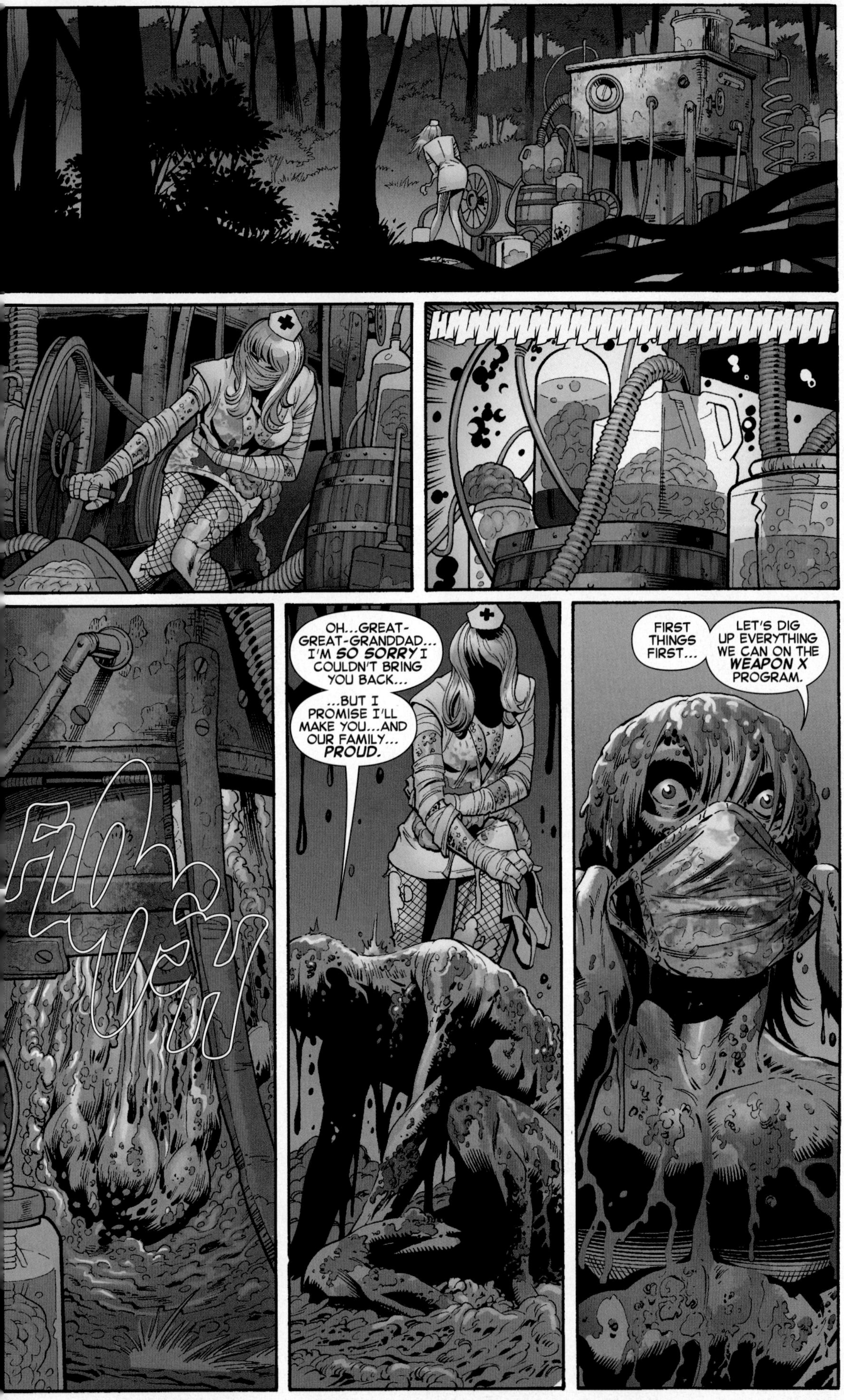
HMMMMMMMMMMMMMMMMMMMMMMMMMMMMMMM
OH...GREAT-GREAT-GRANDDAD... I'M SO SORRY I COULDN'T BRING YOU BACK...
...BUT I PROMISE I'LL MAKE YOU...AND OUR FAMILY... PROUD.
FIRST THINGS FIRST...
LET'S DIG UP EVERYTHING WE CAN ON THE WEAPON X PROGRAM.

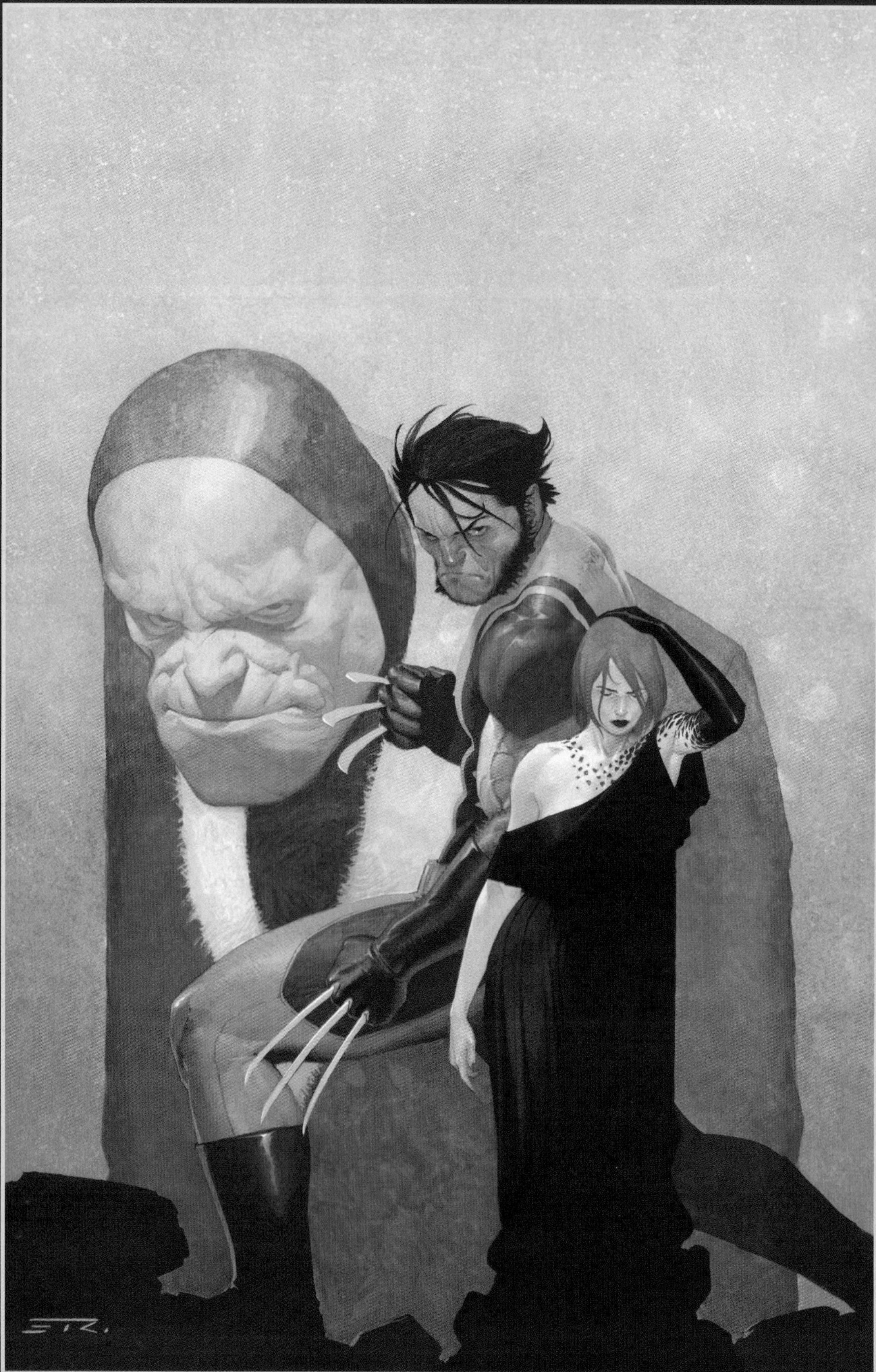

309

Many years ago, a secret government organization abducted the man called Logan, a mutant possessing razor-sharp bone claws and the ability to heal from any wound. In their attempt to create the perfect living weapon, the organization bonded the unbreakable metal Adamantium to his skeleton. The process was excruciating and by the end, there was little left of the man known as Logan. He had become...

WOLVERINE

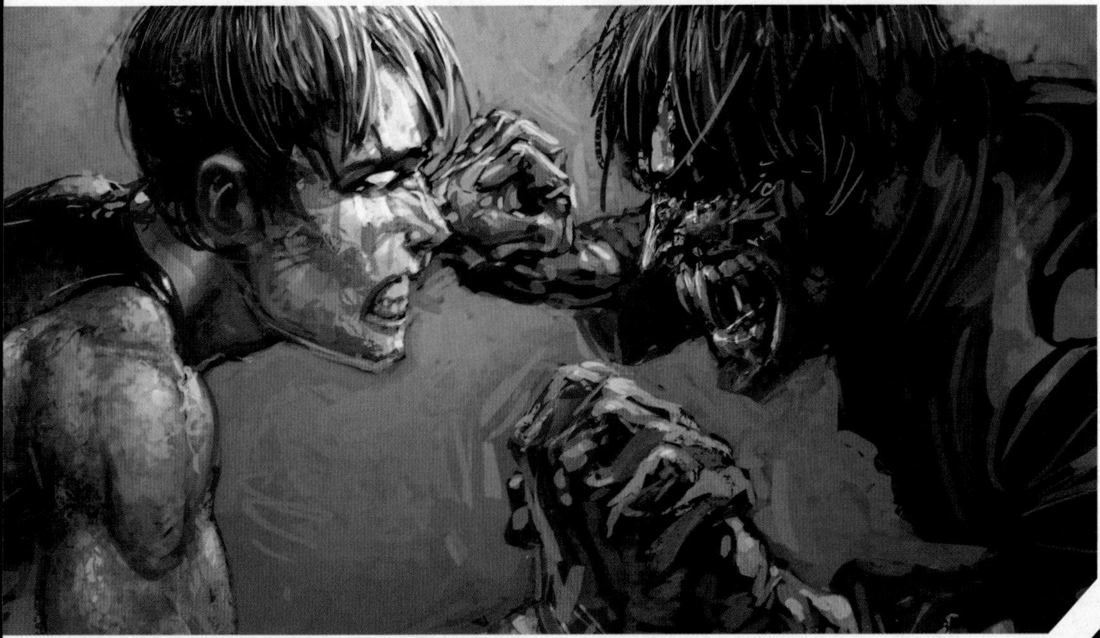

PREVIOUSLY...

Before the Avengers and the X-Men found themselves on opposite sides of a world war, before the X-Men were torn apart by their ideals, Wolverine ran X-Force, a black ops team of mutants, on Cyclops' orders. One of those mutants was Josh Foley, aka Elixir, a teenager with the power to heal.

But after he saw the love of his life killed in front of him, he lost control and his power shifted, became the power to destroy. From then on, he was constantly at war with himself, trying to repress his newfound powers of destruction. After joining X-Force, he put both powers to good use, but was always teetering on the edge of losing control...until a final, climactic battle against teammates that were raised from the dead, in which Elixir utterly decimated a fellow student, and found he wasn't able to heal anymore. Monstrous and devastated, he disappeared.

Now, in the wake of the divide between Wolverine and Cyclops, and Wolverine opening up a school to promote learning and control for younger mutants, Wolverine has time to reflect on one student he wasn't able to save...and what that means for his future and the future of his students...

UNDERNEATH

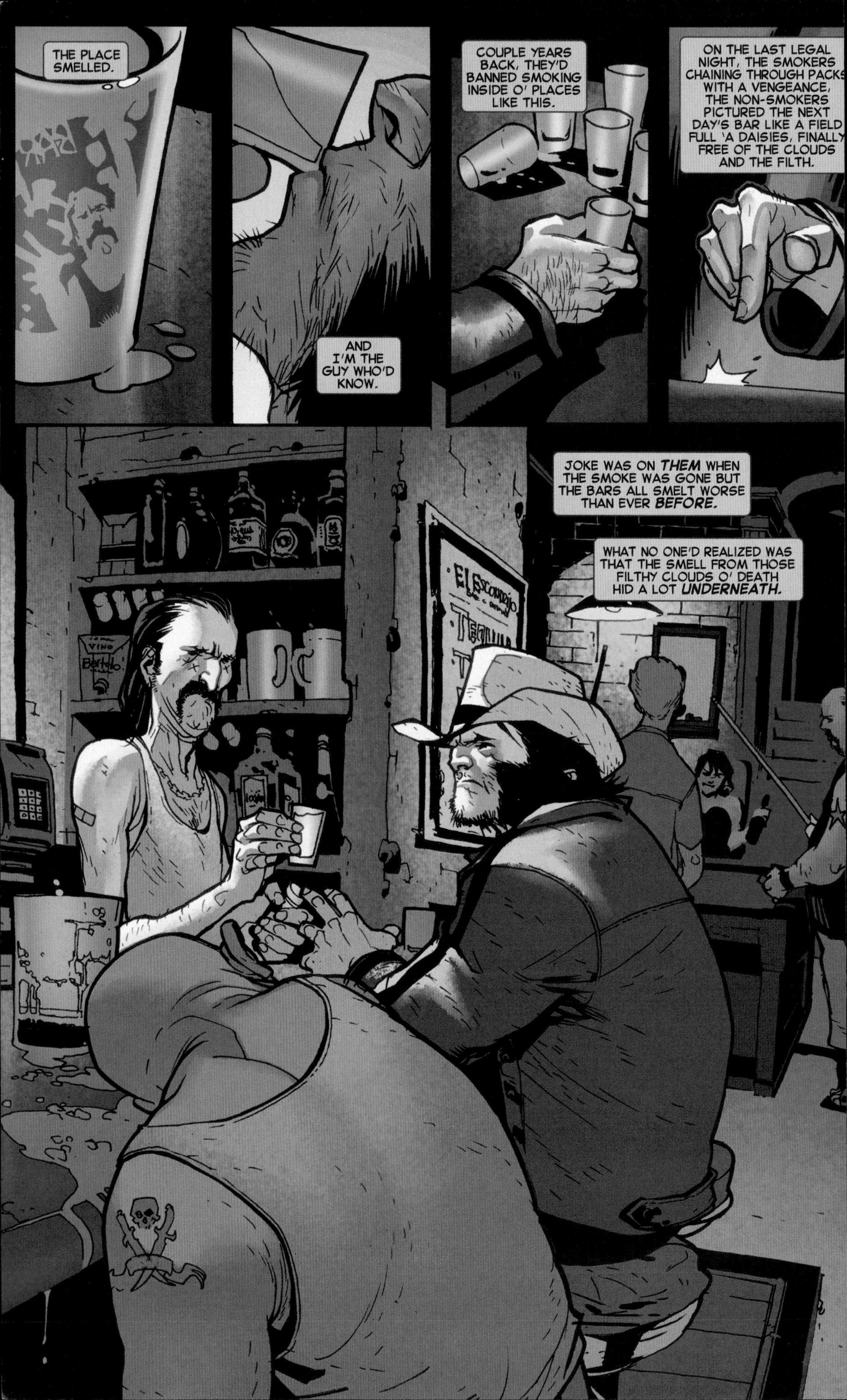

THE PLACE SMELLED.
AND I'M THE GUY WHO'D KNOW.
COUPLE YEARS BACK, THEY'D BANNED SMOKING INSIDE O' PLACES LIKE THIS.
ON THE LAST LEGAL NIGHT, THE SMOKERS CHAINING THROUGH PACKS WITH A VENGEANCE, THE NON-SMOKERS PICTURED THE NEXT DAY'S BAR LIKE A FIELD FULL 'A DAISIES, FINALLY FREE OF THE CLOUDS AND THE FILTH.
JOKE WAS ON *THEM* WHEN THE SMOKE WAS GONE BUT THE BARS ALL SMELT WORSE THAN EVER *BEFORE.*
WHAT NO ONE'D REALIZED WAS THAT THE SMELL FROM THOSE FILTHY CLOUDS O' DEATH HID A LOT *UNDERNEATH.*

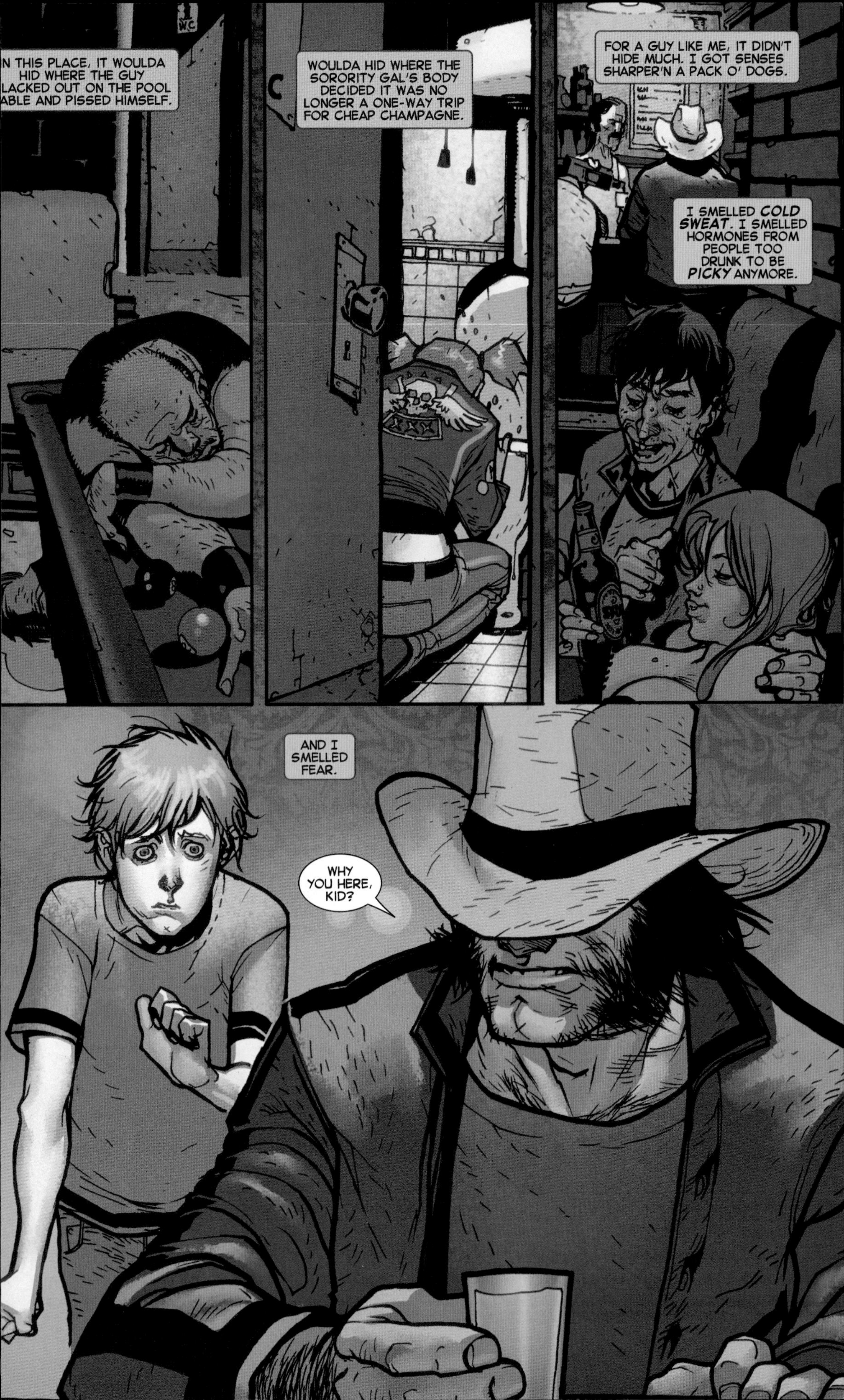

W.C.
N THIS PLACE, IT WOULDA HID WHERE THE GUY LACKED OUT ON THE POOL ABLE AND PISSED HIMSELF.
WOULDA HID WHERE THE SORORITY GAL'S BODY DECIDED IT WAS NO LONGER A ONE-WAY TRIP FOR CHEAP CHAMPAGNE.
FOR A GUY LIKE ME, IT DIDN'T HIDE MUCH. I GOT SENSES SHARPER'N A PACK O' DOGS.
I SMELLED COLD SWEAT. I SMELLED HORMONES FROM PEOPLE TOO DRUNK TO BE PICKY ANYMORE.
AND I SMELLED FEAR.
WHY YOU HERE, KID?

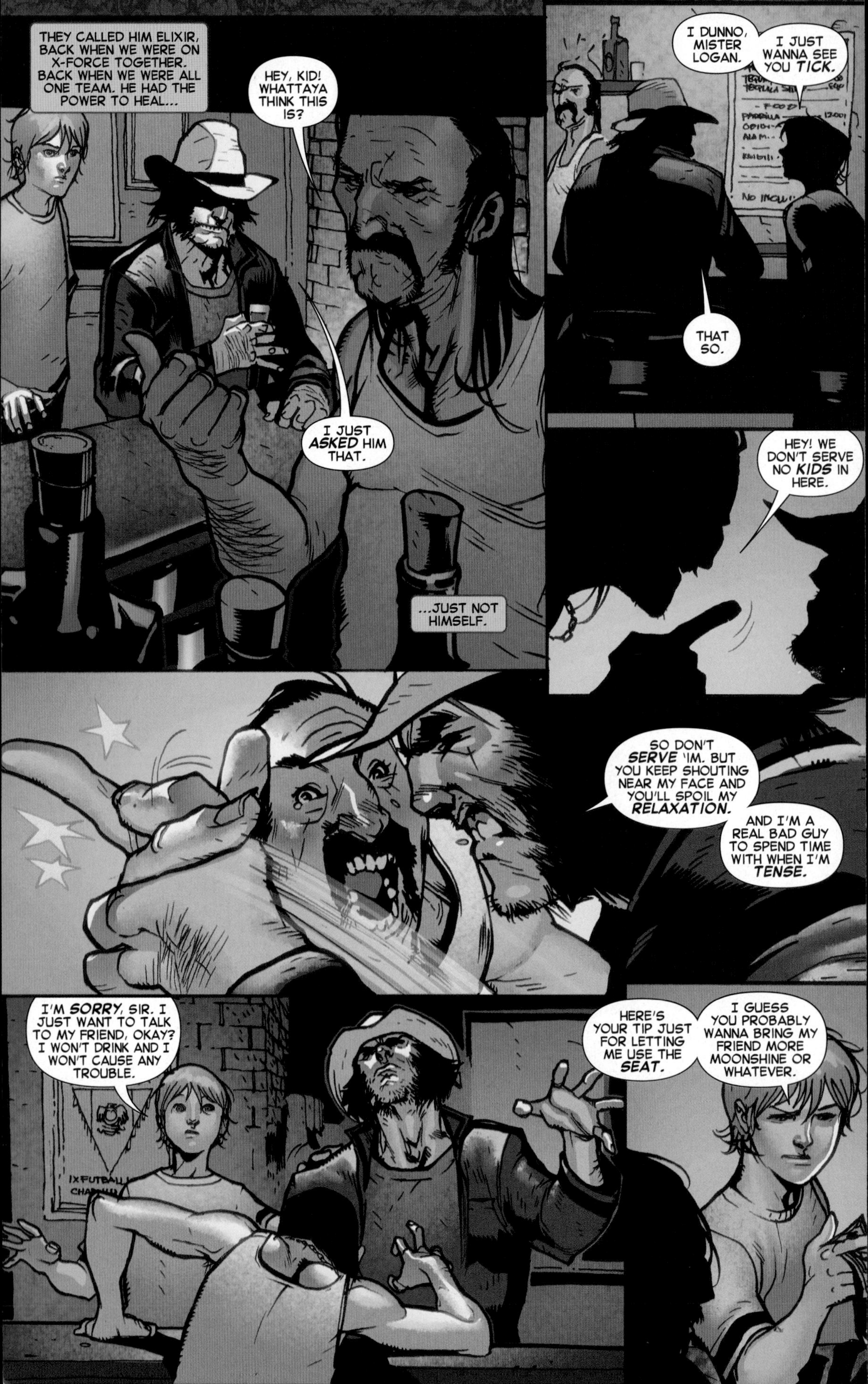

THEY CALLED HIM ELIXIR, BACK WHEN WE WERE ON X-FORCE TOGETHER. BACK WHEN WE WERE ALL ONE TEAM. HE HAD THE POWER TO HEAL...
HEY, KID! WHATTAYA THINK THIS IS?
I JUST ASKED HIM THAT.
...JUST NOT HIMSELF.
I DUNNO, MISTER LOGAN.
I JUST WANNA SEE YOU TICK.
THAT SO.
HEY! WE DON'T SERVE NO KIDS IN HERE.
SO DON'T SERVE 'IM. BUT YOU KEEP SHOUTING NEAR MY FACE AND YOU'LL SPOIL MY RELAXATION.
AND I'M A REAL BAD GUY TO SPEND TIME WITH WHEN I'M TENSE.
I'M SORRY, SIR. I JUST WANT TO TALK TO MY FRIEND, OKAY? I WON'T DRINK AND I WON'T CAUSE ANY TROUBLE.
HERE'S YOUR TIP JUST FOR LETTING ME USE THE SEAT.
I GUESS YOU PROBABLY WANNA BRING MY FRIEND MORE MOONSHINE OR WHATEVER.

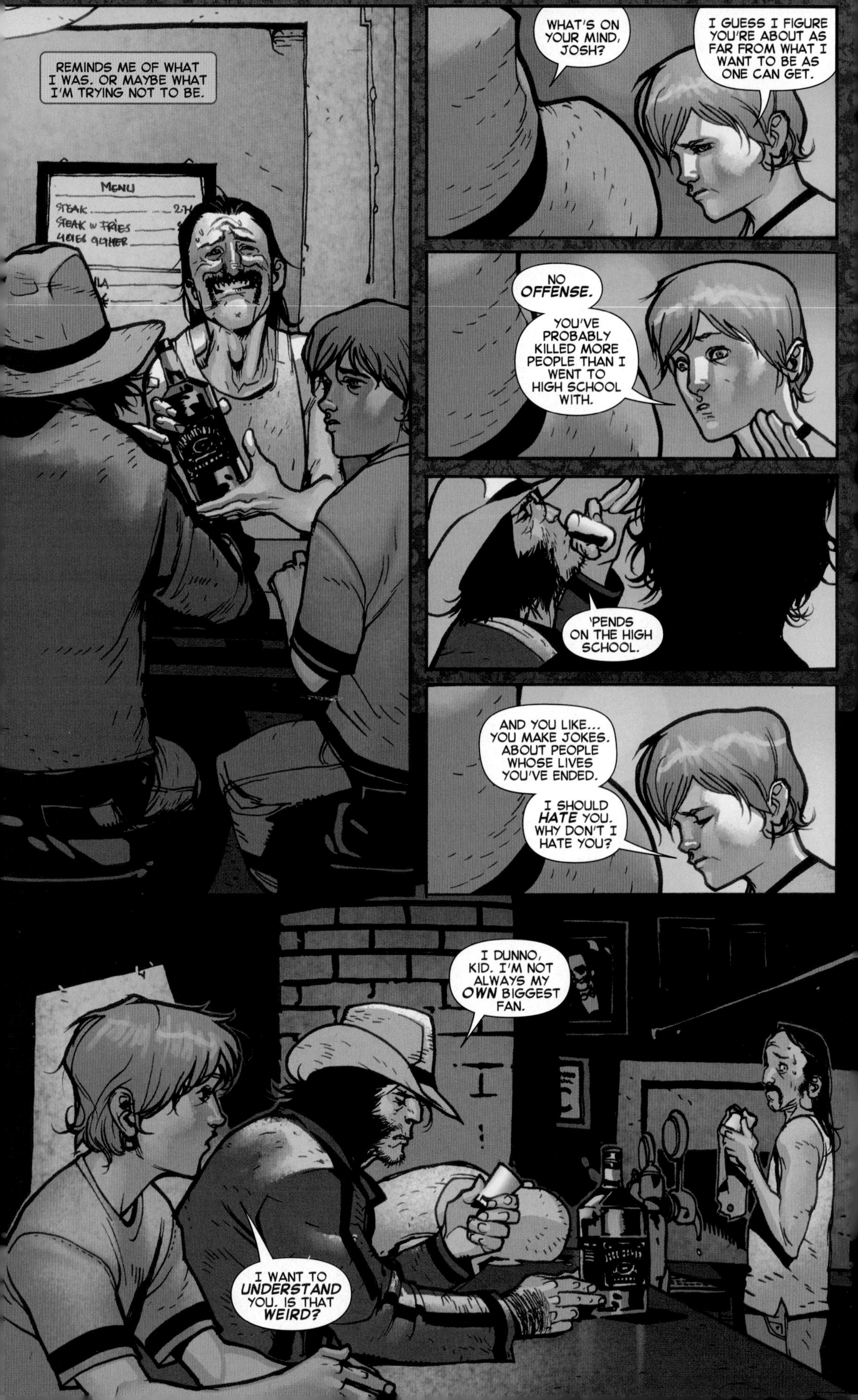
REMINDS ME OF WHAT I WAS. OR MAYBE WHAT I'M TRYING NOT TO BE.
MENU
STEAK
STEAK w FRIES
WHAT'S ON YOUR MIND, JOSH?
I GUESS I FIGURE YOU'RE ABOUT AS FAR FROM WHAT I WANT TO BE AS ONE CAN GET.
NO OFFENSE.
YOU'VE PROBABLY KILLED MORE PEOPLE THAN I WENT TO HIGH SCHOOL WITH.
'PENDS ON THE HIGH SCHOOL.
AND YOU LIKE... YOU MAKE JOKES. ABOUT PEOPLE WHOSE LIVES YOU'VE ENDED.
I SHOULD HATE YOU. WHY DON'T I HATE YOU?
I DUNNO, KID. I'M NOT ALWAYS MY OWN BIGGEST FAN.
I WANT TO UNDERSTAND YOU. IS THAT WEIRD?

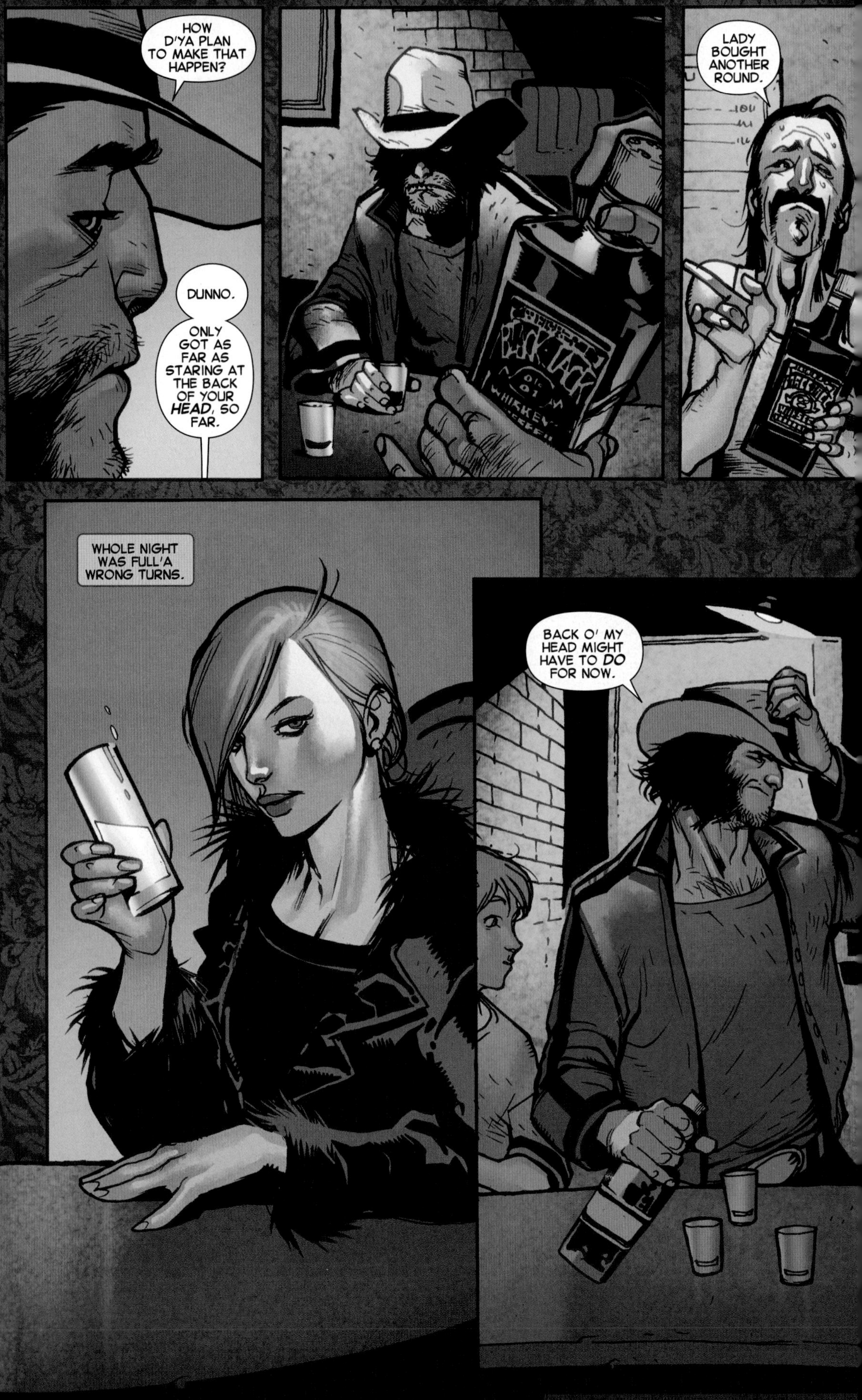
HOW D'YA PLAN TO MAKE THAT HAPPEN?
DUNNO.
ONLY GOT AS FAR AS STARING AT THE BACK OF YOUR *HEAD*, SO FAR.
LADY BOUGHT ANOTHER ROUND.
WHOLE NIGHT WAS FULL'A WRONG TURNS.
BACK O' MY HEAD MIGHT HAVE TO *DO* FOR NOW.

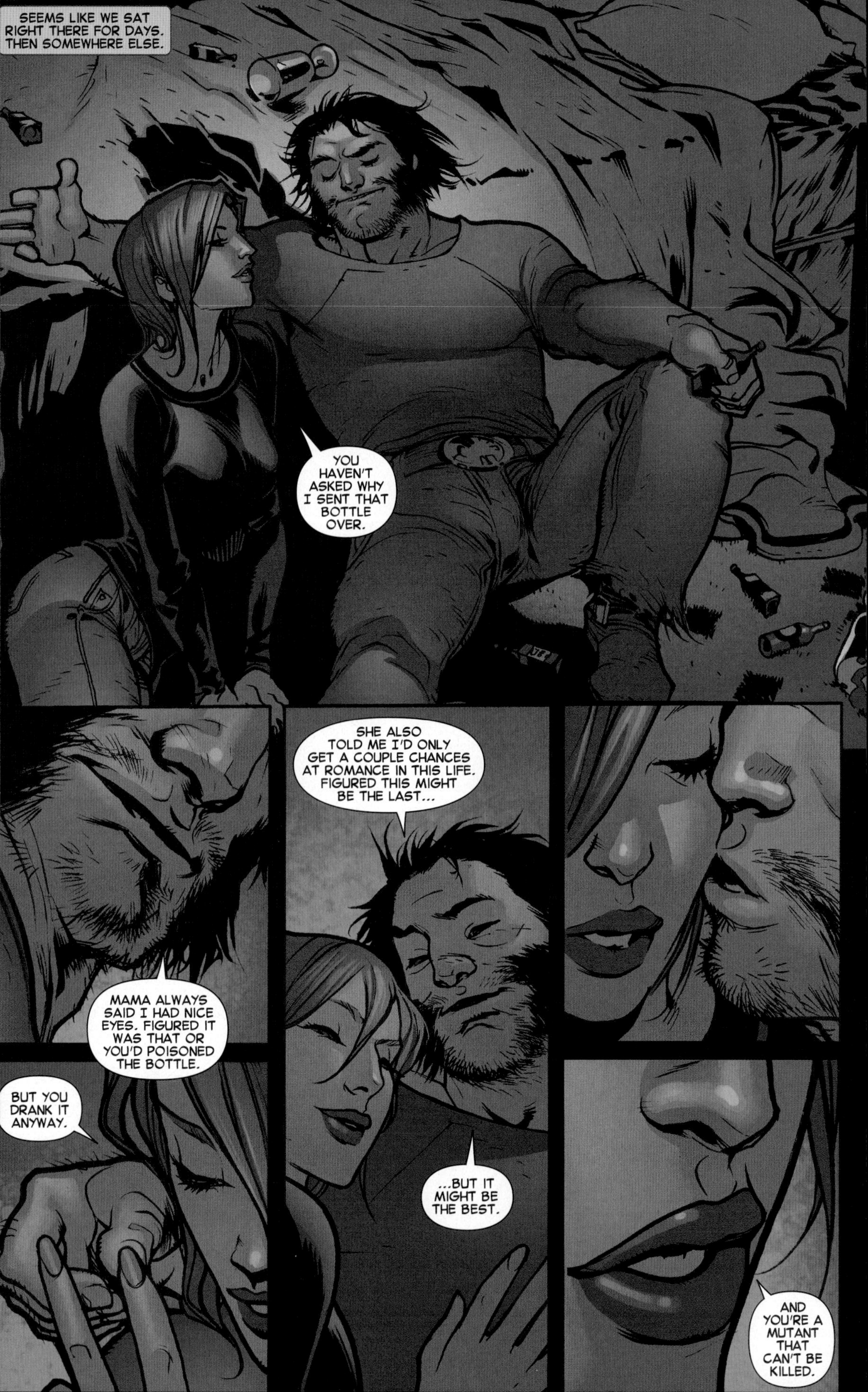
SEEMS LIKE WE SAT RIGHT THERE FOR DAYS. THEN SOMEWHERE ELSE.
YOU HAVEN'T ASKED WHY I SENT THAT BOTTLE OVER.
MAMA ALWAYS SAID I HAD NICE EYES. FIGURED IT WAS THAT OR YOU'D POISONED THE BOTTLE.
BUT YOU DRANK IT ANYWAY.
SHE ALSO TOLD ME I'D ONLY GET A COUPLE CHANCES AT ROMANCE IN THIS LIFE. FIGURED THIS MIGHT BE THE LAST...
...BUT IT MIGHT BE THE BEST.
AND YOU'RE A MUTANT THAT CAN'T BE KILLED.

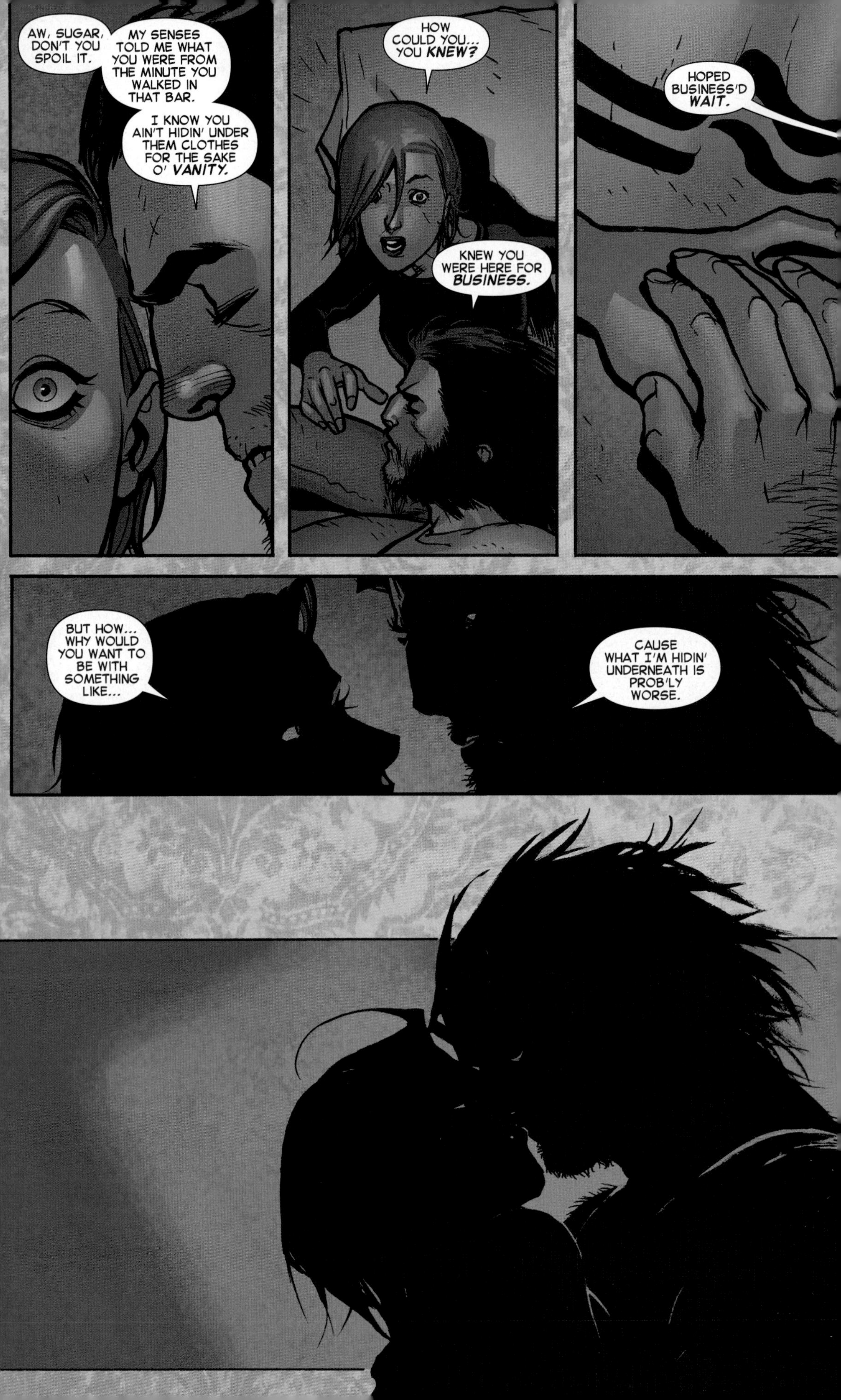

AW, SUGAR, DON'T YOU SPOIL IT.
MY SENSES TOLD ME WHAT YOU WERE FROM THE MINUTE YOU WALKED IN THAT BAR.
I KNOW YOU AIN'T HIDIN' UNDER THEM CLOTHES FOR THE SAKE O' VANITY.
HOW COULD YOU... YOU KNEW?
KNEW YOU WERE HERE FOR BUSINESS.
HOPED BUSINESS'D WAIT.
BUT HOW... WHY WOULD YOU WANT TO BE WITH SOMETHING LIKE...
CAUSE WHAT I'M HIDIN' UNDERNEATH IS PROB'LY WORSE.

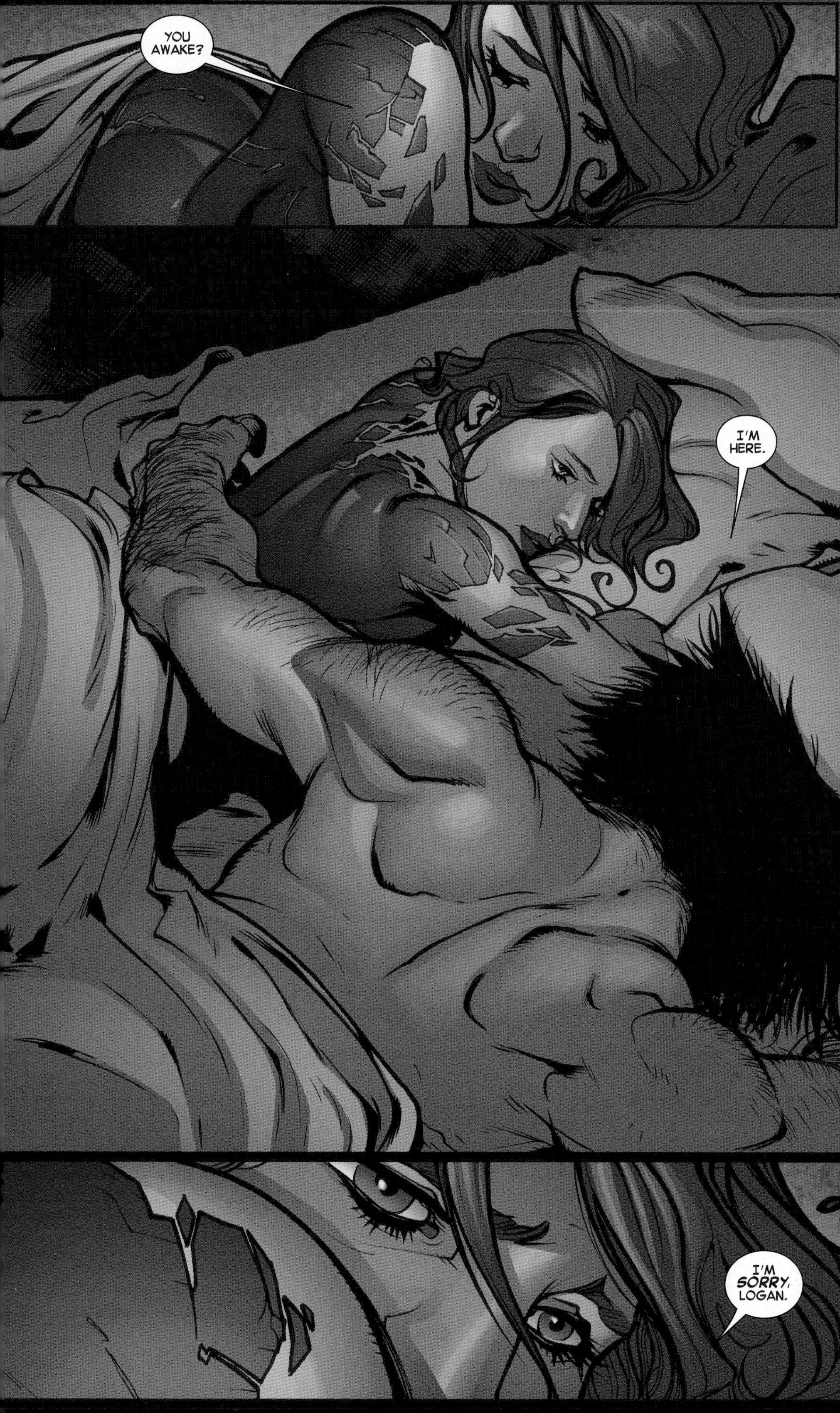
YOU AWAKE?
I'M HERE.
I'M SORRY, LOGAN.

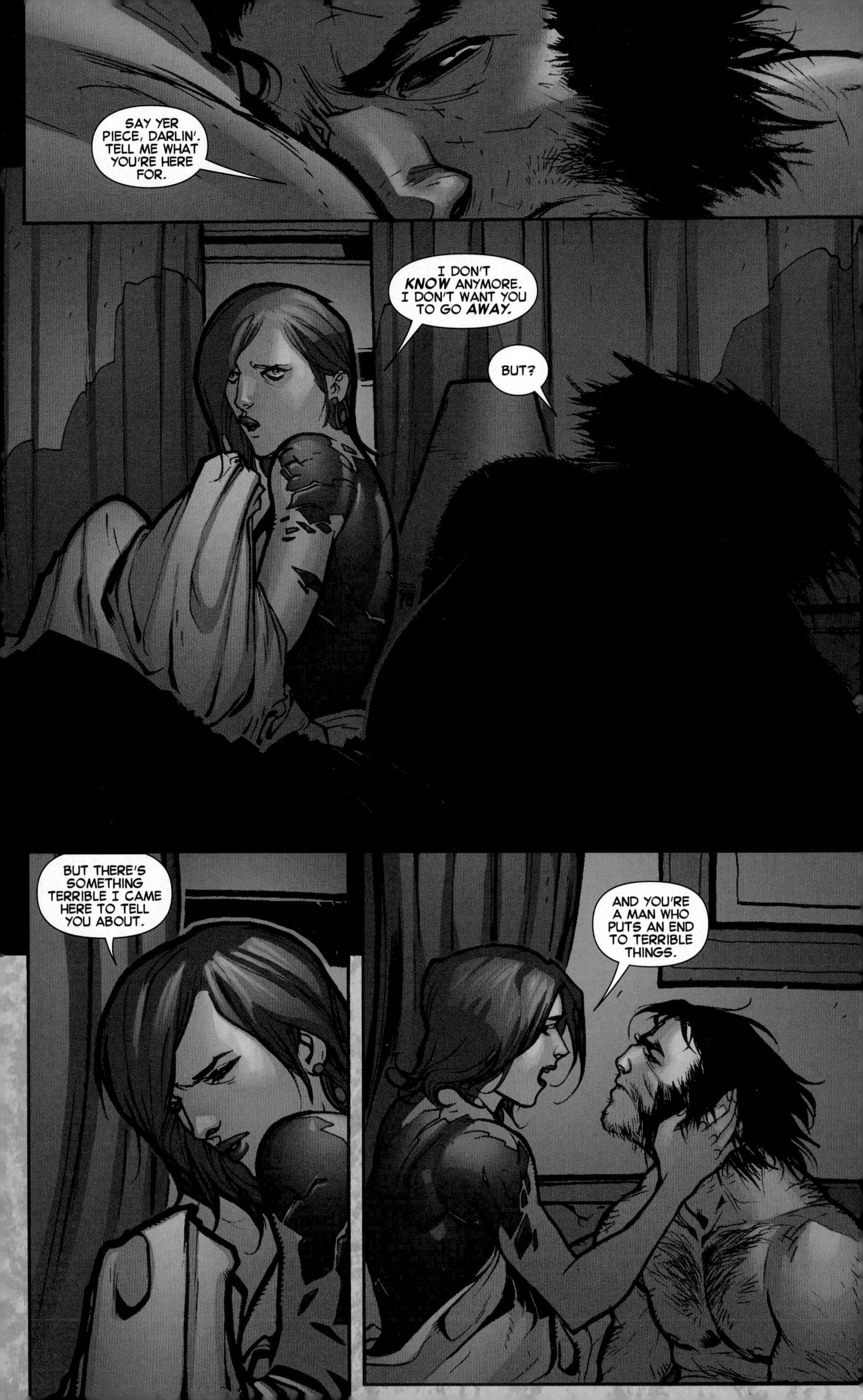
SAY YER PIECE, DARLIN'. TELL ME WHAT YOU'RE HERE FOR.
I DON'T KNOW ANYMORE. I DON'T WANT YOU TO GO AWAY.
BUT?
BUT THERE'S SOMETHING TERRIBLE I CAME HERE TO TELL YOU ABOUT.
AND YOU'RE A MAN WHO PUTS AN END TO TERRIBLE THINGS.

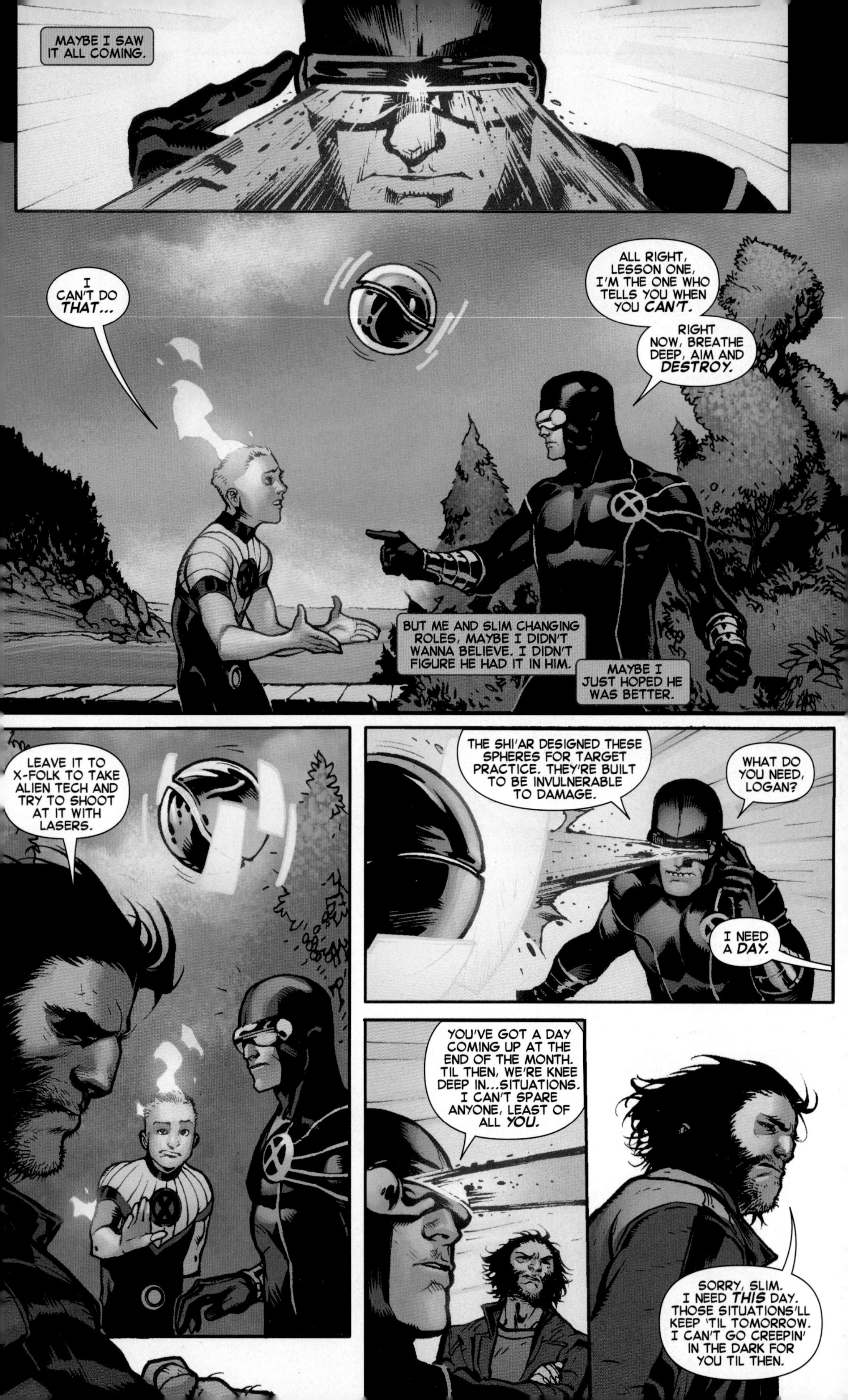
MAYBE I SAW IT ALL COMING.
I CAN'T DO *THAT...*
ALL RIGHT, LESSON ONE, I'M THE ONE WHO TELLS YOU WHEN YOU *CAN'T.*
RIGHT NOW, BREATHE DEEP, AIM AND *DESTROY.*
BUT ME AND SLIM CHANGING ROLES, MAYBE I DIDN'T WANNA BELIEVE. I DIDN'T FIGURE HE HAD IT IN HIM.
MAYBE I JUST HOPED HE WAS BETTER.
LEAVE IT TO X-FOLK TO TAKE ALIEN TECH AND TRY TO SHOOT AT IT WITH LASERS.
THE SHI'AR DESIGNED THESE SPHERES FOR TARGET PRACTICE. THEY'RE BUILT TO BE INVULNERABLE TO DAMAGE.
WHAT DO YOU NEED, LOGAN?
I NEED A *DAY.*
YOU'VE GOT A DAY COMING UP AT THE END OF THE MONTH. TIL THEN, WE'RE KNEE DEEP IN...SITUATIONS. I CAN'T SPARE ANYONE, LEAST OF ALL *YOU.*
SORRY, SLIM. I NEED *THIS* DAY. THOSE SITUATIONS'LL KEEP 'TIL TOMORROW. I CAN'T GO CREEPIN' IN THE DARK FOR YOU TIL THEN.

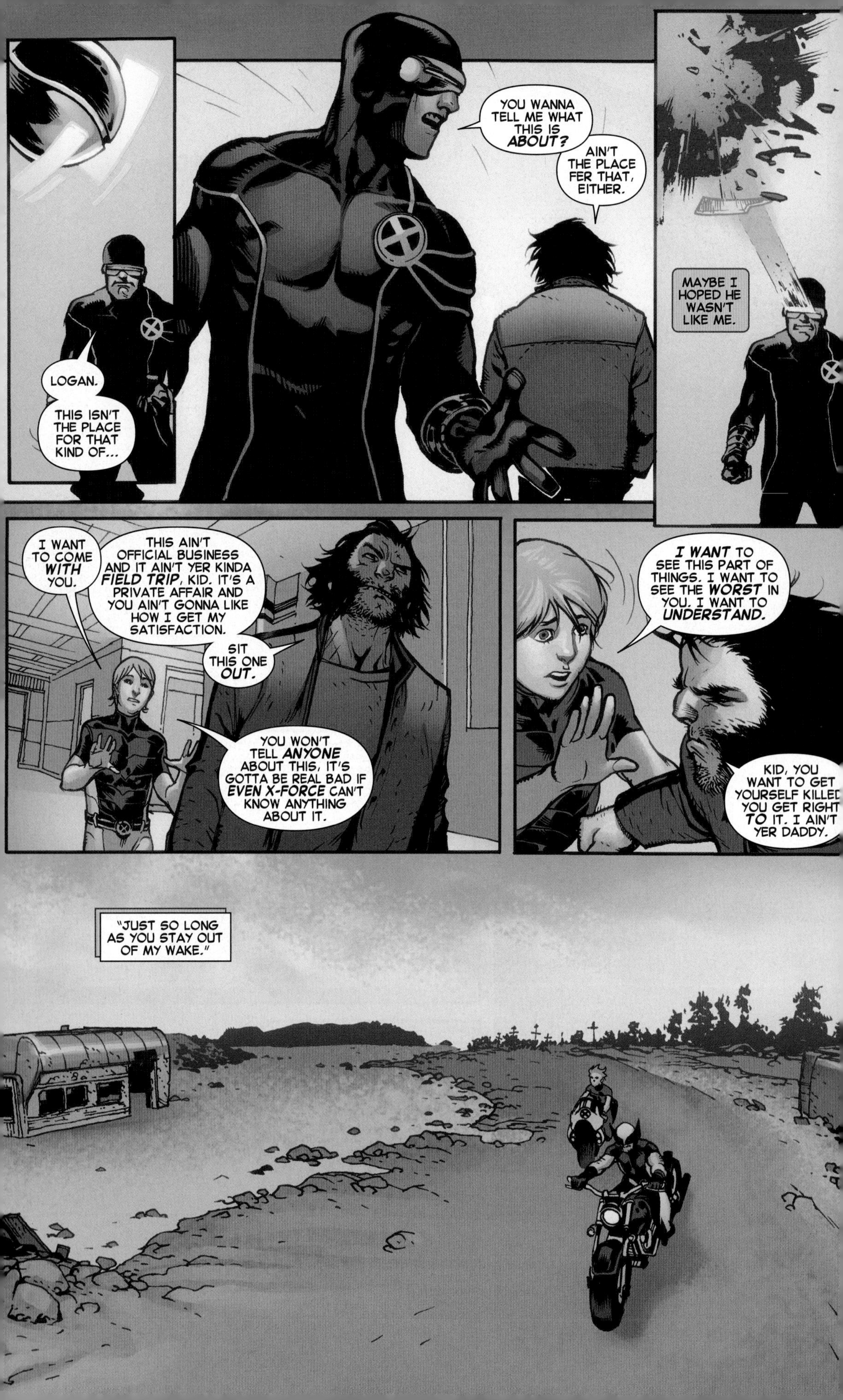
LOGAN.
THIS ISN'T THE PLACE FOR THAT KIND OF...
YOU WANNA TELL ME WHAT THIS IS ABOUT?
AIN'T THE PLACE FOR THAT, EITHER.
MAYBE I HOPED HE WASN'T LIKE ME.
I WANT TO COME WITH YOU.
THIS AIN'T OFFICIAL BUSINESS AND IT AIN'T YER KINDA FIELD TRIP, KID. IT'S A PRIVATE AFFAIR AND YOU AIN'T GONNA LIKE HOW I GET MY SATISFACTION.
SIT THIS ONE OUT.
YOU WON'T TELL ANYONE ABOUT THIS, IT'S GOTTA BE REAL BAD IF EVEN X-FORCE CAN'T KNOW ANYTHING ABOUT IT.
I WANT TO SEE THIS PART OF THINGS. I WANT TO SEE THE WORST IN YOU. I WANT TO UNDERSTAND.
KID, YOU WANT TO GET YOURSELF KILLED YOU GET RIGHT TO IT. I AIN'T YER DADDY.
"JUST SO LONG AS YOU STAY OUT OF MY WAKE."

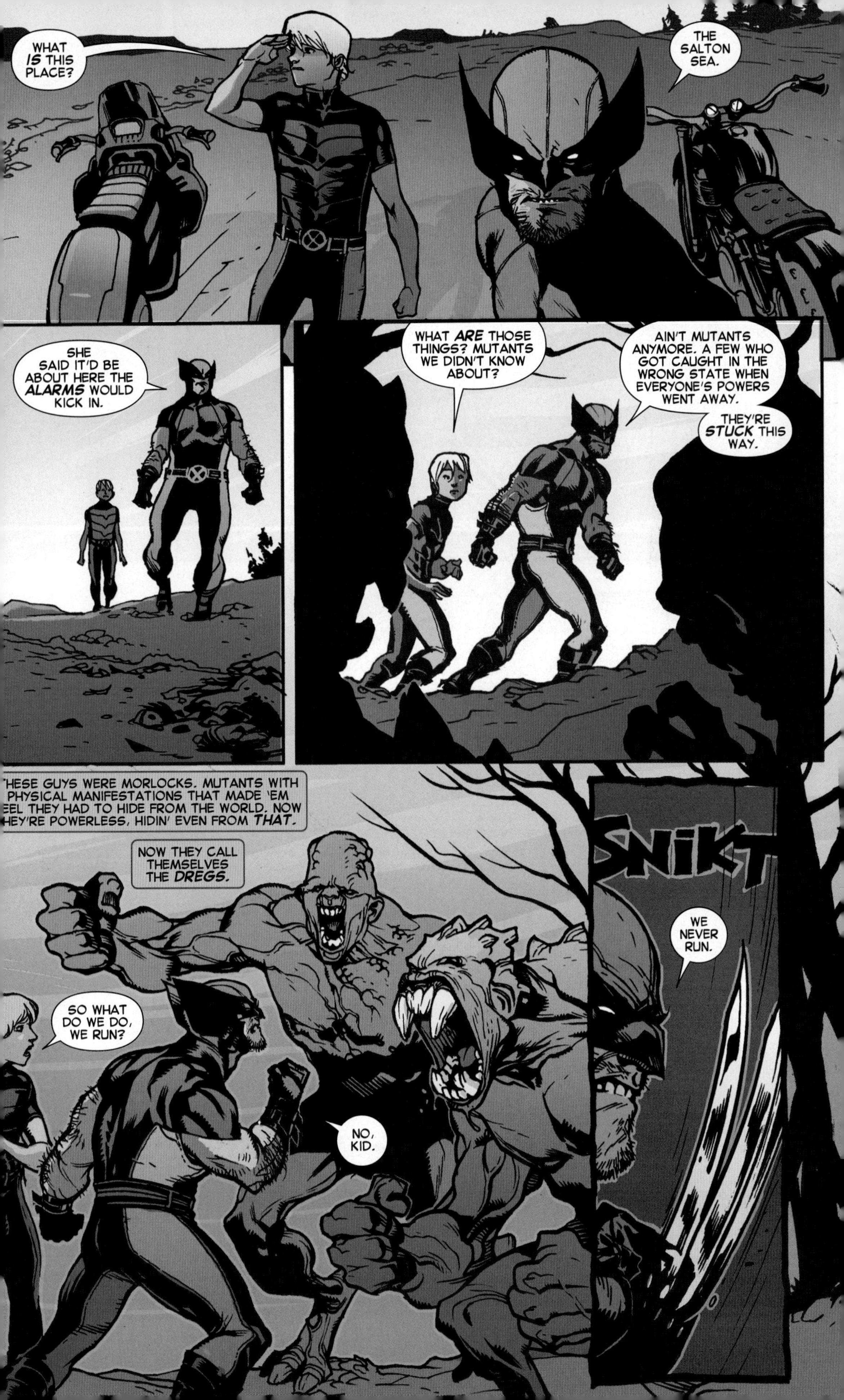
WHAT IS THIS PLACE?
THE SALTON SEA.
SHE SAID IT'D BE ABOUT HERE THE ALARMS WOULD KICK IN.
WHAT ARE THOSE THINGS? MUTANTS WE DIDN'T KNOW ABOUT?
AIN'T MUTANTS ANYMORE. A FEW WHO GOT CAUGHT IN THE WRONG STATE WHEN EVERYONE'S POWERS WENT AWAY.
THEY'RE STUCK THIS WAY.
THESE GUYS WERE MORLOCKS. MUTANTS WITH PHYSICAL MANIFESTATIONS THAT MADE 'EM FEEL THEY HAD TO HIDE FROM THE WORLD. NOW THEY'RE POWERLESS, HIDIN' EVEN FROM THAT.
NOW THEY CALL THEMSELVES THE DREGS.
SNIKT
SO WHAT DO WE DO, WE RUN?
NO, KID.
WE NEVER RUN.

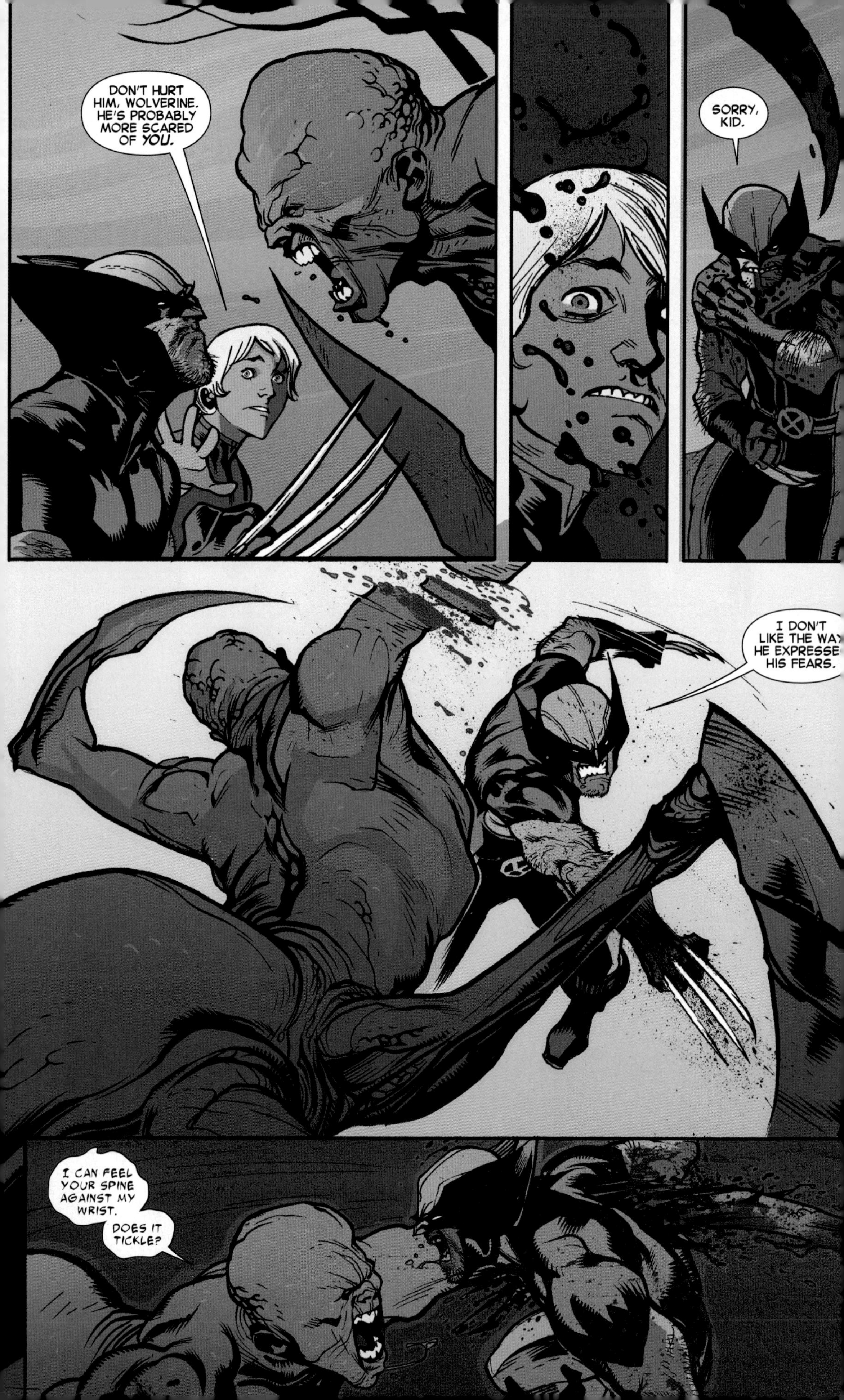
DON'T HURT HIM, WOLVERINE. HE'S PROBABLY MORE SCARED OF *YOU.*
SORRY, KID.
I DON'T LIKE THE WAY HE EXPRESSES HIS FEARS.
I CAN FEEL YOUR SPINE AGAINST MY WRIST.
DOES IT TICKLE?

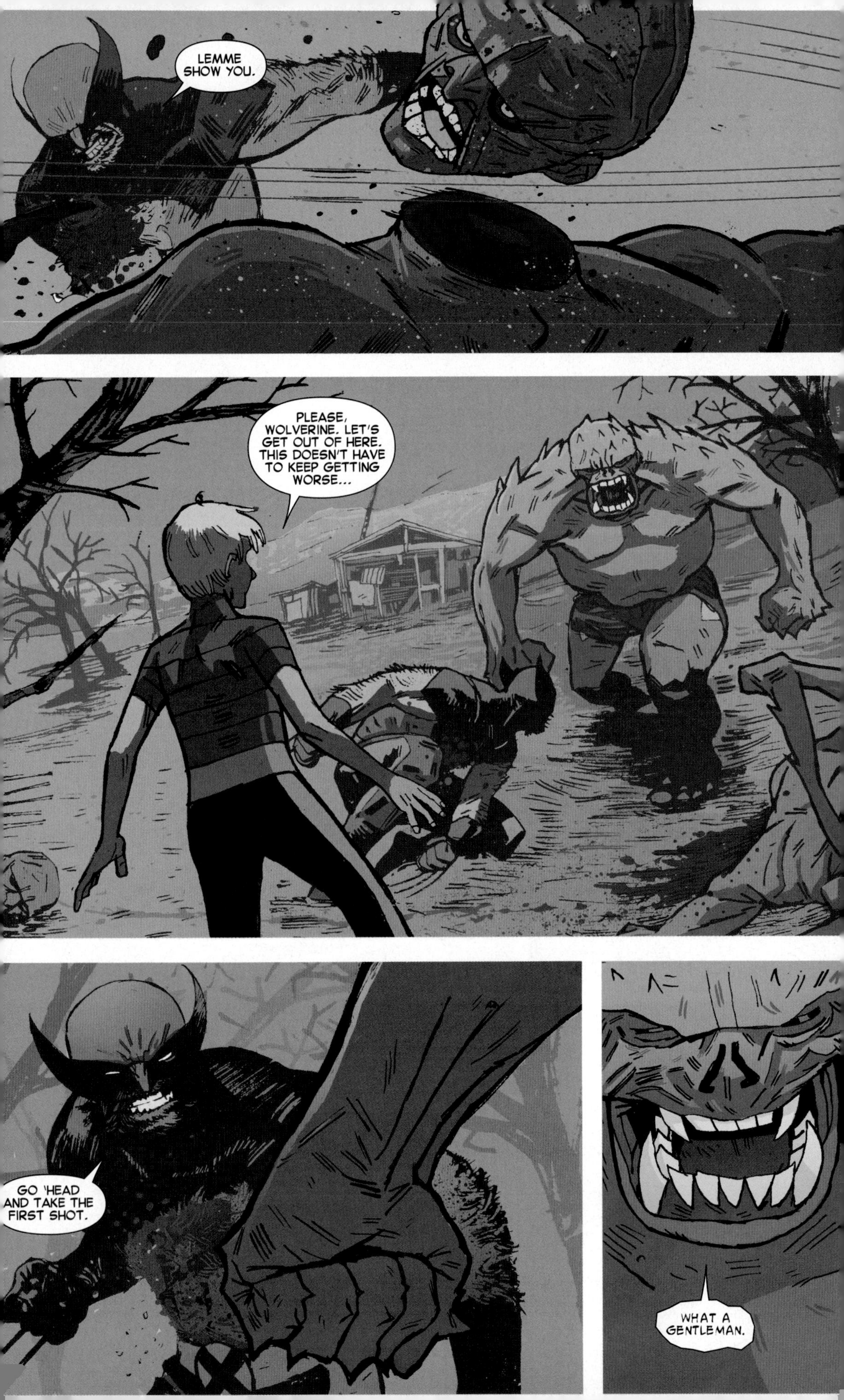
LEMME SHOW YOU.
PLEASE, WOLVERINE. LET'S GET OUT OF HERE. THIS DOESN'T HAVE TO KEEP GETTING WORSE...
GO 'HEAD AND TAKE THE FIRST SHOT.
WHAT A GENTLEMAN.

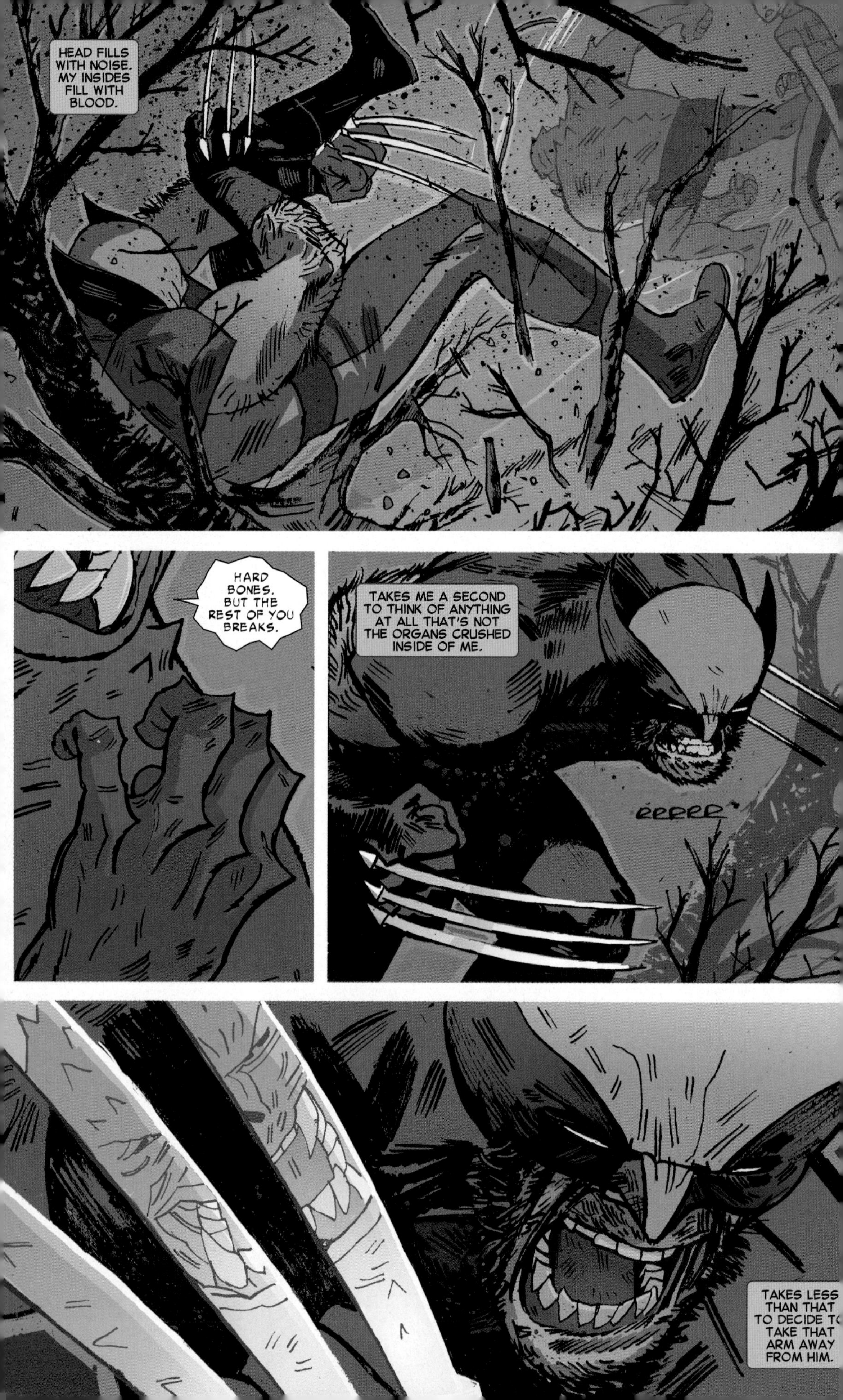
HEAD FILLS WITH NOISE. MY INSIDES FILL WITH BLOOD.
HARD BONES. BUT THE REST OF YOU BREAKS.
TAKES ME A SECOND TO THINK OF ANYTHING AT ALL THAT'S NOT THE ORGANS CRUSHED INSIDE OF ME.
RRRRR
TAKES LESS THAN THAT TO DECIDE TO TAKE THAT ARM AWAY FROM HIM.

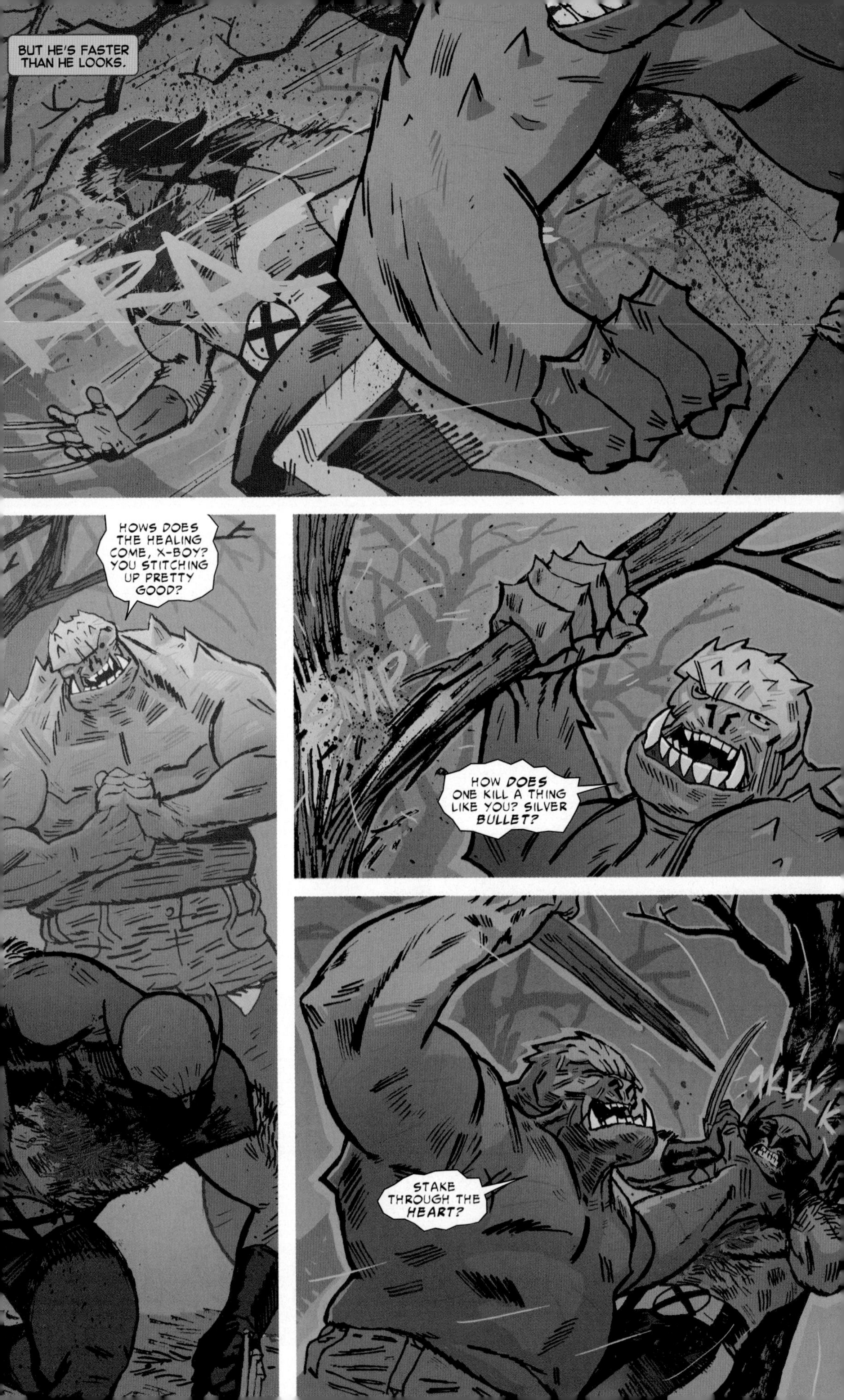
BUT HE'S FASTER THAN HE LOOKS.
HOWS DOES THE HEALING COME, X-BOY? YOU STITCHING UP PRETTY GOOD?
SNAP
HOW DOES ONE KILL A THING LIKE YOU? SILVER BULLET?
STAKE THROUGH THE HEART?
SKKKK

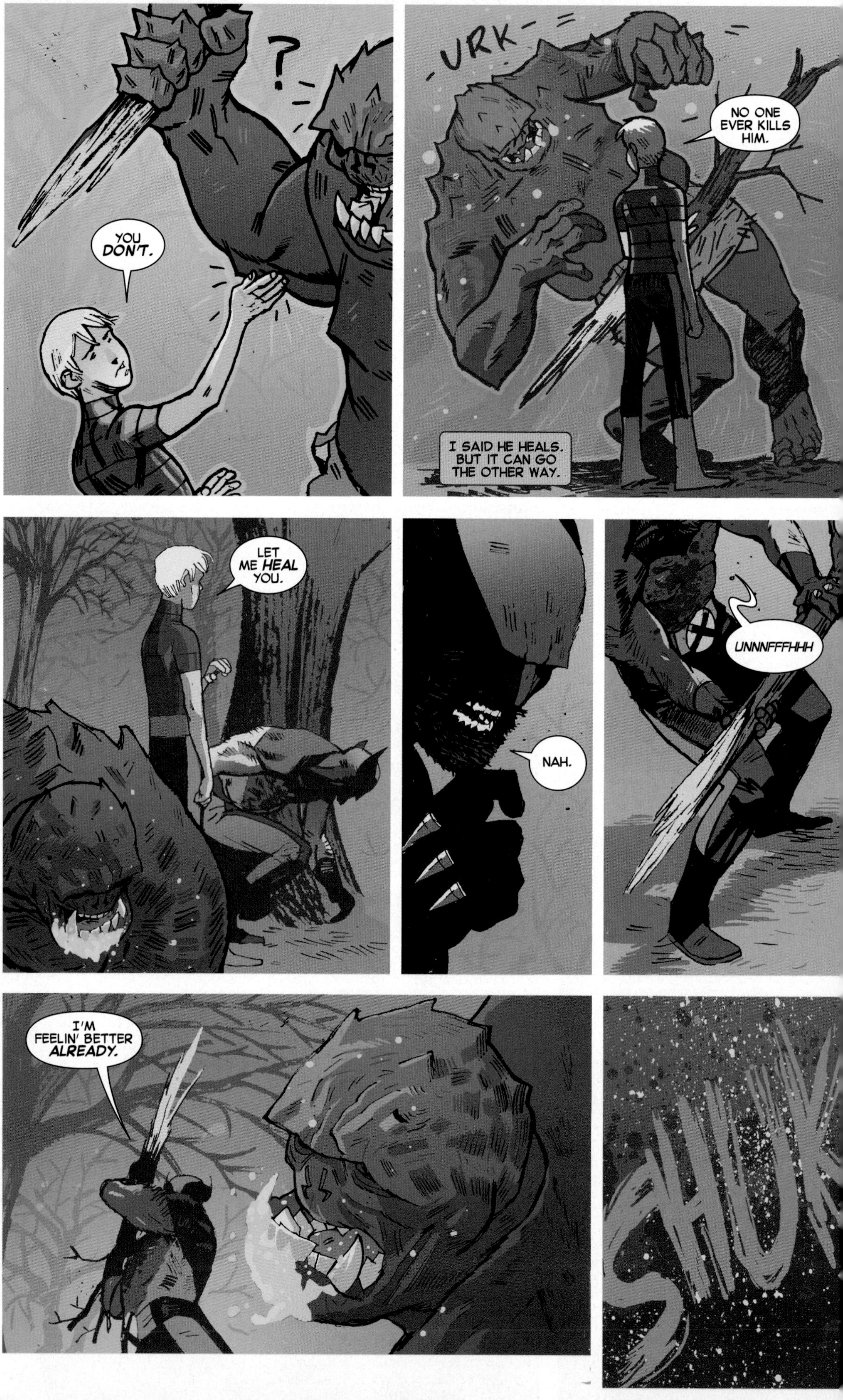
?
YOU DON'T.
URK
NO ONE EVER KILLS HIM.
I SAID HE HEALS. BUT IT CAN GO THE OTHER WAY.
LET ME HEAL YOU.
NAH.
UNNNFFFHHH
I'M FEELIN' BETTER ALREADY.
SHUK

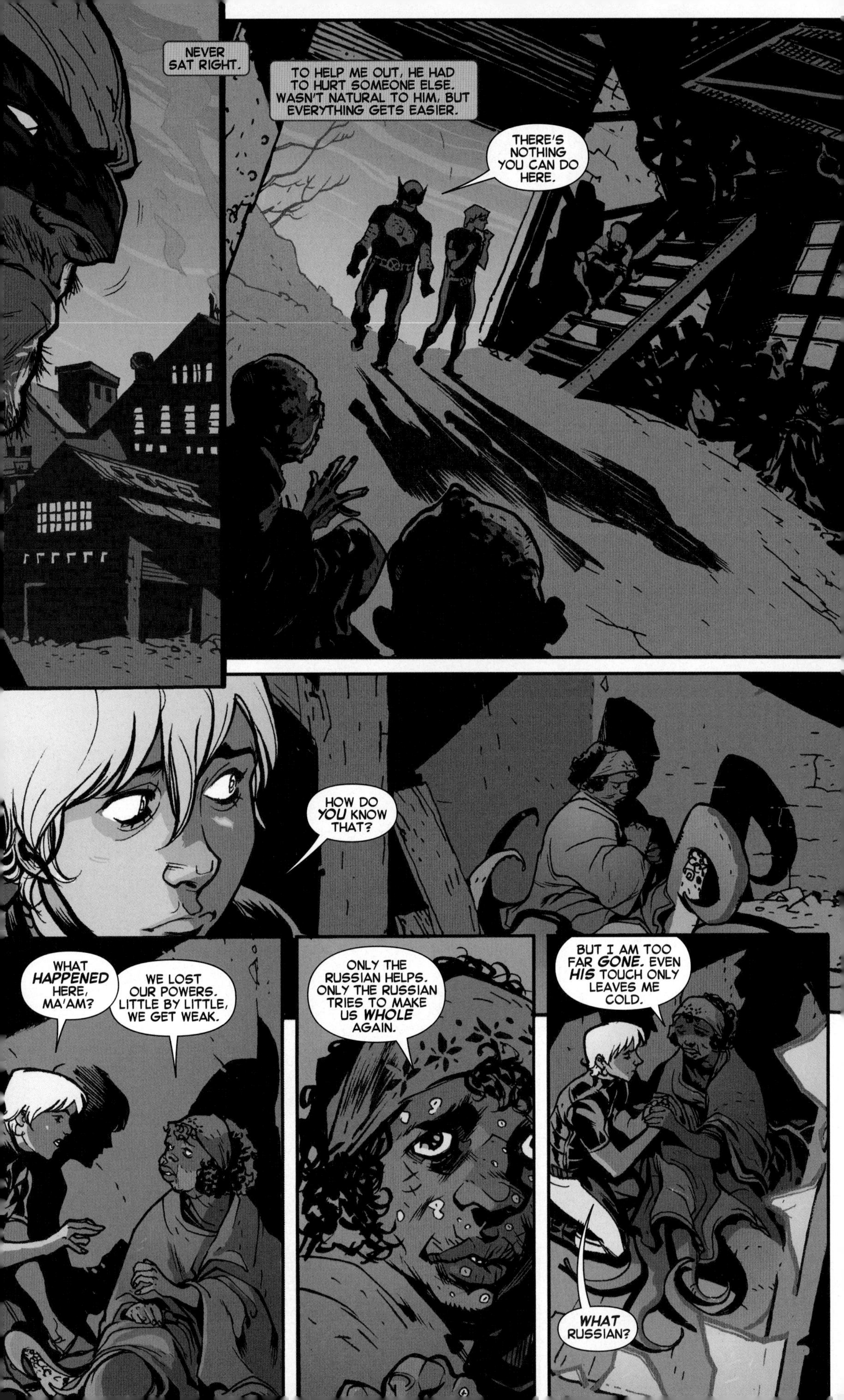
NEVER SAT RIGHT.
TO HELP ME OUT, HE HAD TO HURT SOMEONE ELSE. WASN'T NATURAL TO HIM, BUT EVERYTHING GETS EASIER.
THERE'S NOTHING YOU CAN DO HERE.
HOW DO *YOU* KNOW THAT?
WHAT *HAPPENED* HERE, MA'AM?
WE LOST OUR POWERS. LITTLE BY LITTLE, WE GET WEAK.
ONLY THE RUSSIAN HELPS. ONLY THE RUSSIAN TRIES TO MAKE US *WHOLE* AGAIN.
BUT I AM TOO FAR *GONE*. EVEN *HIS* TOUCH ONLY LEAVES ME COLD.
WHAT RUSSIAN?

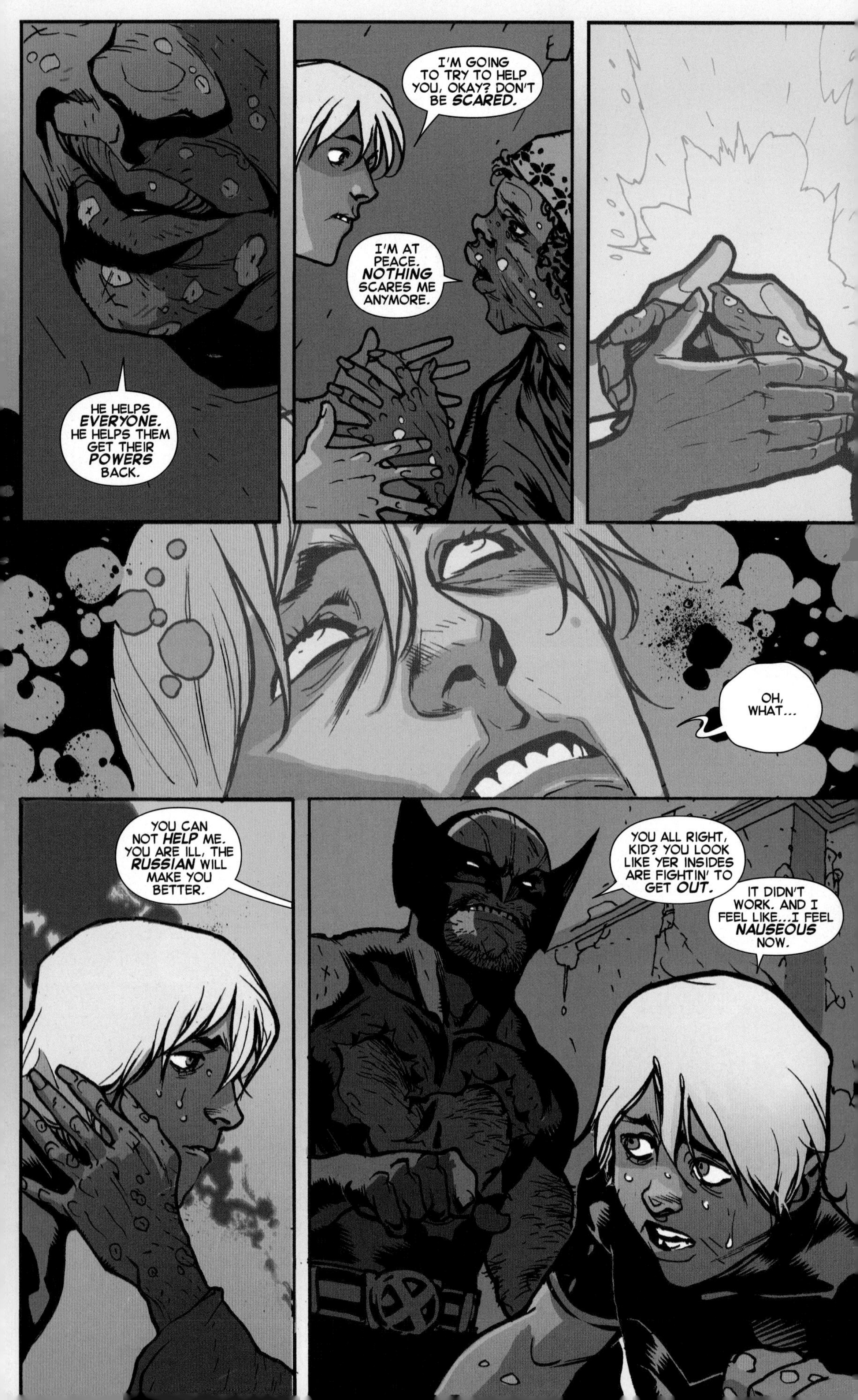
HE HELPS EVERYONE. HE HELPS THEM GET THEIR POWERS BACK.
I'M GOING TO TRY TO HELP YOU, OKAY? DON'T BE SCARED.
I'M AT PEACE. NOTHING SCARES ME ANYMORE.
OH, WHAT...
YOU CAN NOT HELP ME. YOU ARE ILL, THE RUSSIAN WILL MAKE YOU BETTER.
YOU ALL RIGHT, KID? YOU LOOK LIKE YER INSIDES ARE FIGHTIN' TO GET OUT.
IT DIDN'T WORK. AND I FEEL LIKE...I FEEL NAUSEOUS NOW.

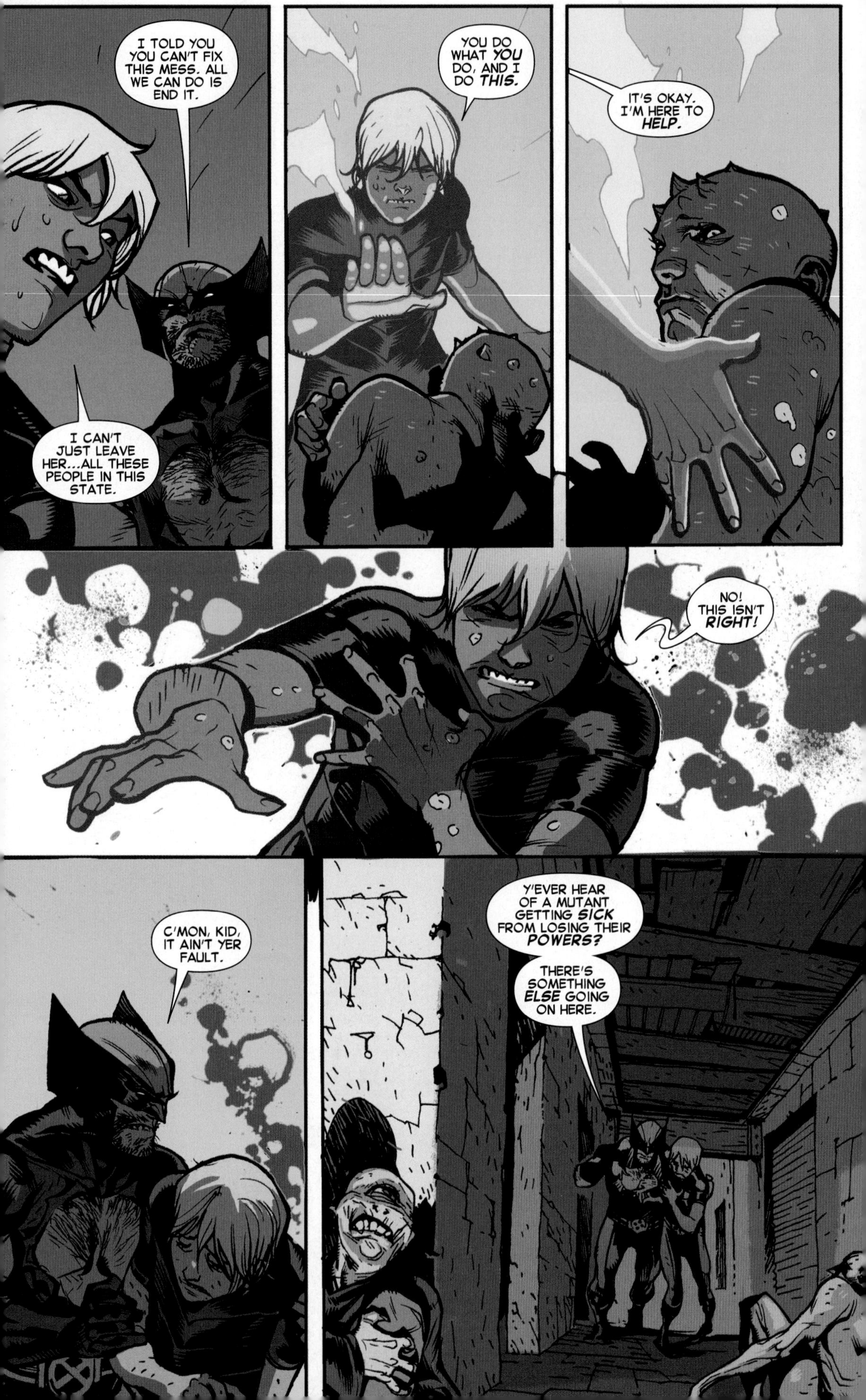
I TOLD YOU YOU CAN'T FIX THIS MESS. ALL WE CAN DO IS END IT.
I CAN'T JUST LEAVE HER...ALL THESE PEOPLE IN THIS STATE.
YOU DO WHAT YOU DO, AND I DO THIS.
IT'S OKAY. I'M HERE TO HELP.
NO! THIS ISN'T RIGHT!
C'MON, KID, IT AIN'T YER FAULT.
Y'EVER HEAR OF A MUTANT GETTING SICK FROM LOSING THEIR POWERS?
THERE'S SOMETHING ELSE GOING ON HERE.

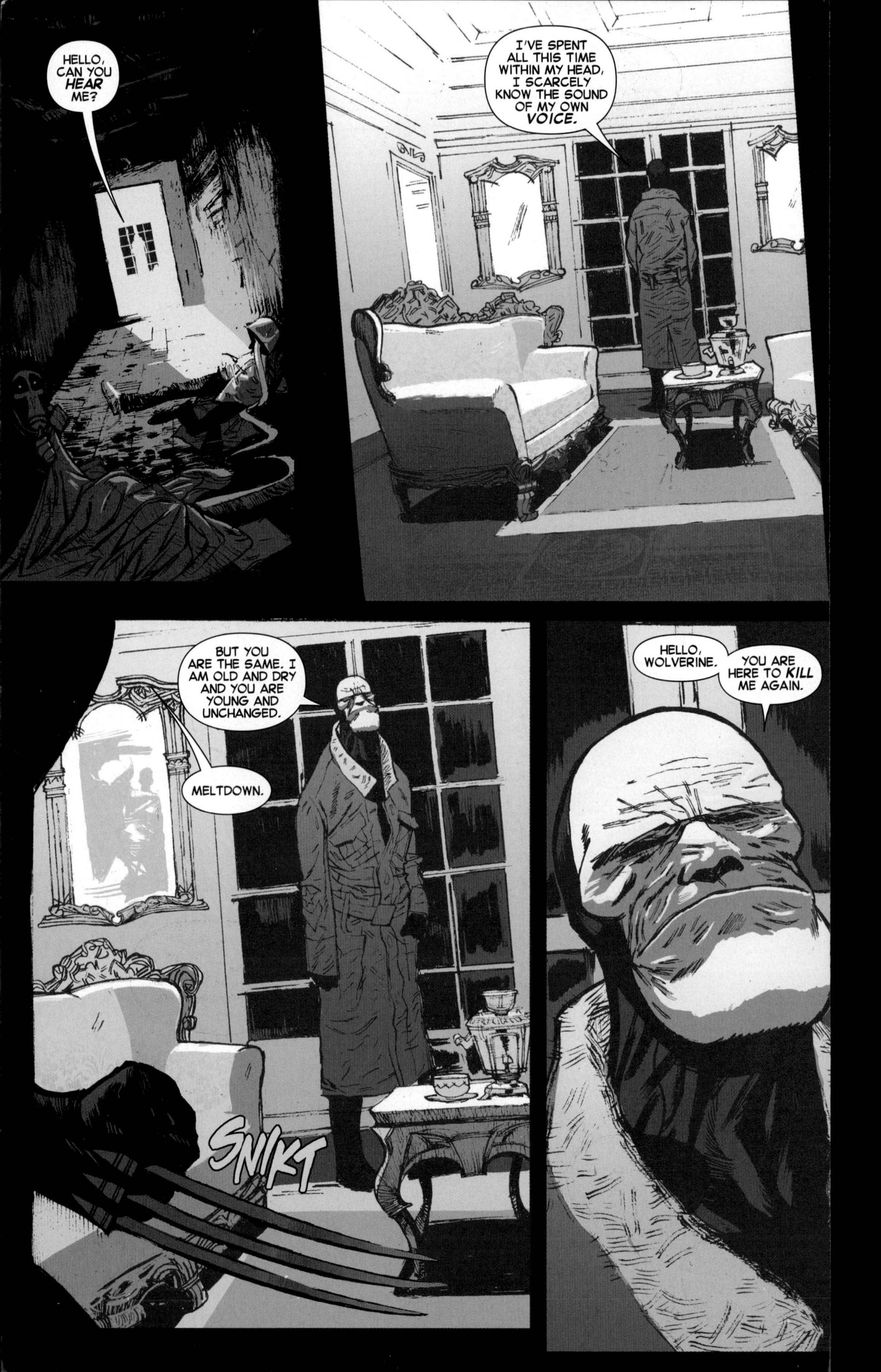
HELLO, CAN YOU HEAR ME?
I'VE SPENT ALL THIS TIME WITHIN MY HEAD, I SCARCELY KNOW THE SOUND OF MY OWN VOICE.
BUT YOU ARE THE SAME. I AM OLD AND DRY AND YOU ARE YOUNG AND UNCHANGED.
MELTDOWN.
SNIKT
HELLO, WOLVERINE.
YOU ARE HERE TO KILL ME AGAIN.

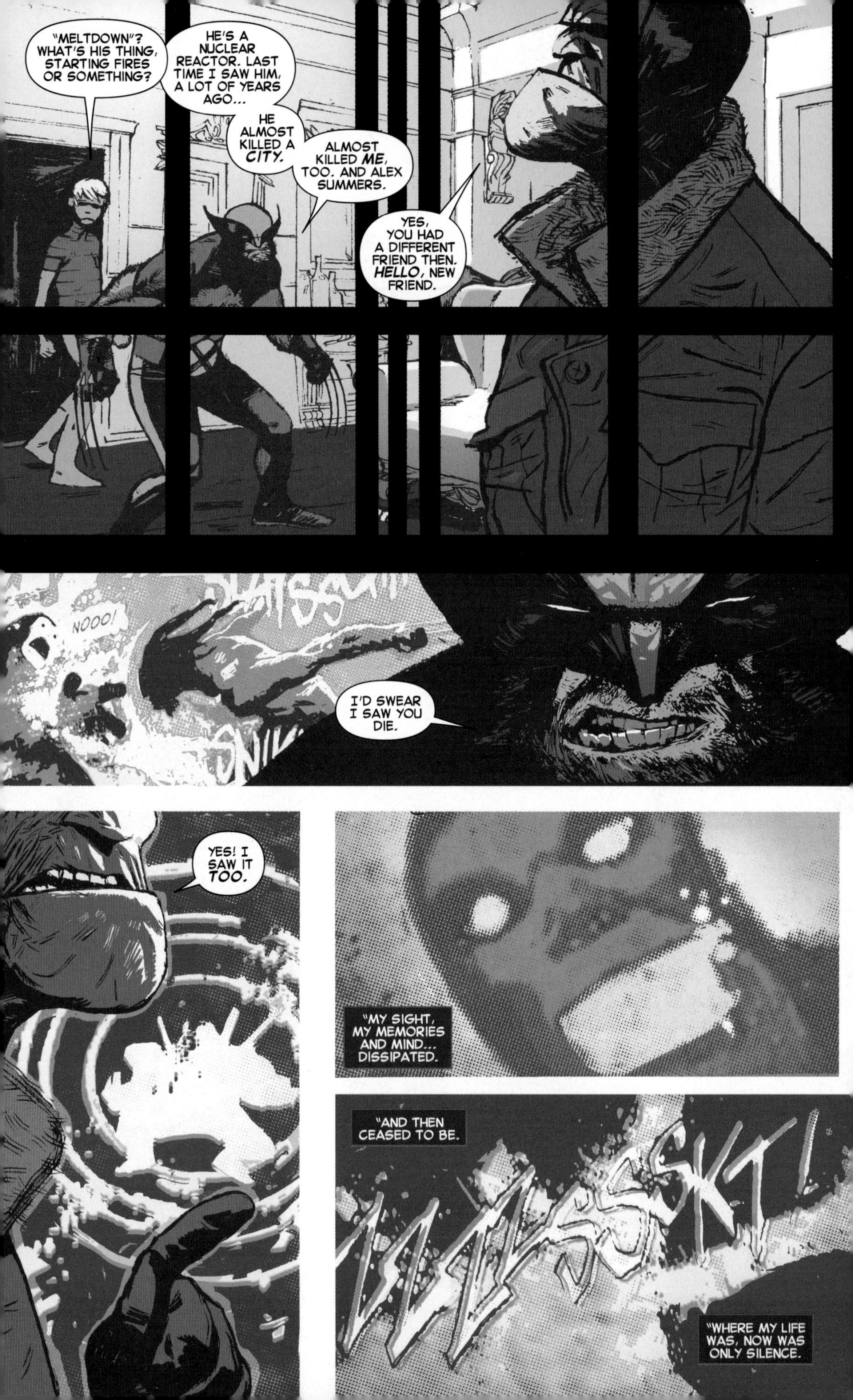
"MELTDOWN"? WHAT'S HIS THING, STARTING FIRES OR SOMETHING?
HE'S A NUCLEAR REACTOR. LAST TIME I SAW HIM, A LOT OF YEARS AGO...
HE ALMOST KILLED A CITY.
ALMOST KILLED ME, TOO. AND ALEX SUMMERS.
YES, YOU HAD A DIFFERENT FRIEND THEN. HELLO, NEW FRIEND.
NOOO!
I'D SWEAR I SAW YOU DIE.
YES! I SAW IT TOO.
"MY SIGHT, MY MEMORIES AND MIND... DISSIPATED.
"AND THEN CEASED TO BE.
"WHERE MY LIFE WAS, NOW WAS ONLY SILENCE.

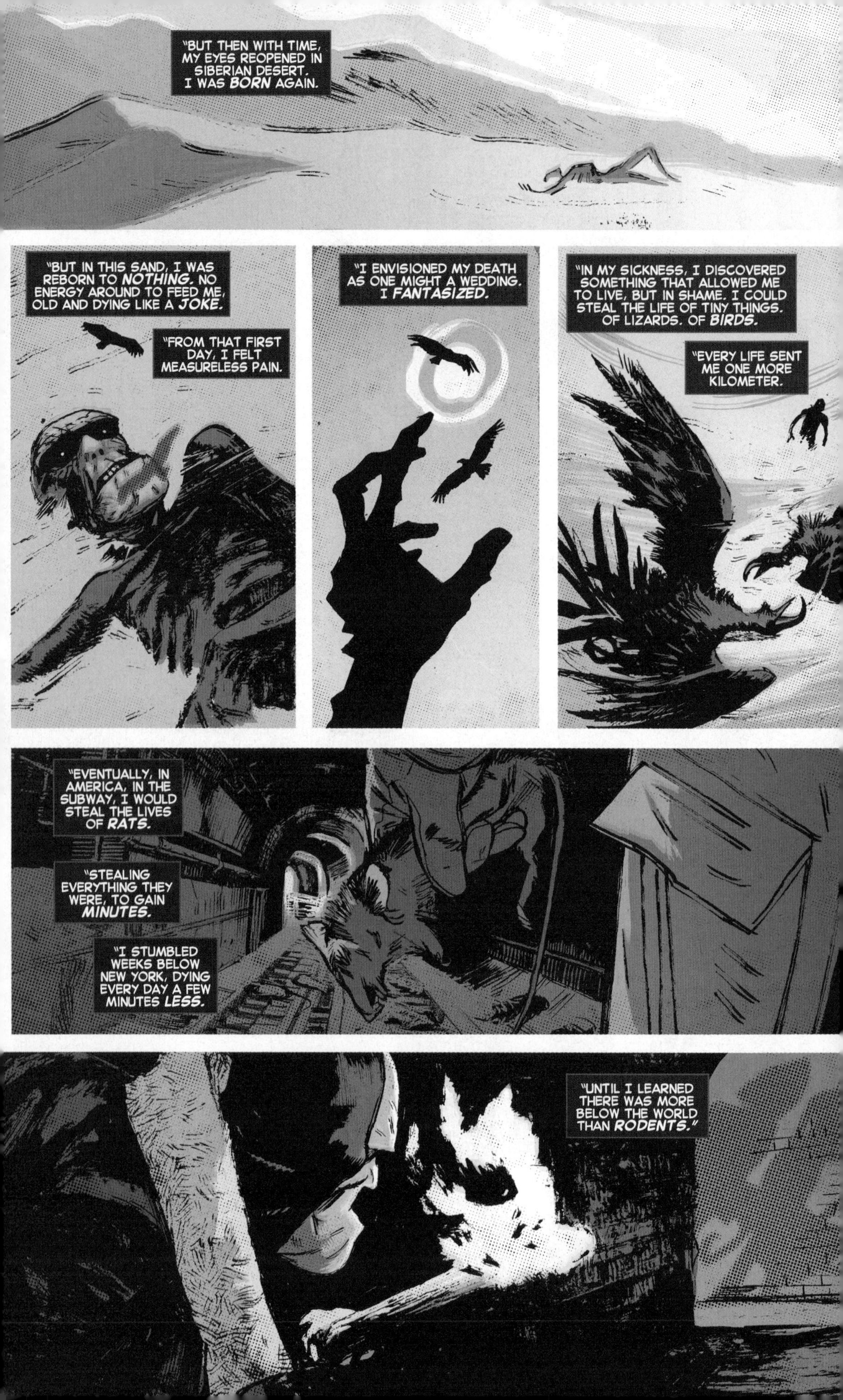
"BUT THEN WITH TIME, MY EYES REOPENED IN SIBERIAN DESERT. I WAS BORN AGAIN.
"BUT IN THIS SAND, I WAS REBORN TO NOTHING. NO ENERGY AROUND TO FEED ME, OLD AND DYING LIKE A JOKE.
"FROM THAT FIRST DAY, I FELT MEASURELESS PAIN.
"I ENVISIONED MY DEATH AS ONE MIGHT A WEDDING. I FANTASIZED.
"IN MY SICKNESS, I DISCOVERED SOMETHING THAT ALLOWED ME TO LIVE, BUT IN SHAME. I COULD STEAL THE LIFE OF TINY THINGS. OF LIZARDS. OF BIRDS.
"EVERY LIFE SENT ME ONE MORE KILOMETER.
"EVENTUALLY, IN AMERICA, IN THE SUBWAY, I WOULD STEAL THE LIVES OF RATS.
"STEALING EVERYTHING THEY WERE, TO GAIN MINUTES.
"I STUMBLED WEEKS BELOW NEW YORK, DYING EVERY DAY A FEW MINUTES LESS.
"UNTIL I LEARNED THERE WAS MORE BELOW THE WORLD THAN RODENTS."

HE FOUND THE MORLOCKS. THE *DREGS*. HE FOUND *ME*.

EVA.

YOU'VE COME BACK TO ME, I THOUGHT THAT I HAD *LOST* YOU.

WE'D ALL LOST OUR ABILITIES AT THE WRONG TIME. WE WERE ALL *DEFORMED*, DESPERATE.

TILL WE ALL LOST OUR POWERS, I'D CHANGE INTO THIS DARK LIQUID STONE AND IT WAS *PERFECT*.

I FELT IMMACULATE. NO ONE COULD HURT ME. NO ONE *ELSE* COULD BE WHAT I WAS.

AND THEN ONE DAY I'M CHANGING *BACK* AND RIGHT IN THE MIDDLE, SOMETHING *HAPPENS*.

NOT JUST TO *ME*. ALL *OVER*, PEOPLE CAN'T DO THE THINGS THEY USED TO DO.

"THERE'S A GUY THAT LOOKED JUST LIKE A DRAGON...HE COULD FLY, HE SPOKE FIRE...IT SOUNDS SCARY BUT HE WAS *MAGNIFICENT*.

"HE WAS FLYING WHEN THAT DAY CAME AND HE FELL OUT OF THE SKY. BROKE HIS LEGS, HIS SPINE...HE WAS POWERLESS EVEN TO CHANGE BACK TO HIS HUMAN FACE.

"THEY DIDN'T EVEN TURN HIM AWAY AT THE HOSPITAL. THEY *EVACUATED*, THEY THOUGHT THEY WERE UNDER *ATTACK*.

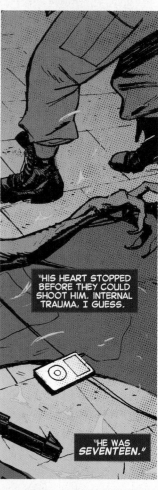

"HIS HEART STOPPED BEFORE THEY COULD SHOOT HIM. INTERNAL TRAUMA, I GUESS.

"HE WAS *SEVENTEEN*."

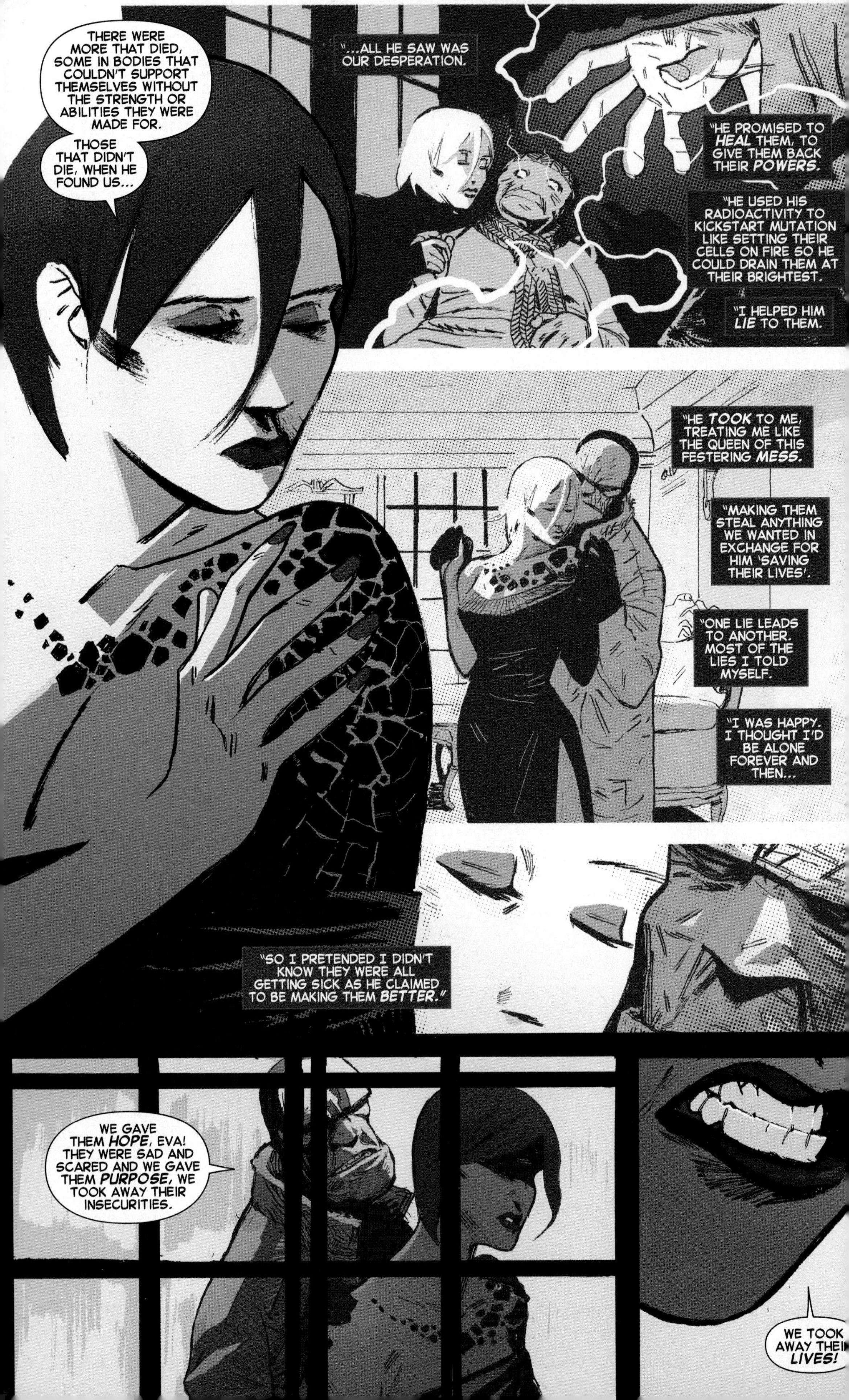

THERE WERE MORE THAT DIED, SOME IN BODIES THAT COULDN'T SUPPORT THEMSELVES WITHOUT THE STRENGTH OR ABILITIES THEY WERE MADE FOR.
THOSE THAT DIDN'T DIE, WHEN HE FOUND US...
"...ALL HE SAW WAS OUR DESPERATION.
"HE PROMISED TO *HEAL* THEM, TO GIVE THEM BACK THEIR *POWERS.*
"HE USED HIS RADIOACTIVITY TO KICKSTART MUTATION LIKE SETTING THEIR CELLS ON FIRE SO HE COULD DRAIN THEM AT THEIR BRIGHTEST.
"I HELPED HIM *LIE* TO THEM.
"HE *TOOK* TO ME, TREATING ME LIKE THE QUEEN OF THIS FESTERING *MESS.*
"MAKING THEM STEAL ANYTHING WE WANTED IN EXCHANGE FOR HIM 'SAVING THEIR LIVES'.
"ONE LIE LEADS TO ANOTHER. MOST OF THE LIES I TOLD MYSELF.
"I WAS HAPPY. I THOUGHT I'D BE ALONE FOREVER AND THEN...
"SO I PRETENDED I DIDN'T KNOW THEY WERE ALL GETTING SICK AS HE CLAIMED TO BE MAKING THEM *BETTER.*"
WE GAVE THEM *HOPE*, EVA! THEY WERE SAD AND SCARED AND WE GAVE THEM *PURPOSE*, WE TOOK AWAY THEIR INSECURITIES.
WE TOOK AWAY THEI *LIVES!*

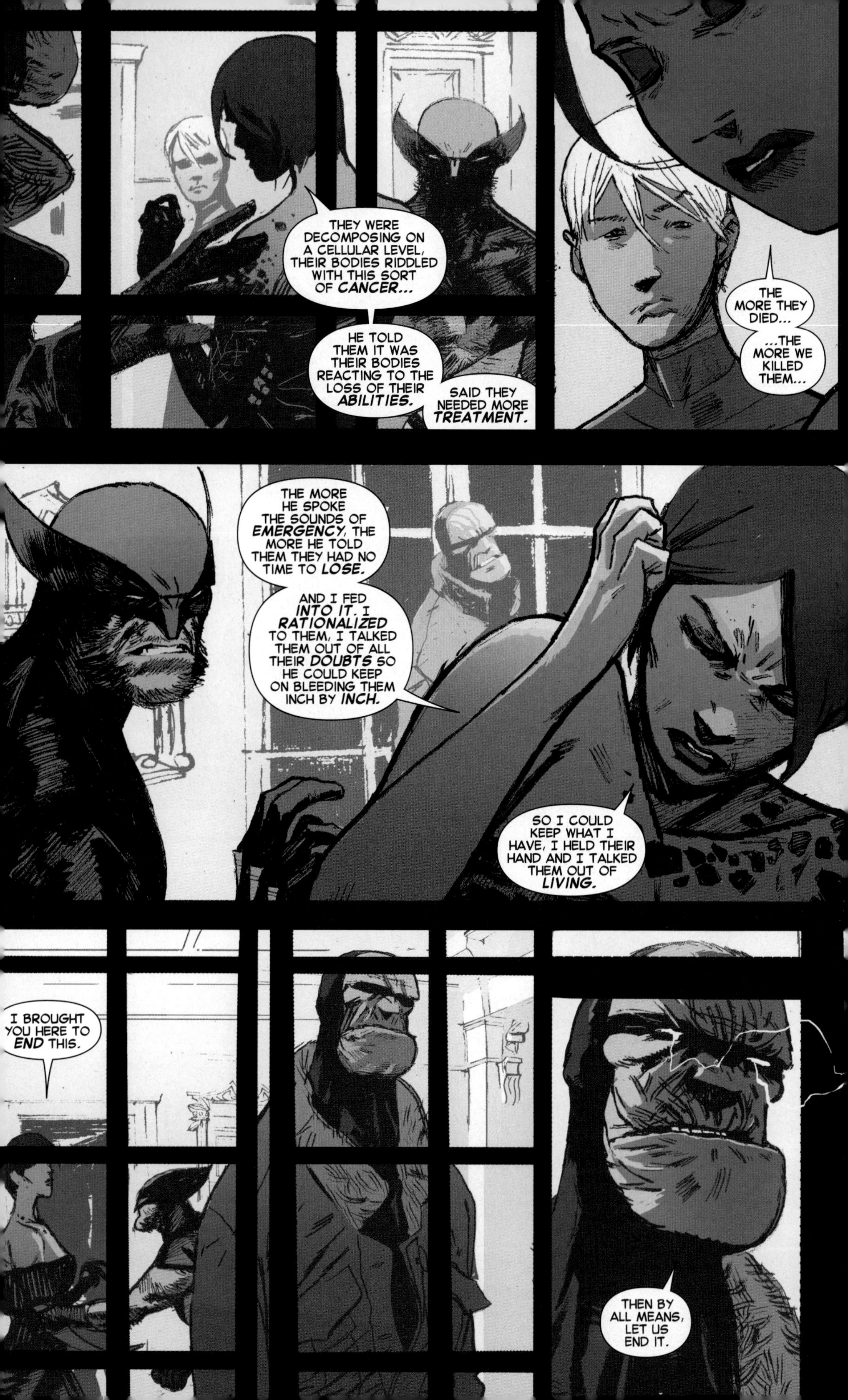
THEY WERE DECOMPOSING ON A CELLULAR LEVEL, THEIR BODIES RIDDLED WITH THIS SORT OF CANCER...
HE TOLD THEM IT WAS THEIR BODIES REACTING TO THE LOSS OF THEIR ABILITIES.
SAID THEY NEEDED MORE TREATMENT.
THE MORE THEY DIED...
...THE MORE WE KILLED THEM...
THE MORE HE SPOKE THE SOUNDS OF EMERGENCY, THE MORE HE TOLD THEM THEY HAD NO TIME TO LOSE.
AND I FED INTO IT. I RATIONALIZED TO THEM, I TALKED THEM OUT OF ALL THEIR DOUBTS SO HE COULD KEEP ON BLEEDING THEM INCH BY INCH.
SO I COULD KEEP WHAT I HAVE, I HELD THEIR HAND AND I TALKED THEM OUT OF LIVING.
I BROUGHT YOU HERE TO END THIS.
THEN BY ALL MEANS, LET US END IT.

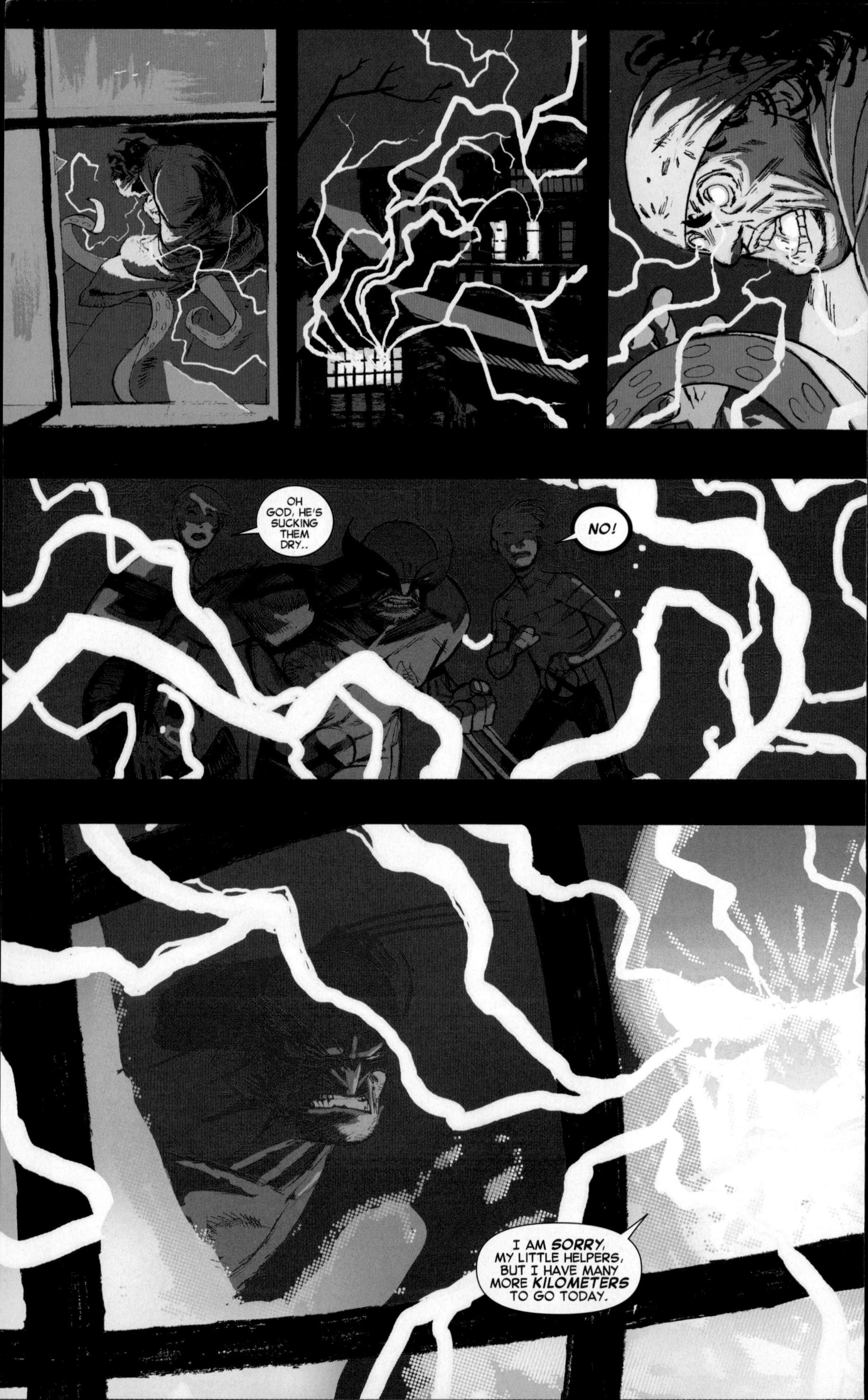
OH GOD, HE'S SUCKING THEM DRY..
NO!
I AM SORRY, MY LITTLE HELPERS, BUT I HAVE MANY MORE KILOMETERS TO GO TODAY.

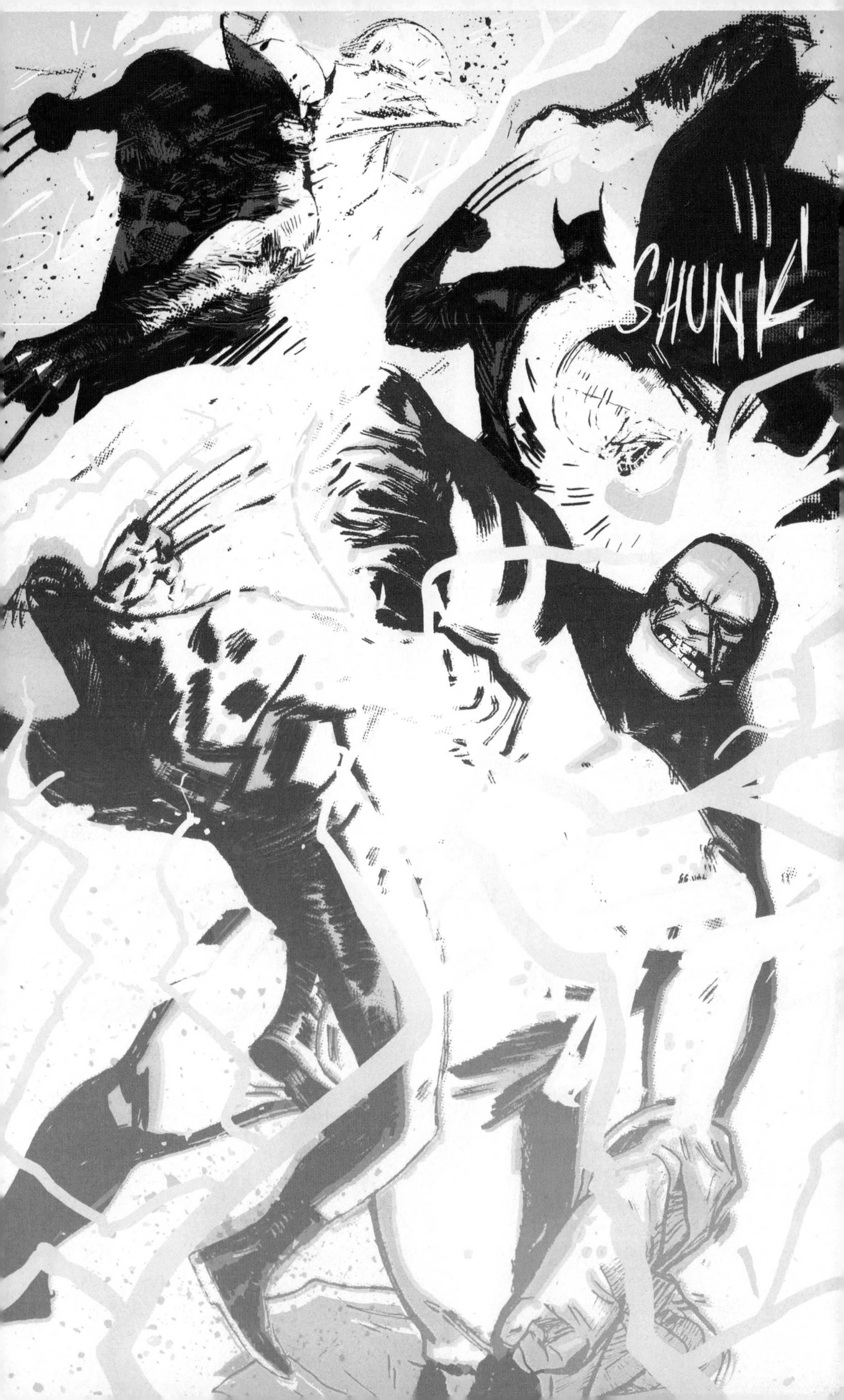
SHUNK!

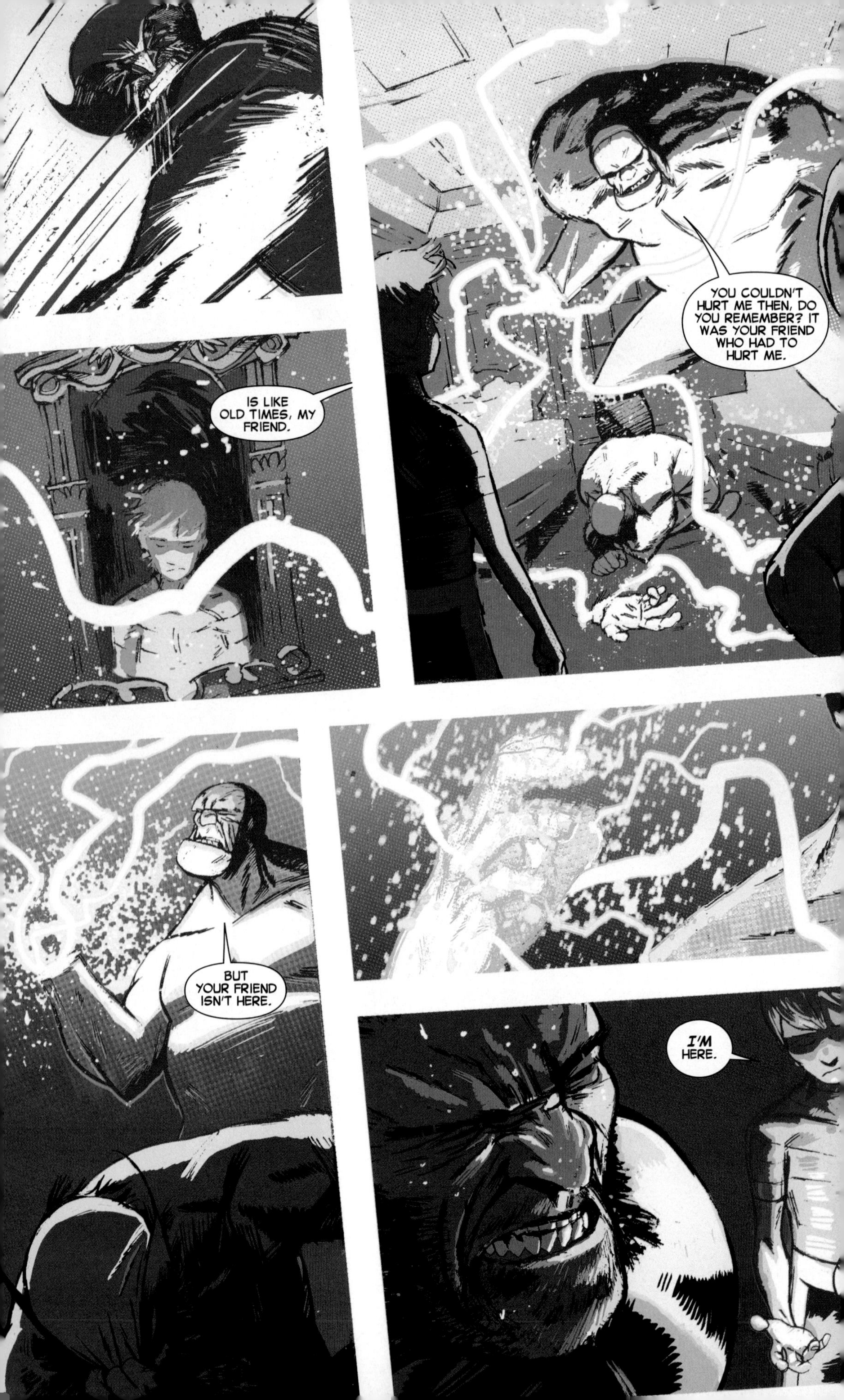
IS LIKE OLD TIMES, MY FRIEND.
YOU COULDN'T HURT ME THEN, DO YOU REMEMBER? IT WAS YOUR FRIEND WHO HAD TO HURT ME.
BUT YOUR FRIEND ISN'T HERE.
I'M HERE.

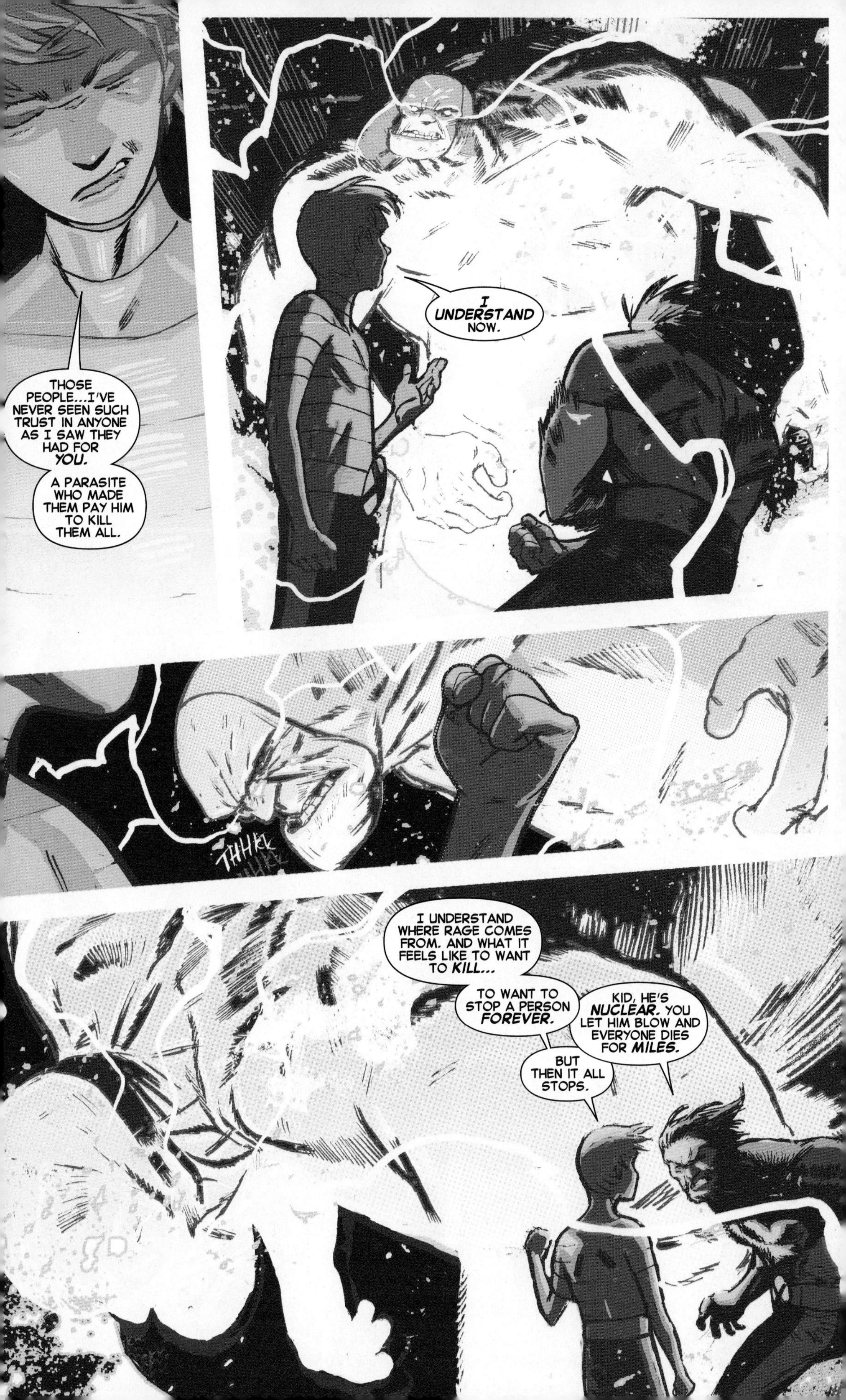
THOSE PEOPLE...I'VE NEVER SEEN SUCH TRUST IN ANYONE AS I SAW THEY HAD FOR YOU.
A PARASITE WHO MADE THEM PAY HIM TO KILL THEM ALL.
I UNDERSTAND NOW.
THHKK
I UNDERSTAND WHERE RAGE COMES FROM. AND WHAT IT FEELS LIKE TO WANT TO KILL...
TO WANT TO STOP A PERSON FOREVER.
KID, HE'S NUCLEAR. YOU LET HIM BLOW AND EVERYONE DIES FOR MILES.
BUT THEN IT ALL STOPS.

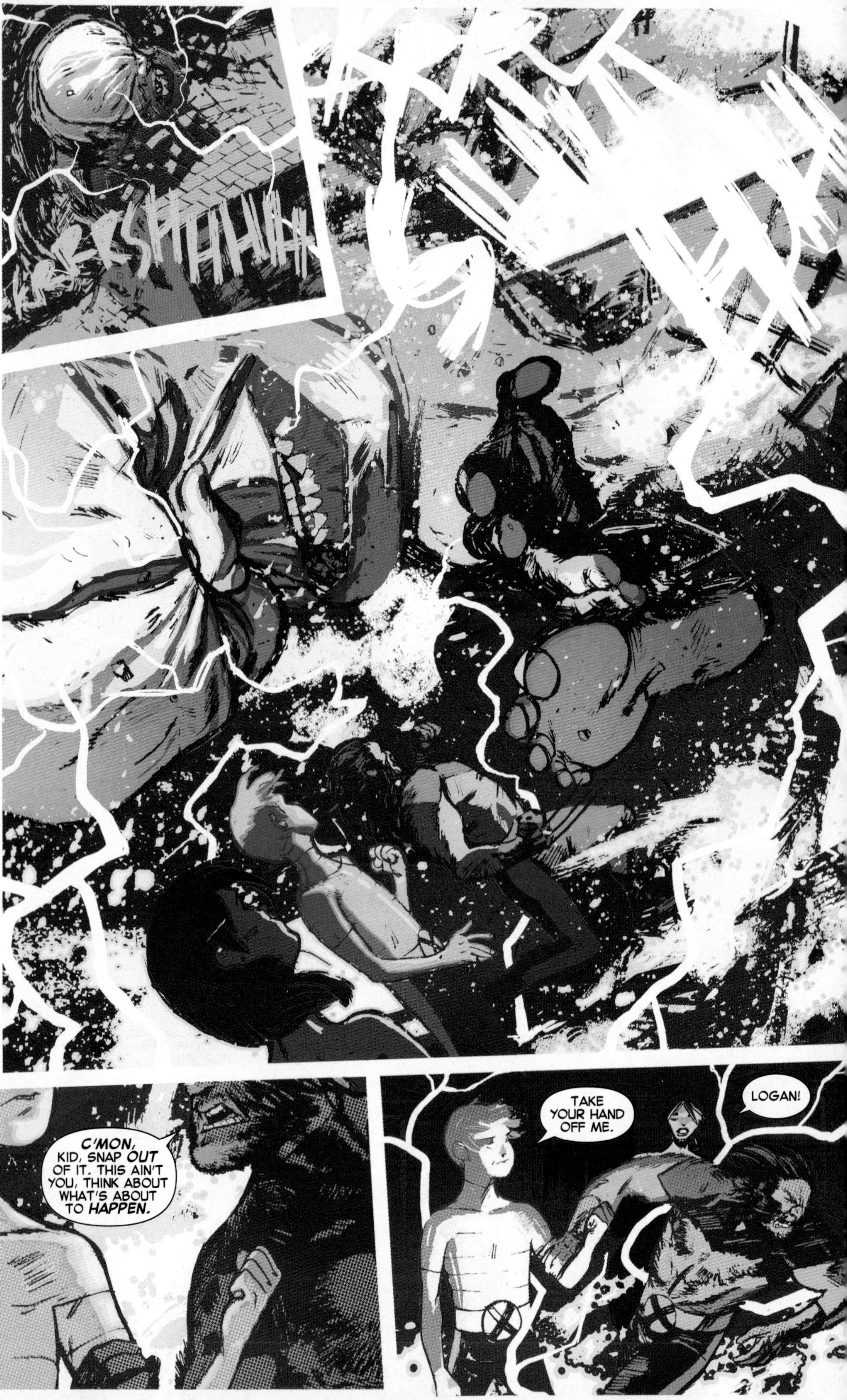
C'MON, KID, SNAP OUT OF IT. THIS AIN'T YOU, THINK ABOUT WHAT'S ABOUT TO HAPPEN.
TAKE YOUR HAND OFF ME.
LOGAN!

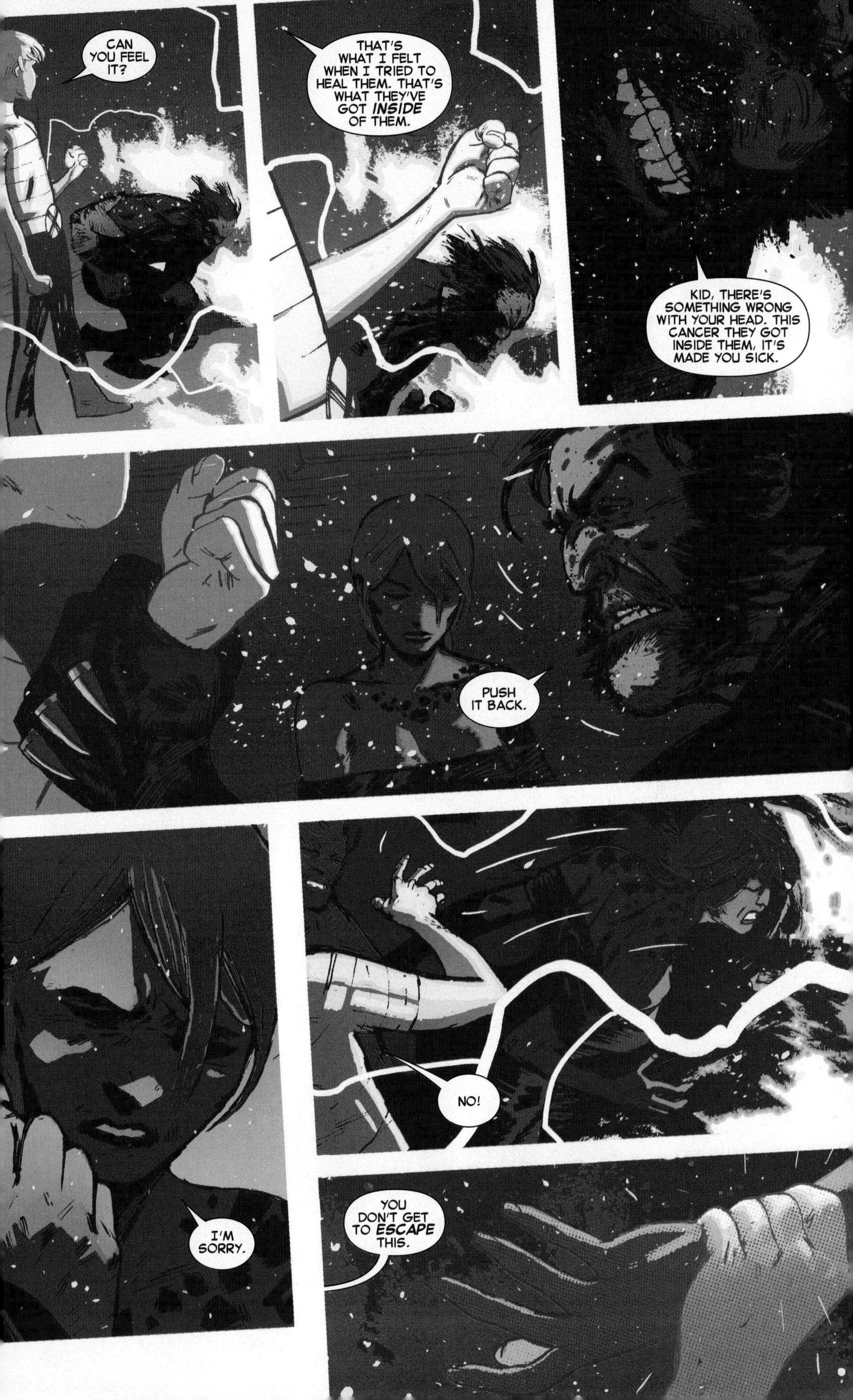
CAN YOU FEEL IT?
THAT'S WHAT I FELT WHEN I TRIED TO HEAL THEM. THAT'S WHAT THEY'VE GOT *INSIDE* OF THEM.
KID, THERE'S SOMETHING WRONG WITH YOUR HEAD. THIS CANCER THEY GOT INSIDE THEM, IT'S MADE YOU SICK.
PUSH IT BACK.
I'M SORRY.
NO!
YOU DON'T GET TO *ESCAPE* THIS.

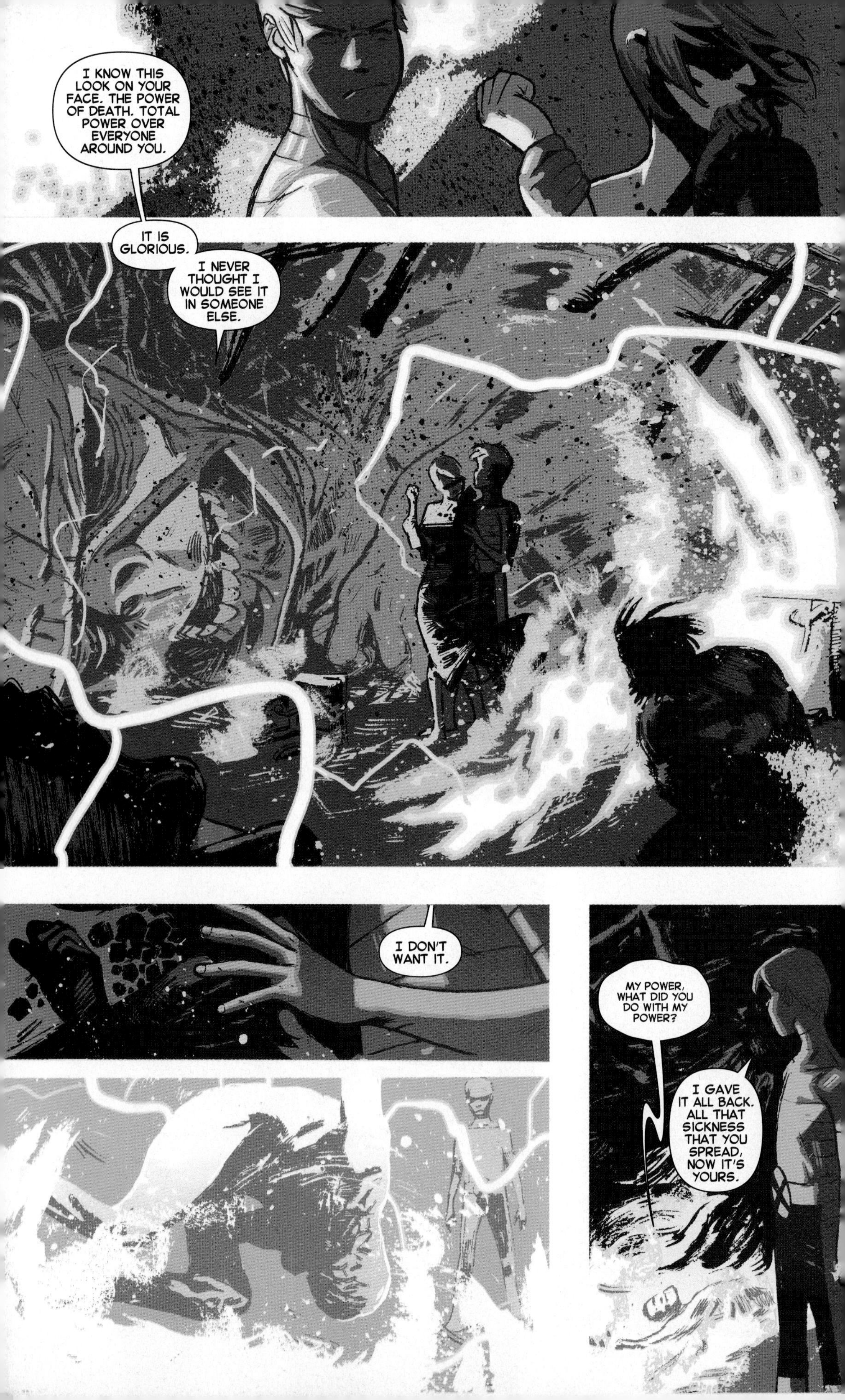
I KNOW THIS LOOK ON YOUR FACE. THE POWER OF DEATH. TOTAL POWER OVER EVERYONE AROUND YOU.
IT IS GLORIOUS.
I NEVER THOUGHT I WOULD SEE IT IN SOMEONE ELSE.
I DON'T WANT IT.
MY POWER, WHAT DID YOU DO WITH MY POWER?
I GAVE IT ALL BACK. ALL THAT SICKNESS THAT YOU SPREAD, NOW IT'S YOURS.

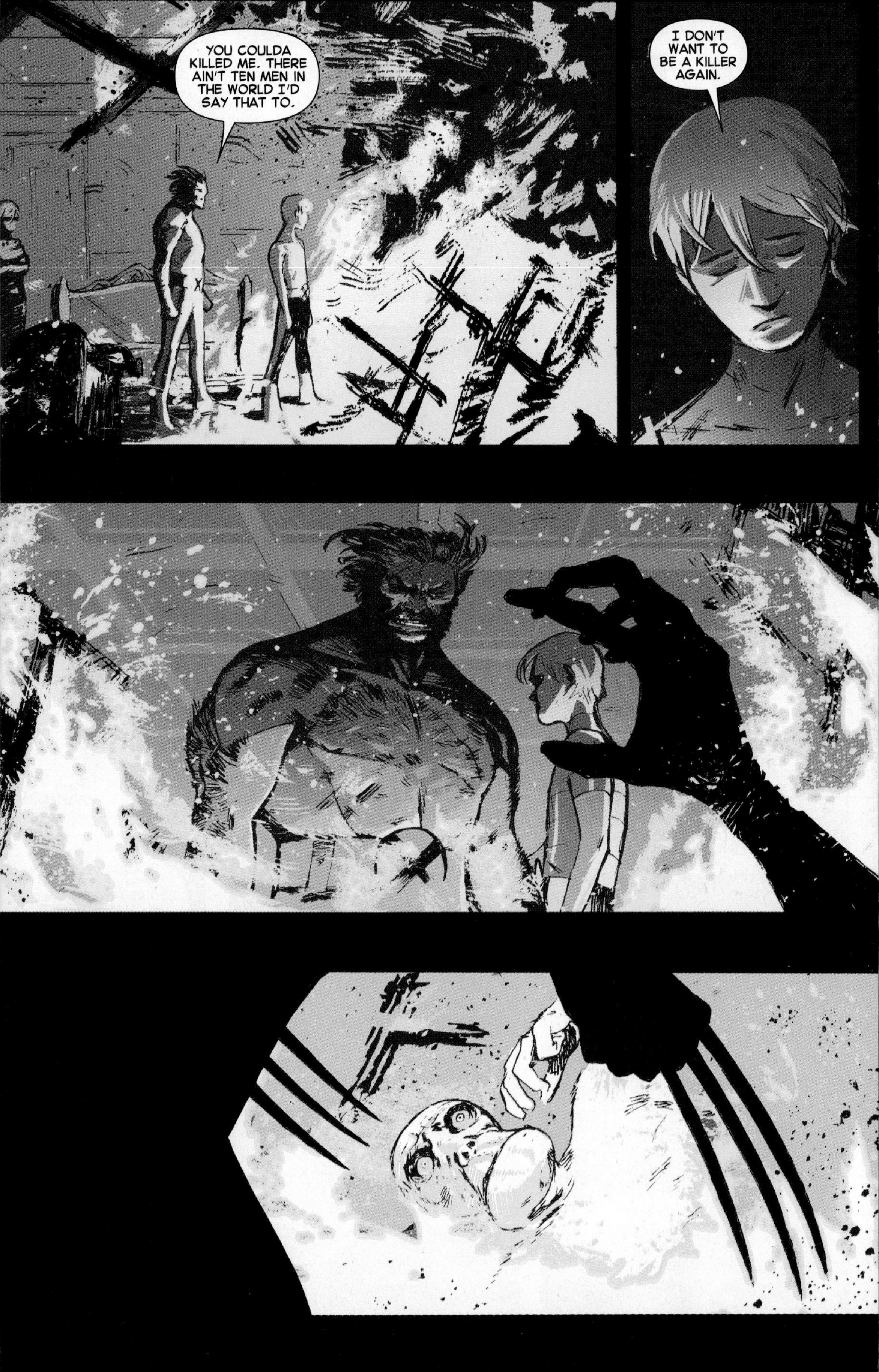
YOU COULDA KILLED ME. THERE AIN'T TEN MEN IN THE WORLD I'D SAY THAT TO.
I DON'T WANT TO BE A KILLER AGAIN.

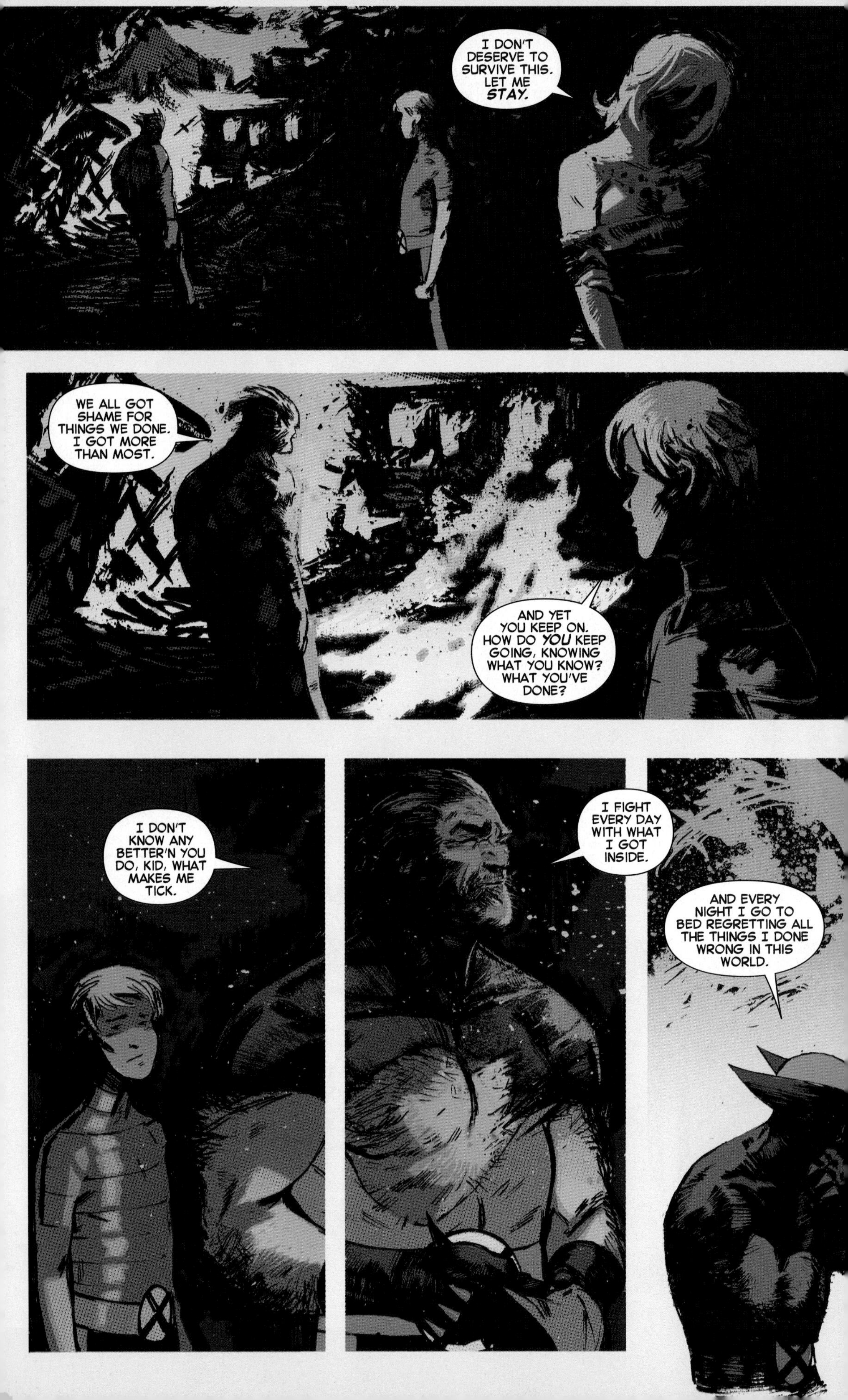
I DON'T DESERVE TO SURVIVE THIS. LET ME *STAY.*
WE ALL GOT SHAME FOR THINGS WE DONE. I GOT MORE THAN MOST.
AND YET YOU KEEP ON. HOW DO *YOU* KEEP GOING, KNOWING WHAT YOU KNOW? WHAT YOU'VE DONE?
I DON'T KNOW ANY BETTER'N YOU DO, KID, WHAT MAKES ME TICK.
I FIGHT EVERY DAY WITH WHAT I GOT INSIDE.
AND EVERY NIGHT I GO TO BED REGRETTING ALL THE THINGS I DONE WRONG IN THIS WORLD.

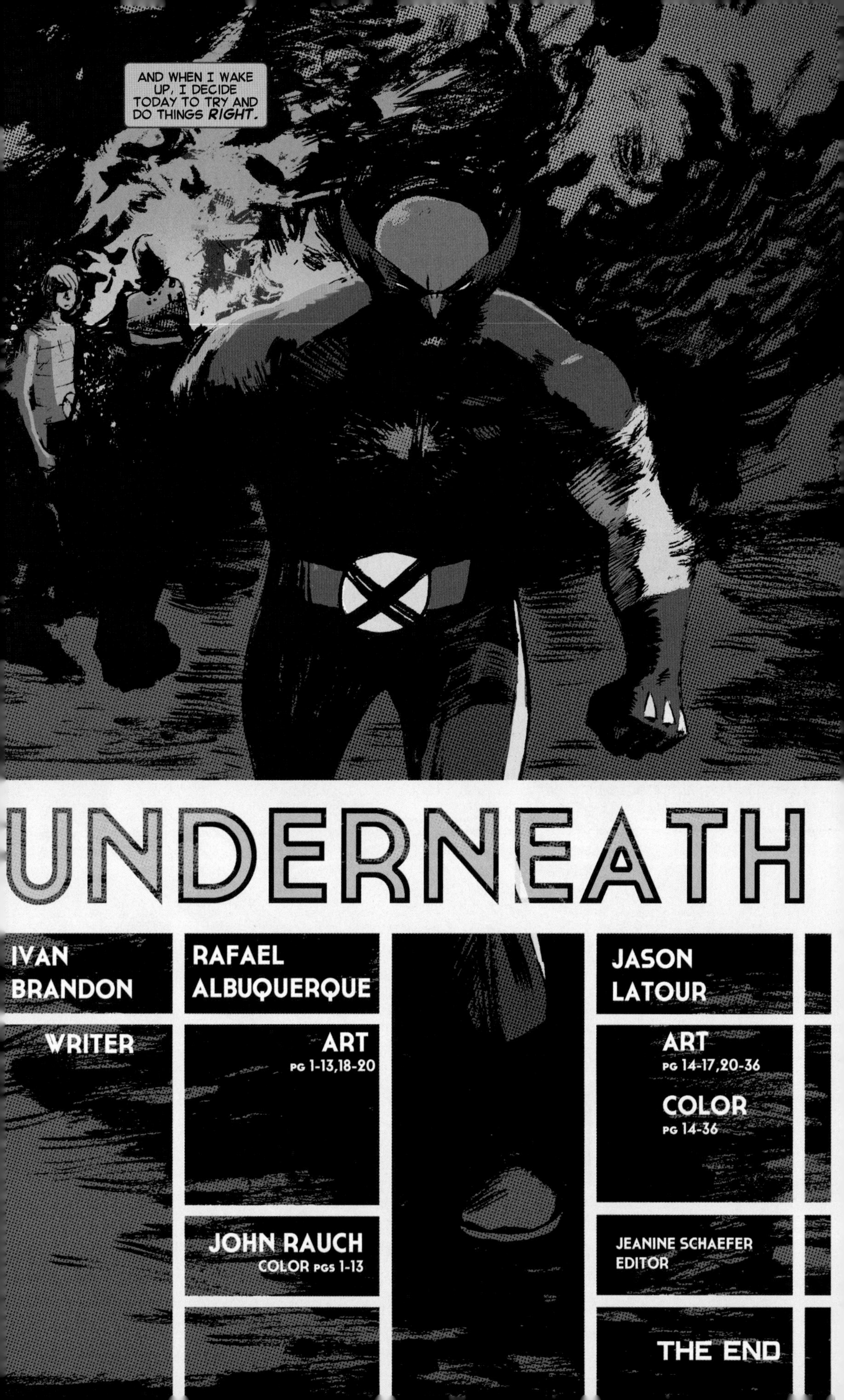
AND WHEN I WAKE UP, I DECIDE TODAY TO TRY AND DO THINGS RIGHT.
UNDERNEATH
IVAN BRANDON
WRITER
RAFAEL ALBUQUERQUE
ART PG 1-13,18-20
JOHN RAUCH
COLOR PGS 1-13
JASON LATOUR
ART PG 14-17,20-36
COLOR PG 14-36
JEANINE SCHAEFER
EDITOR
THE END

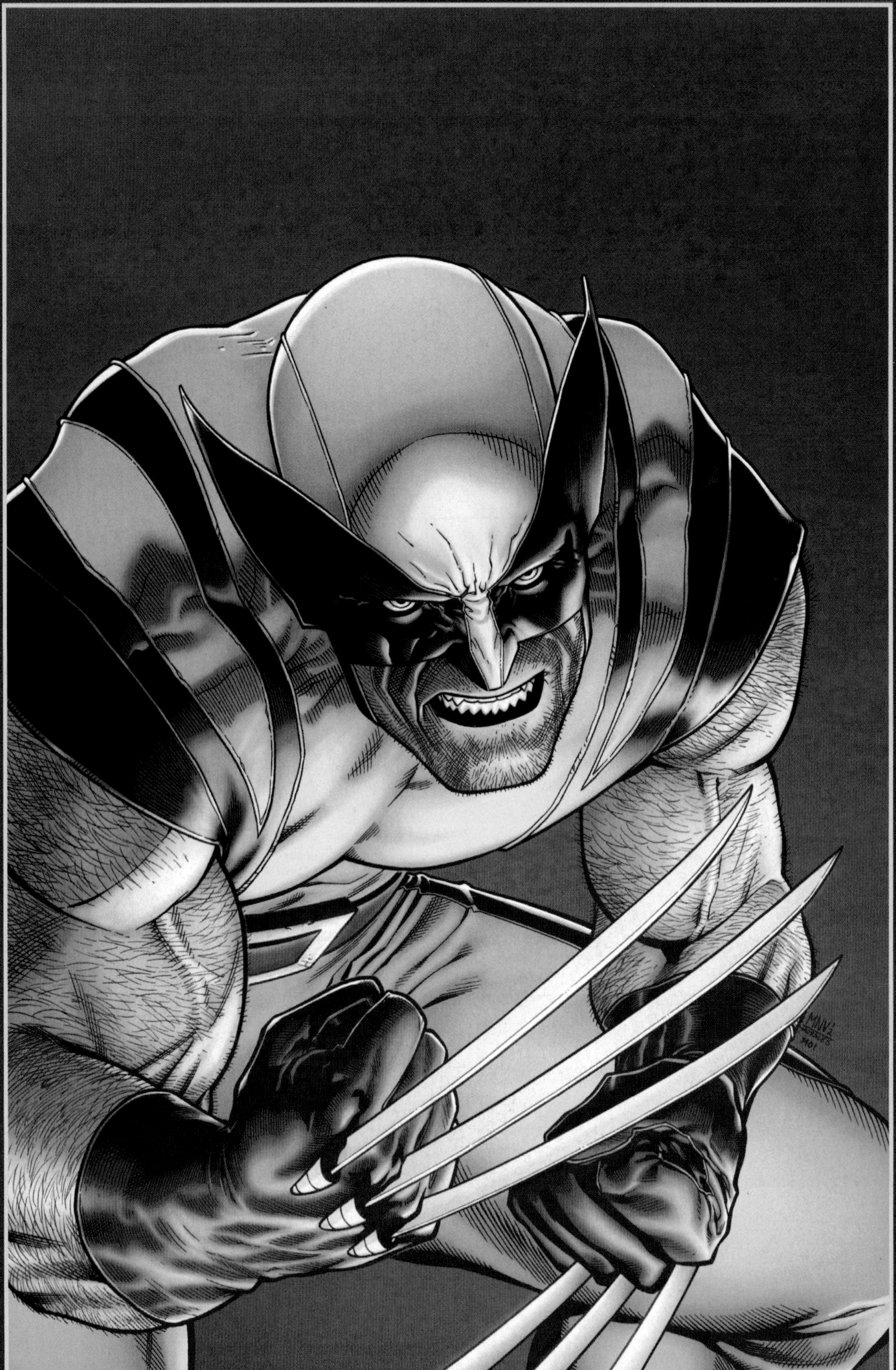

#305 VARIANT
BY STEVE McNIVEN, MARK MORALES & MORRY HOLLOWELL

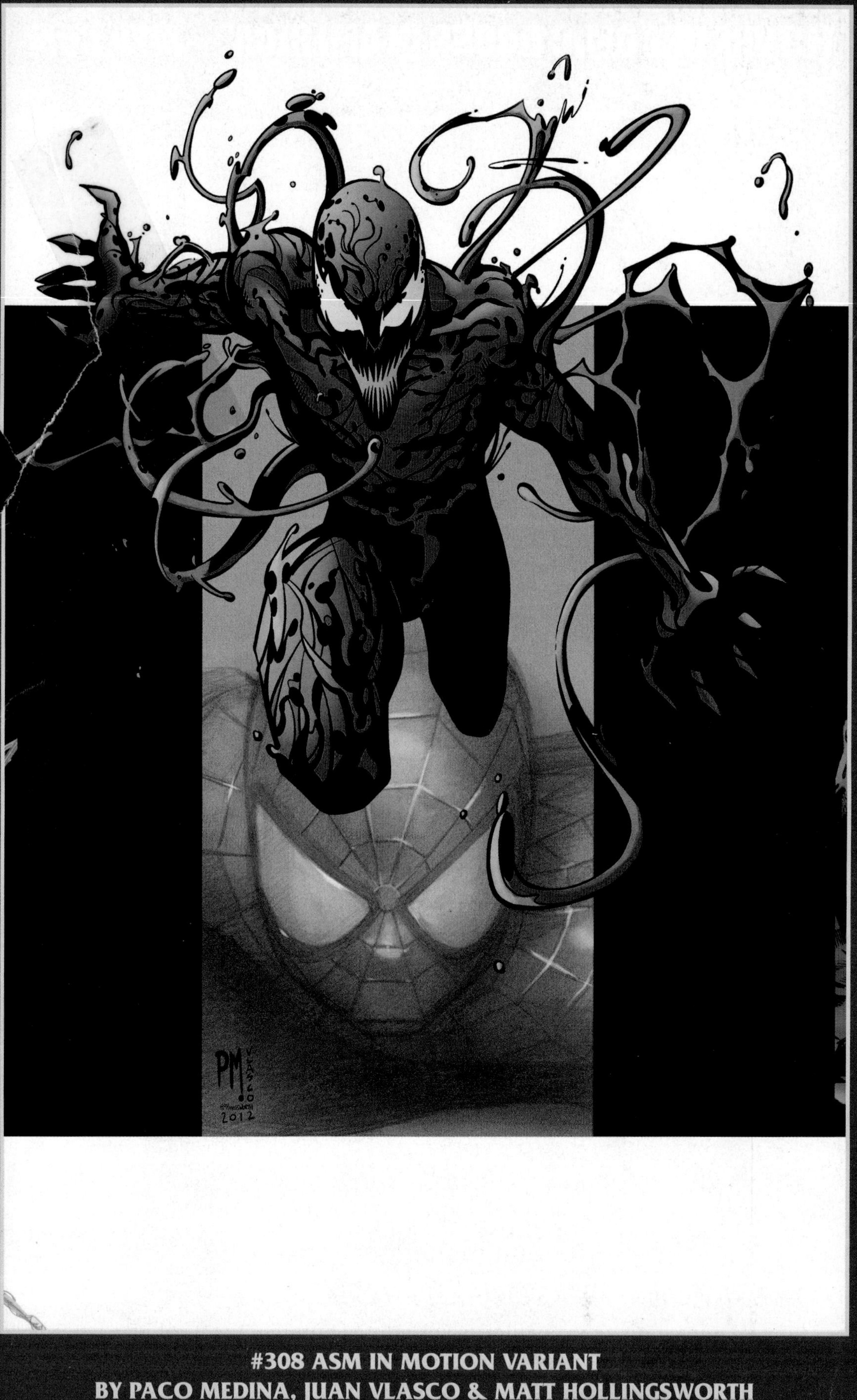

#308 ASM IN MOTION VARIANT
BY PACO MEDINA, JUAN VLASCO & MATT HOLLINGSWORTH

"WOLVERINE & THE X-MEN...MAKES ME HOPEFUL FOR THE FUTURE OF COMIC BOOKS IN AMERICA" – *MTV.COM*

WOLVERINE and the
X-MEN
AARON
BACHALO
BRADSHAW
MARVEL

WOLVERINE & THE X-MEN BY JASON AARON VOL. 1 PREMIERE HC
978-0-7851-5679-6

ALSO AVAILABLE

MARVEL
AARON
GUEDES
WOLVERINE
GOES TO HELL

WOLVERINE: WOLVERINE GOES TO HELL PREMIERE HC
978-0-7851-4784-8

AARON
ACUÑA
PALO
WOLVERINE VS. THE X-MEN

WOLVERINE: WOLVERINE VS THE X-MEN PREMIERE HC
978-0-7851-4786-2

MARVEL
AARON
GUEDES
SUDZUKA
WOLVERINE
WOLVERINE'S REVENGE

WOLVERINE: WOLVERINE'S REVENGE PREMIERE HC
978-0-7851-5279-8

WOLVERINE
AARON • GARNEY • GUEDES
SAN FRANCISCO
CITY LIMITS
GOODBYE, CHINATOWN

WOLVERINE: GOODBYE, CHINATOWN PREMIERE HC
978-0-7851-6141-7

Available Wherever Books Are Sold

To Find A Comic Shop Near You Visit www.comicshoplocator.com

MARVEL

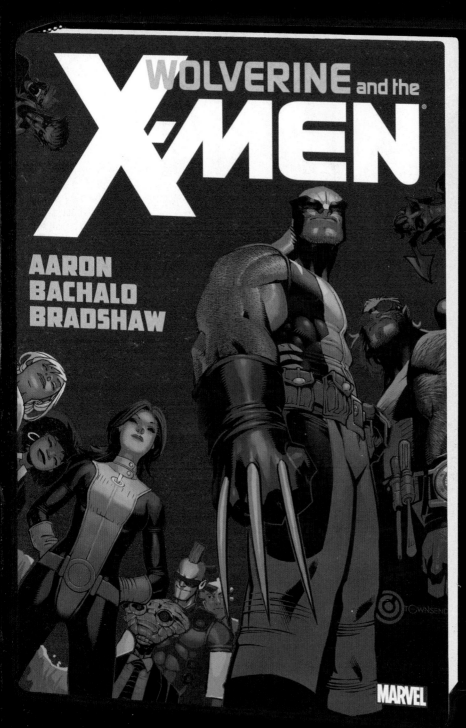

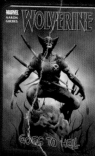

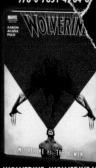

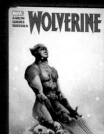

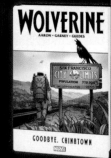